Leading for Regeneration

This book presents the regenerative leadership framework that has emerged from doctoral research and consulting work with successful sustainability leaders and their organizations in business, education, and community. The framework synthesizes the levels of awareness, the leadership styles and behaviors, and the organizational arrangements that correlate most significantly across these domains. Most importantly, the overwhelming majority of the leaders in this work agree that individual and collective consciousness development is critical to transforming the culture of organizations for sustainability and beyond.

The term regenerative has not been chosen arbitrarily, but to provide an alternative to the notion of sustainability, which many of the leaders featured here indicate has become insufficient to describe what needs to be done, economically, socially, and environmentally, if we are to ensure a flourishing world for present and future generations. This work in turn has led to the development of the Regenerative Capacity Index (RCI), a tool designed to assess an organization's readiness to engage in regenerative practice. From this evaluation of an organization's regenerative capacity, it becomes possible to design a strategy for regeneration that considers all levels of its environmental, social, and economic impact, both internally and externally, in the local and global community.

Among its major findings, the book argues that the more evolved sustainability leaders are becoming increasingly dissatisfied with the construct of sustainability, and indicate the need for a profound cultural shift toward regenerative human systems. In this framework, regenerative organizations are driven by a sense of higher purpose, and leadership is exercised horizontally and collaboratively. Leaders and followers engage in generative conversations to create desirable futures which are then "backcasted" to eliminate unanticipated consequences. Throughout, leaders emphasize the critical importance of engaging in personal and collective consciousness development or "inner work" in order to make regenerative practices possible.

John Hardman specializes in training leaders and facilitating the shift of their organizations toward sustainability and regenerative practice in business, community, and education. He is the founder and CEO of Regenerative Organizations, a process consulting firm that brings together a network of experts in sustainability leadership, legislation, construction, engineering, energy efficiency, and community and business development. John is a licensed facilitator of the AtKisson Group's ISIS Accelerator for sustainability strategic planning. He is also licensed as a sustainability business professional in S-CORE (Sustainability – Competency, Opportunity & Rating Evaluation).

Leading for Regeneration

Going beyond sustainability in business, education, and community

John Hardman

LONDON AND NEW YORK

First published 2012
by Earthscan
2 Park Square, Milton Park, Abingdon, Oxon OX14 4RN

Simultaneously published in the USA and Canada
by Earthscan
711 Third Avenue, New York, NY 10017

Routledge is an imprint of the Taylor & Francis Group, an informa business

British Library Cataloguing in Publication Data
A catalogue record for this book is available from the British Library

Library of Congress Cataloging in Publication Data
Hardman, John, 1953–
Leading for regeneration: going beyond sustainability in business, education, and community / John Hardman.
p. cm.
Includes bibliographical references and index.
1. Reengineering (Management) 2. Leadership—Psychological aspects.
3. Sustainable development. 4. Organizational effectiveness. I. Title.
HD58.87.H367 2012
658.4'092—dc23
2011022091

ISBN 978-1-84971-460-0 (hbk)
ISBN 978-0-415-69245-8 (pbk)
ISBN 978-0-203-15528-8 (ebk)

Typeset in Times New Roman
by Book Now Ltd, London

Contents

Illustrations

Figures

Tables

Acknowledgments

As with most good things in life, my own journey to regenerative leadership has been traveled in inspiring company. This work would not have been possible without the support and tolerant good humor of advisors and innumerable colleagues, friends, and students in the colleges and schools at Florida Atlantic University, whose encouragement led me to venture far beyond the walls of academia. For the content and intrinsic value of the regenerative leadership framework, I have to thank the extraordinary leaders in business, community, government, and education who have shared their eventful journeys to sustainability and beyond. These experiences have been instrumental in shaping my own consciousness and practice. Above all, I owe a debt of gratitude to my wife and companion Patricia, whose steadfast love and far seeing wisdom made it possible for us to weather profound changes in lifestyles, career paths, and countries in order to build a purposeful life, more fulfilling than we could ever have envisioned when we began our own journey in Patagonia close to 30 years ago. The final chapter on meditation in organizations could not have been written without her professional background, credentials, and practical expertise.

John Hardman
Delray Beach, Florida, April 2011

Preface

> We see the world piece by piece, as the sun, the moon, the animal, the tree; but the whole, of which these are shining parts, is the soul.
>
> (Ralph Waldo Emerson)

> I hesitate to relate it to The Matrix, but it's a little like taking the red pill. You suddenly wake up. It's not easy. In the nineteenth century, Goethe was already beginning to say, what do you need to do to jump out of old constructs? How do you stop, as Otto Scharmer (2007) would say, the download of habitual patterns of thinking? How do you begin, in a sense, to wake consciousness up? It's not so much about the emerging future as beginning to look at the deeper geometry, at what consciousness really is.
>
> Having spent a number of years looking at Hegel's logic, I agree with him that we have barely touched the surface of knowing how to road test the equipment. And it's funny how much the present state reflects that, the present economy, the present government, the present way of doing business. I'm really down on the Academy these days, because they keep teaching the same frameworks since the 1600s, still that old Cartesian linear frame that people just don't seem to want to climb out of (Gregor Barnum, Director of Corporate Consciousness, Seventh Generation, the mission of which is "To inspire a more conscious and sustainable world by being an authentic force for positive change").
>
> (Interview with the author)

I have chosen this brief account, including that of (main character) Neo's awakening and his connection to a real community in order to embark on the search for a real purpose in life, to illustrate the starting point of the journey proposed by this book. This describes the processes by which successful leaders engaged in sustainability work in business, education, and community have managed to go beyond conventional ways of thinking and acting in order to engage a deeper, more conscious approach to their work and that of their organizations. These evolutionary processes, and the behaviors they engender, have emerged because they have learned to acknowledge that real, sustainable change and development is rooted, first and foremost, in the quality of our consciousness, in our ability to perceive reality as it is rather than how we have been taught to see it. In consequence, regenerative leaders as defined here are becoming more successful in cultivating the capacity of their organizations to work towards the triple top line: how to grow prosperity, celebrate community, and enhance the health of all species for all time (Cuginotti, Miller, & van der Pluijm, 2008).

In the more advanced organizations, the deeply felt sense of the interdependence of all living and nonliving things has led to a more mindful, highly ethical interaction with others and with the environment. In consequence, those organizations that have "come of age" in sustainability terms no longer differentiate between the financial bottom line, preserving natural resources, or supporting their local and the global community. These are all integral aspects of what they do, and environmental conservation, corporate social responsibility, philanthropy, community engagement, environmental and social governance are no longer marketing buzzwords but have become second nature, as vital to their mission as income generation. In fact, the notion of charity or philanthropy is complemented and even replaced through the leveraging of their core business and their workforce as very real agents for positive change within their communities at the local and the global level.

Given the complexity inherent in understanding and managing these processes, the purpose of this book is to collect and describe the journeys of these leaders and their organizations in a coherent theoretical framework that I have called regenerative leadership, with the supporting evidence that has emerged from doctoral research and ongoing case work in the field. This work in turn has led to the development of the Regenerative Capacity Index (RCI), a tool designed to assess an organization's readiness to engage in sustainability efforts and beyond. The term regenerative has not been chosen arbitrarily but to provide an alternative to the notion of sustainability, which many of the leaders featured here indicate has become insufficient to describe what needs to be done, economically, socially, and environmentally, if we are to ensure a flourishing world for present and future generations.

Simply expressed, before we can live in a sustainable society, locally and globally, we must undergo (another) profound paradigm shift similar to those that have allowed us throughout the ages to divest ourselves of beliefs that could no longer explain reality, that no longer worked for us, in order to seek out and adopt a more satisfactory new set of beliefs (Kuhn, 1962). As will be seen here, a paradigm shift at this time in history requires a radical upward gear change in our consciousness, the search for a higher level of understanding and practice that will make the change possible. This includes the engagement of other faculties to balance the reductionist tendency of reason in the search for a more holistic understanding of who we are and of our place in the grand scheme of things. From the experience gained from ongoing research and the work reported here, I argue that this is the necessary and critical first step in the journey to profoundly redesigning all human systems in an economically viable manner in such a way that we can restore, preserve, and even increase the planet's natural health while fostering lasting social prosperity and well-being. This is the challenge for regenerative leaders.

If we accept this premise, we must also accept that it brings with it profound implications for our behaviors, for how we educate our young, conduct business, make, use, and dispose of things, and how we treat ourselves, each other, and the world around us. While this may appear obvious to those already engaged in sustainability work, it is also true that the results we have seen at this time fall far short from where we need to be. There is a growing and excellent body of work that shows us how to "do" sustainability, with comprehensible and comprehensive frameworks, and increasingly sophisticated tools that can track, measure, and report on environmental and social impact, and the best of this makes reference to issues of personal and collective transformation. However, little of the sustainability literature is grounded in actual research, theory development, and practice on consciousness development and how this may take us to more effective and rapid change, and even less of it has compared effective sustainability leadership across different fields of human endeavor. While conducting research and consulting work over the past 5 years with successful business, community, and university leaders engaged in sustainability efforts, this notion of the need for a radical rebooting of our inner selves, both individually and collectively, has been raised repeatedly, and this has led to the development of the construct of regenerative leadership presented here.

Our behaviors, upon which many of us focus our attention when engaging in sustainability work, can be no more, and no less, than the visible manifestation of our beliefs at any given time. So what myths might be driving our behaviors today that present very real hazards for us and other living things, even when their critics continue to be ridiculed in boardrooms, university departments, and political seats of power? British economist Tim Jackson (2009) tells us that one of the more serious of these is the increasingly foolish belief that prosperity is grounded in economic growth and expansion. Our ignorance regarding how to do things differently, for example for competing organizations to learn to succeed by collaborating with each other to optimize resource use and financial efficiency, points to what Scharmer (2007, 2009; Scharmer et al., 2002) calls the "blind spot" from which our consciousness (or unconsciousness) operates. This links to the myth, still widely held, of the real meaning of what Darwin (1859) defined in *Origin of Species* as survival of the fittest. In the process of natural selection described in his theory of evolution, Darwin refers to the success in the struggle for life as a result of the capacity of a species to adapt to its environment, not its strength to overcome competition or challenges, as Ron Heifetz has so successfully taught at Harvard (see Sparks, 2005). And by species, it is absolutely critical to understand that we must regain the sense of interdependence and community that we have allowed to erode in our fast-paced contemporary lives. While our inner work as individuals is central to our awakening, the productive interaction with others is essential if we are to adapt successfully to the challenges before us.

It is becoming increasingly obvious that we cannot continue to hold onto our present-day myths without impoverishing the quality of life for present and especially future generations. Recent events, such as the 2011 nuclear power plant disaster in Japan and the 2010 BP oil spill in the Gulf of Mexico, and even supposedly enlightened forums such as the Conferences of the Parties (CoP) on Climate Change, make this abundantly clear. However, they are also revealing of our shortsightedness and our inability to set aside agendas in search of the common good. Hopefully, these events will remain sufficiently present in our minds to help increase the global momentum in the right direction, as we not only need to make profound changes to how we do things but we can no longer afford to waste any further time before we make them. However, while behavior modification can be induced by external stimuli such as governmental regulation and social pressure, this is not where the most positive changes originate. As has been repeated by sages throughout history and by the leaders reported here, this shift must come from within. Accessing, developing, and acting from this deeper source of human consciousness is the single, most effective approach to managing the baser aspects of human nature in order to find ways to resolve historical conflicts across political, religious, cultural, economic, ethnic, and ideological divides, and to create a shared vision of desirable futures at the individual, local, and global level, to replace the current multitude of narrow-minded agendas. To paraphrase the words of Lao Tse, for there to be peace in the world, in the nations, in the cities, and in the homes, there must first be peace in the heart. In this acknowledgment and in the resulting behaviors lies the work of regenerative leaders and, in consequence, the coming of age of regenerative practice and eventual sustainability as a global phenomenon.

To provide a sense of the commonalities operating in the mindsets of regenerative leaders across different professional fields, the following narratives present the perspectives of two of them, one in higher education and the other in government, both of whom have been recognized as highly successful in driving sustainable change in their own fields.

Tony Cortese is President of Second Nature, a nonprofit organization whose mission is to catalyze sustainable strategies in higher education. He is a founding board member of the American College and University Presidents' Climate Commitment, and a member of the board of the Association for the Advancement of Sustainability in Higher Education (AASHE). Dr Cortese brings virtue into his conceptualization of the sustainability mindset, and he refers here to the moral responsibility that comes with knowledge.

> I think that one of the most important solutions for me is to understand that by trying to live a virtuous life I have a positive impact that is far beyond any negative consequence that I had ever conceptualized. Knowing that the way that I live has a negative impact on many other people in the world as well as many biological species leaves me with a deeper sense of responsibility. Now that I know what I know, I feel that I have an ethical duty to try to

> live my life in a way that will minimize the negative impact that I have by virtue of my life, and to help others to do the same.

Charged with overseeing Leadership for Energy and Environmental Design (LEED) certified constructions and retrofitting of the city's public buildings, Eve Williams, Program Architect for the City of Tallahassee, Florida's state capital, is an acknowledged sustainability leader. Eve criticizes the fact that "we have become so gluttonous, so decadent." This present state of affairs, she asserts, is very different from her memory of what she and society were like at the time of her childhood and adolescence.

> When I was in school in the 70s and 80s, there were so many of us who were so energy conscious. The more we read about it, the more we talked about it, the more it tied in with me in the 80s, when I first started having my children. I started doing things like using cloth diapers. I intuitively knew that manufactured diapers would take a very long time to break down in the landfill and knew this couldn't be good. I reused everything I could so I wouldn't have to throw it away. I had read about a family of four out west that was able to conserve, reuse and compost so much of their garbage that they only had 4 bags of garbage in a year. I thought if they could do this, then so could I. I made my own baby food, conserved water and stayed away from chemicals as much as I could. I owe it to the upbringing of my mom who used to (and still does) reuse, recycle, and collect rain water ever since I can remember. My mom came from the Depression era. She was always conserving everything.

From this reflection, Eve concludes that the inner dimension of the human experience needs to be brought back in order to make sustainability possible. In herself, this has allowed her to become less self-centered, which in turn has brought about a new understanding of how her actions affect others.

> The inner self and the spiritual, it's got to come back to make us say that it may not be the best thing for all of us, the whole world, to live in this way. This process has helped me to get outside myself, to quit worrying so much about me, to looking outward to seeing how my actions are affecting everything around me. I'm stopping myself every time I start to make changes. I look at everything I do and I think about how this is going to affect something else. What kind of consequences is this going to have?

This strong correlation of how a personal ethics informs best practices among sustainable leaders in different contexts will be seen to emerge repeatedly throughout the book, and it is the consistency of this shared perspective that serves to validate the construct of regenerative leadership. While the reader may be familiar with some or all of its individual components as described in Chapter 2, the real value of the framework can be explored from two perspectives. First, the theory that has emerged from the shared themes in diverse professional and civic domains has been organized within a coherent framework that is easy to understand and assimilate. Concepts that may be less familiar to some are carefully defined and placed within a context that makes them readily accessible. Second, the framework has been translated into an effective assessment instrument capable of measuring an organization's capacity to engage in regenerative change internally, and within the local, national, and global community.

Structure of the book

This work collects, interprets, and offers practical applications of the findings of research and consulting work with effective sustainability leaders in companies, communities, government, nonprofit organizations, universities, and schools. For those still unfamiliar with the topic, Chapter 1 provides key aspects of the historical background to the development of the concepts of sustainability and sustainable development. It also discusses some of the more important leadership constructs of the past decades and how they relate to sustainability. Chapter 2 presents and discusses the regenerative leadership framework that emerged from the research, and from facilitating sustainability strategic planning efforts in companies, communities, and at a midsized public university in Florida. This framework synthesizes the mindsets and behaviors of individuals and organizations engaged in building a culture of regenerative practice. It also presents the most effective style of leadership for sustainability and beyond to have emerged from the research, from subsequent teaching in higher education, and from process consulting, and describes how this is applied within and across organizations. The framework is then translated into the RCI, the self-assessment tool that measures a team or organization's capacity to engage in regenerative practice (see Appendix 1). This identifies gaps in individuals' and teams' mindset and worldview for effective sustainability work, leading to the identification of training and development needs and strategies. Chapter 3 lays out the inner journeys of the leaders involved in the research, supported by the experiences of the leaders themselves. Chapter 4 presents the journeys of the organizations to greater degrees of sustainability and beyond, described from personal experience by these "sustainability champions," as Bob Willard (2009) defines them. Chapter 5 highlights the most effective aspects of the inner and outer dimensions of the regenerative leadership mindset, and presents recent cases and lessons from the field, focusing not so much on outcomes as on the underlying processes that are critical to success in building regenerative cultures in organizations. Chapter 6 helps to connect the regenerative leadership framework to specific relaxation and meditation techniques that may be applied in organizations as a method for cultivating higher levels of consciousness and performance. Finally, a list and brief bios of the regenerative leaders who have participated in the development of the regenerative leadership framework are presented in Appendix 2. For those who may be interested in understanding more about the research process itself, the complete dissertation can be downloaded from the Internet (see http://regenerativeorganizations.com). Also available at this site are the reports of ongoing projects in higher education, community, and business.

1 Introduction

Leadership for the twenty-first century

In view of the limited success that efforts to attain and scale up sustainability have shown to date, this books argues that leaders in the twenty-first century cannot rely on traditional approaches to leadership to find effective solutions to current problems which, in the words of Lester Brown (2006), are bringing global civilization close to "overshoot-and-collapse mode" (p. 5). In essence, the leadership challenges of sustainability are contained in the need to balance complex and sometimes conflicting demands for economically, socially, and environmentally sustainable solutions (Ferdig, 2007), which require skills and behaviors that have gone unrecognized or have not been necessary in more stable organizational and social environments.

Traditional leadership models are understood to refer to the accepted roles that leaders adopt when establishing strategies for coping with change within their organizations. Within this paradigm, from the perspective of the pioneers of the time such as the social scientist Kurt Lewin (1951), change is promoted through a transformation strategy where an organization, and people's resistance to change, is unfrozen, changed, and refrozen. This implication of a well-managed linear transition from an outdated to a new and improved state of equilibrium, in a process where outcomes are predicted in a prior planning process, derives naturally from a rational worldview initially established during the Enlightenment (Gould, 2003; Wheatley, 2004; Wilber, 2000). An extreme example of this perspective may be found in the work of Frederick Taylor in the scientific management of industrial processes, which sought to increase productivity and profit through incremental improvements in assembly line efficiency (Taylor, 2004). The search for profit through efficiency at the expense of other considerations was legitimate at the time. In this context, the potential long-term natural and social impacts of exponential growth in industrial productivity would not have been a factor of concern.

More recently, developmental models of leadership have brought leaders and followers into a more balanced relationship, as in the case of the uplifting nature of the moral paradigm of transforming leadership of James MacGregor Burns (1978), or servant leadership of Robert Greenleaf (1977), where the leader is viewed in a nonhierarchical supporting role for the empowerment of followers in an organization. In rebutting critics (Gronn, 1995; Keeley, 1995) who affirm that transformational leadership may border on the unethical in self-serving leaders, or for being manipulative and undemocratic, Bass, Adams, and Webster (1997) argue that this form of leadership requires a high degree of moral maturity and "trust among leaders and followers," and that it was conceived to "avoid the tragedy of the commons" (p. 1), a concept closely associated with sustainability and sustainable development (Hardin, 1968).

Spiritual approaches to leadership have become evident in the renewal and sacrifice cycles researched and described as resonant leadership by Boyatzis and McKee (2005); in leadership as "presence in the moment" derived from in-depth interviews with corporate leaders applying what is termed as deep listening (Senge, Scharmer, Jaworski, & Flowers, 2004); or leadership as inspired pragmatism, that combines Eastern philosophy and Western practicality to drive effective decision making and organizational change (Link, 2006).

Perhaps one of the most comprehensive analyses of evolution and human society can be found in the work of Ken Wilber. Wilber has devised an *Integral Vision* (2007) that presents a comprehensive, chronological map of evolution of the biosphere, the individual, and society, since the beginning of time. In this map, which he defines as presenting all quadrants, all levels, all states, and all lines, Wilber has overlaid religion, psychology, sociology, and Eastern and Western philosophy, to present an integral perspective on what he calls, quite simply, everything we know (Wilber, 2000). Using Wilber's framework in part to support his own work, Otto Scharmer has developed a six-stage process that offers a means by which it becomes possible to create prototypes of desirable futures that offer a clean break from the obsolete patterns of thought and behavior of the past (Scharmer, 2007). These patterns are imbued with assumptions that affect science, society and how we think about systems, and condemn us to applying increasingly inadequate solutions to emerging problems that we have never experienced before as a global species. However, no single theory, whether directed at leadership or at social or organizational development, can respond effectively by itself to the challenges leaders face today. In education, if there were no schools, universities, or educational systems and we knew everything we now know about learning and development, what sort of an educational system would we build? The problem for many of us is that we carry the baggage of having gone through a school system, which predisposes us to replicate something similar to our own experience. The key to this particular conundrum lies in finding a method that will allow us to disengage from all previous assumptions in order to embrace an entirely new way of doing things. But how to do this?

The twenty-first century has brought with it a greater degree of complexity, uncertainty, and ambiguity to virtually everything that we do. This is true of our family life, our workplace, our communities, and local, state, and national governments. In a dynamic paradigm such as this, merely rational models of leadership are no longer viable. We must look even more deeply "within ourselves" (Ferdig, 2007, p. 26) for the leadership that responds to a complex, highly fluid reality (Stacey, 2002). Margaret Wheatley (2004) defines the current state of reality thus: "This is the era of many messes. Some of these we've created (although not intentionally) because we act on assumptions that can never engender healthy, sustainable societies and organizations" (p. 2).

In this context, "pre-conceived strategic plans, or [...] the mandate of any single individual boss" (Wheatley & Frieze, 2006, p. 3), go against nature and are therefore unsustainable. On the other hand, change that allows local actions to connect, interact, and engage each other following natural patterns of behavior is far more likely to be transformed into networks, and then systems, a process that Wheatley and Frieze define as emergent phenomena. The resilience and sustainability of these systems, as mentioned before, result from fostering the greatest number of connections and interactions between and among their multiple living and nonliving components (Capra, 1996, 2002). From this perspective, leadership is no longer a position, nor is it limited to a single person or team symbolically located at the top of an organizational chart. Leadership is therefore the natural behavior of every leader in a self-organizing system that is inherently too complex, too unstable, and unpredictable for any one individual to control.

From this multidimensional organizational systems thinking perspective (Bertalanffy, 1950; Senge, 1990; Senge, Cambron, McCabe, Lucas, & Kleimer, 2000; Capra, 2002; Wheatley, 2004), it may be assumed that leaders must approach change and innovation differently. Ferdig (2007) describes the following leadership capacities engaged in promoting sustainability. Sustainability leaders

> Create opportunities for people to come together and generate their own answers – to explore, to learn, and devise a realistic course of action to address sustainability challenges. Instead of giving direction, sustainability leaders develop and implement actions in collaboration with others, modifying them as needed to adapt to unforeseen changes in the environment over time ... Sustainability leaders recognize that the experience of change itself, and the dissonance it creates, fuels new thinking, discoveries, and innovations that can revitalize organizations.
>
> (p. 31)

In organizational environments that recognize the unpredictable nature of reality, leaders relinquish the prerogative for control. Rather, they accept a reality that shifts each and every day, and yet they cultivate skills and actions that are reasonable within a flexible framework that allows for continual correction and improvement. Ferdig (2007) goes on to indicate that:

> Sustainability leaders make the notion of sustainability personally relevant, grounding action in a personal ethic that reaches beyond self-interest. They recognize that all of us can co-create the future through individual ways of seeing, understanding, interacting and doing. Sustainability leaders are

> informed, aware, realistic, courageous, and personally hopeful in ways that genuinely attract others to the business of living collaboratively.
>
> (p. 32)

From this perspective, it is possible to define sustainability leadership as purposeful action driven from a position of enlightened self-interest, where benefiting others and the planet as a whole means the same as benefiting oneself (Capra, 2002). This follows logically from a mindset that conceives a universe where all things are interconnected, where every personal action affects other actions elsewhere in a ripple effect over a very long period of time. At first glance, this growing awareness of the consequences of our actions can appear overwhelming, and requires leadership capable of mobilizing organizational decisions that balance the common good against personal needs and desires. In the words of Marianne Williamson, attributed to Nelson Mandela, "Our deepest fear is not that we are inadequate. Our deepest fear is that we are powerful beyond measure. It is our light, not our darkness, that most frightens us" (Williamson, 1992, p. 190).

The dilemmas of leadership at this time become more complex and challenging as conflicting actions and reactions interact. Leaders can no longer depend on the successes of the past to provide solutions for the problems of today, as they discover when diverse cultures are brought into the organizational mix. Trompenaars and Hampden-Turner (2002) indicate that, as a leader today:

> You are supposed to inspire and motivate yet listen, decide yet delegate, and centralize business units that must have locally decentralized responsibilities. You are supposed to be professionally detached yet passionate about the mission of the organization, be a brilliant analyst when not synthesizing others' contributions, and be a model and rewarder of achievement when not eliciting the potential of those who have yet to achieve. You are supposed to develop priorities and strict sequences, although parallel processing is currently all the rage and saves time. You must enunciate a clear strategy but never miss an opportunity even when the strategy has not anticipated it. Finally, you must encourage participation while not forgetting to model decisive leadership.
>
> (p. 2)

This dilemma-fraught reality fosters the emergence of sustainability leaders who possess a spirit of inquiry and learning (Ferdig, 2007), who share what they learn along the way, and are not daunted by unexpected turns of events. They "take informed and calculated risks; they unashamedly learn from their mistakes and tell others about what they discovered in the process" (p. 33). Far from discarding the approaches of traditional leaders, sustainability leaders take strategic thinking, planning, communicating, galvanizing others, and evaluating results to a new level of awareness. Recognizing the impossibility of commanding and controlling organizational goals and objectives, they engage all followers as leaders in a common enterprise.

Their initiatives are serving to promote more responsible practices related to environmental preservation, to the education of upcoming generations in sustainability, and to the development of a more just and sustainable world. However, all too often these initiatives plateau, or fail to evolve to the next level (Doppelt, 2003; McDonough & Braungart, 1991, 2002). There have been numerous studies over the years of different aspects of leadership in the corporate world, in education, and in community (Waters, Marzano, & McNulty, 2003; Leithwood, Seashore Louis, Anderson, & Wahlstrom, 2004; Laszlo, 2005; Seelos & Mair, 2005b; Esty & Winston, 2006; McEwen & Schmidt, 2007; Quinn, 2007). Some of these, such as McEwen and Schmidt's (2007) *Mindsets in Action*, have begun to explore in some depth the developmental experiences of leaders across these different domains to identify those that are most powerful in implementing and sustaining sustainable development initiatives. However, Doppelt (2003) indicates that "discussions about *what* to do ... dominate the public dialogue on sustainability" (p. 16). Little emphasis, he indicates, is placed on "*how* organisations can change their internal thought processes, assumptions and ingrained behavior to embrace the new tools and techniques" (p. 16). Shortly after his groundbreaking study into what he came to define as Level 5 leaders (Collins, 2001a), a model of leadership that hypothetically could be considered transferable to sustainability leaders, Jim Collins admitted that

> We would love to be able to give you a list of steps for getting to Level 5, but we have no solid research data that would support a credible list. We could speculate on what that inner box might hold, but it would mostly be just that, speculation.
>
> (Collins, 2001b, p. 76)

This admission of the inability to map the leadership development process beyond a definition of what makes a leader what he or she is, coupled to the increasing scientific evidence that the human race is rapidly driving nature and society to a state of overshoot and collapse, highlighted the importance of exploring this critical area at this time.

The most comprehensive, if not the only, research to have compared leadership for sustainability across domains was conducted in the late nineties and first part of the century by Bob Doppelt (2003). Doppelt's qualitative study, revised and updated in 2009, reviewed the "core principles of success" (p. 19) of business corporations, government, and civic society. From working with companies and governments over a period of 20 years, Doppelt identified factors that may lead organizations either to fail or plateau in their sustainability efforts, and to those contrasting factors that underpin successfully evolving sustainability initiatives. Among the factors contributing to failure, he identified what he has called the seven sustainability blunders, which relate, he indicates, to the patterns of behavior that drive leadership decision-making processes, that "poison efforts to reduce and eliminate adverse environmental and socioeconomic impacts" (p. 30).

Doppelt states that the "key to transforming the governance system of an organisation so that it embraces sustainability is *leadership*" (Doppelt, 2003, p. 37). The organizations he studied demonstrated time after time that this key is found in a leadership style that "kept the organisation focused on its long-term goal of becoming sustainable while encouraging employees to take it upon themselves to work together diligently toward that end" (p. 37). Central to this approach is the notion that a "skillful and equitable distribution of power and authority throughout the organisation unlocks the doors to deep-seated commitment by employees and stakeholders and is a key to changing outdated and harmful beliefs and assumptions" (p. 37). In one of his more recent works, Doppelt (2008) asserts the need for organizations to change their internal thought processes, assumptions, and ingrained behaviors. The regenerative leadership framework presented here is intended to build on this conceptual understanding by delving more deeply into the subjective realm of consciousness development in leaders at all levels that results in engaging organizations in regenerative practices that go beyond mere sustainability. This understanding of the nature of human consciousness and how its development influences our worldview is critical to personal and organizational change. With the appropriate mindset, our minds, hearts, and hands are far more easily aligned with regenerative behaviors. This book therefore offers a map of those aspects of human consciousness and resulting leadership behaviors and organizational strategies which the leaders in the study consistently identified as critical to sustainability process.

Historical background to sustainability

The more recent history of international concern for social, economic, and environmental sustainability can be traced to the United Nation's Universal Declaration of Human Rights (1948), the Convention on the Rights of the Child (1989), the United Nations' Agenda 21 (1992), particularly Chapter 36, which focuses on education, and the Millennium Development Goals (2000), the tenth anniversary review of which concluded recently with mixed results. Education, considered a fundamental factor in eradicating poverty, was brought further into the limelight at the World Conference on Education for All (1990). In 2000, UNESCO launched the Education for All program (2000), with particular responsibility for pursuing the United Nations Priorities in Education, which led to the so-called Decade on Education for Sustainable Development (2005–2015). Parallel to these efforts have been the international climate initiatives that led to the Kyoto Protocol in 1997 and most recently the disappointing Copenhagen Climate Change Conference in 2009 followed by an equally ineffective outcome of the Cancun summit in November, 2010.

These international initiatives have had important impacts, many of them positive. However, it is also clear that the desired outcomes have not been fully attained, and that the leaders of governments, international coalitions, and organizations are ill-prepared to design and implement long-term solutions to global issues that will ensure an equitable, sustainable, and prosperous society for all. What is also clear is that focusing on the behaviors that should have served to resolve these issues has not worked, indicating that we must look elsewhere if we are to find both short- and long-term solutions to our most pressing problems. The findings contained in this book serve to open up a new approach. From my research and further work with sustainability leaders in corporations, nonprofit organizations, higher education, and government, I have found that the most sustainable outcomes have come from leaders who have been willing to explore the nature and role of their own human consciousness in order to develop a clearer understanding of their place, and that of their organizations, in the greater scheme of things.

2 The regenerative leadership framework

The original research that gave rise to the interest in writing this book was conducted with business, educational, political, and community leaders who were recognized by their peers as becoming increasingly effective in moving themselves and others in their organizations toward more comprehensive or sophisticated approaches to sustainability. This study led to the generation of a substantive theory that sought to conceptualize leadership for sustainability in a manner that made it accessible to those interested in gaining a deeper understanding of how this increasingly important notion could be applied in their own organizations and communities. By applying the qualitative approach known as grounded theory, the first purpose of the study focused on the developmental experiences or personal journeys of these leaders, and their responses are collected in Chapter 3. The second purpose explored the strategies they have found most effective in moving their organizations in the direction of sustainability or sustainable development, and these are reported in Chapter 4.

Expressed very simply, sustainability can be defined as the ability of natural and social systems to continue doing what they are doing indefinitely, whereas sustainable development is the process that is undertaken so that sustainability may be achieved (AtKisson, 2008). As will be seen here, however, for a number of these leaders, the concepts of sustainability and sustainable development no longer provide a satisfactory explanation for what they were seeking to accomplish, particularly for those who are more deeply aware of the human factors involved in issues of sustainability. It is therefore worth noting the reasoning behind the adoption of the term regenerative rather than sustainability leadership. While this may seem a minor matter in the context of the urgency of current events, this distinction is important due to the profound shift in perspective it proposes. From a focus on reaching a sustainable state as defined by sustainable development for sustainability, regenerative leadership and practice propose that we must first heal and restore, in essence regenerate currently damaged ecological and social systems if we are to evolve toward a truly desirable future.

As the study progressed, it became apparent that much of the research, the existing literature, and the strategic plans of people and organizations focused overwhelmingly on the behaviors that produced certain effects rather than on the causes of unsustainable practices and conditions linked to environmental degradation, social injustice, and poor economics. For example, in the literature on climate change, population growth and poverty, free market economics, among others, authors and researchers offered powerful frameworks and strategies for the alleviation of poverty and suffering (Sachs, 2005), restoration of natural environments (Brown, 2006; Meadows, Randers & Meadows, 2004), replicating natural processes in design manufacturing (Benyus, 2002; McDonough & Braungart, 2002), and turning environmental issues to profit through approaches described as "green to gold" and natural capitalism (Esty & Winston, 2006; Hawken, Lovins, & Lovins, 1999). Only a few studies looked at the underlying human factors responsible for unsustainable practices, and the role of leadership in addressing the issues emerging from the dysfunctional relationship between individual and collective consciousness and sustainability (Amodeo, 2005; AtKisson, 2008; Ferdig, 2007; Ferdig & Ludema, 2005; McEwen & Schmidt, 2007; Quinn, 2007; Seelos & Mair, 2005b).

Even these studies, however, while successfully describing the major attributes of sustainability leaders, did little to reveal the process by which leaders came to be aware of and engaged in the shift toward a new paradigm in the way they operated as individuals and within their organizations and communities. This pointed to a gap in our understanding of the developmental experiences that leaders had undergone in their personal or professional lives that had prepared them for this undertaking. Anthony Giddens (1986) preceded Wilber (2001) and Scharmer (2007) in addressing this dynamic in his theory of structuration, which describes a duality of structure between the realm of the subject (the knowledgeable human agent) and object (society), where he recommends that "social theory should be concerned first and foremost with reworking conceptions of human being and human doing, social reproduction and human transformation" (p. xx).

This led to the adoption of a term which, while not entirely new, served the purpose of shifting the focus away from the consequences of human action on sustainable development to the underlying causes and potential solutions to the problems. The decision to adopt this concept of regenerative leadership came about quite naturally. Further to discussion with a number of the leaders involved in the study, we concluded that the term regenerative leadership and the framework that emerged from the research to explain it served to capture the more holistic perspective emerging in the more recent leadership practices for sustainability.

The belief in the importance of understanding this dynamic as it related to sustainability and sustainable development framed the present study, and informed the research questions and the most appropriate methodology. What follows are the conclusions drawn from the findings that emerged from the 24 structured interviews conducted with the study's leaders.

To begin with, leaders showed strong consensus in their definition of sustainability. The majority shared the basic premise of the Brundtland Commission Report of 1987, which defined sustainability as "development that meets the needs of the present without compromising the ability of future generations to meet their own needs" (World Commission on Environment and Development, 1987, p. 54). For this to occur, they also agreed that the greatest challenge lay in people's ignorance and resistance to change, grounded in their inability to engage in systems thinking, to recognize the place and role of the human species within the broader context of the biosphere, and the unintended consequences of maintaining current unsustainable practices. The majority of the leaders agreed that the solution lay in awakening people's awareness to the problems through the development of personal and collective mindsets for sustainability. Then again, if a positivist-rational epistemology has brought us to the present situation of unsustainability, it followed that we cannot resolve the issues that threaten our natural and social environments from this mechanistic perspective. Therefore, in order to perceive and make sense of reality as it is, we must engage other faculties in addition to our capacity to reason. To embed sustainability in every human action as a natural rather than an artificial behavior, we must develop a more complete or integral vision of reality as it is, not as we think it is or are conditioned to see it. The implication for sustainability leaders, as Jeffrey Hollender, CEO of Seventh Generation expressed it in conversation with Otto Scharmer, is that this "is about being better able to listen to the whole than anyone else" (Scharmer, 2007, p. 20). Scharmer himself defines this as "the need to go beyond the concept of leadership," asserting that, "we must discover a more profound and practical integration of the head, heart, and hand – of the intelligences of the open mind, open heart, and open will – at both an individual and collective level" (p. 20).

This imperative for going beyond current practice, of seeking new ways to resolve ongoing problems that in many cases have taken on global proportions, and the urgency with which we must respond to some of these in order to maintain the quality of life for present and future generations, requires that we prepare the upcoming generation of leaders with a new perspective. Given that a coherent approach to leadership does not appear in the literature as a perfect match for the author's findings, this book offers the regenerative leadership framework as a starting point from which to respond to this demand.

Regenerative leadership: a model for the twenty-first century

The regenerative leadership framework is presented in Figure 2.2. This style is applied by formal and informal leaders at all levels of organizations who engage groups of people in the development of higher levels of awareness that translate into behaviors that seek not merely to preserve existing natural and social resources while ensuring a healthy bottom line but to restore and create new resources that have become depleted through overuse or misuse. Sustainability can be defined colloquially, as Melaver, Inc., real estate company CEO Martin Melaver told me, citing John Abrams, as "doing what you are doing so that you can keep on doing what you're doing." On the other hand, regenerative leadership can be said to be about putting back more than we took out, and doing it in entirely new ways unconditioned by prior assumptions.

In essence, regenerative leaders operate in one of two principal ways. Some work to restore man-made linear systems to cyclical systems that respect the natural or synthetic cycle, as McDonough and Braungart (2002) have described it. This includes recovery of brownfields; restoring topsoil to its original state; retrofitting construction, transportation, and industrial manufacturing systems; and facilitating community regeneration at the grassroots level. Others work to shift the culture in their organizations. They do this by enabling cross-disciplinary conversations within and across the boundaries of their organizations, leading to the design and implementation of radically innovative ways of doing things that are not affected by unanticipated consequences in the short and the long term.

Whether regenerative leadership is believed to be economically viable or idealistic foolishness, there is a strong case for the construct to be given serious consideration. Among numerous scientific and sociological studies offering current statistics on the state of the world (Intergovernmental Panel on Climate Change, 2007; International Geosphere-Biosphere Programme, 2007), Meadows et al. (2004) provide the following evidence to show how far we are reaching the point of overshoot and collapse:

> - Sea level has risen 10–20 cm since 1900. Most nonpolar glaciers are retreating, and the extent and thickness of Arctic sea ice is decreasing in summer.
> - In 1998, more than 45 percent of the globe's people had to live on incomes averaging $2 a day or less. Meanwhile, the richest one fifth of the world's population has 85 percent of the global GNP (gross national product). And the gap between rich and poor is widening.
> - In 2002, the Food and Agriculture Organization of the UN estimated that 75 percent of the world's oceanic fisheries were fished at or beyond capacity. The North Atlantic cod fishery, fished sustainably for hundreds of years, has collapsed, and the species may have been pushed to biological extinction.
> - The first global assessment of soil loss, based on studies of hundreds of experts, found that 38 percent, or nearly 1.4 billion acres, of currently used agricultural land has been degraded.
> - Fifty-four nations experienced declines in per capita GDP (gross development product) for more than a decade during the period 1990–2001.
>
> These are symptoms of a world in overshoot, where we are drawing on the world's resources faster than they can be restored, and we are releasing wastes and pollutants faster than the Earth can absorb them or render them harmless. They are leading us toward global environmental and economic collapse – but there may still be time to address these problems and soften their impact.
>
> (p. 3)

In face of scenarios such as these, it was not surprising to find that a number of the leaders in the research were no longer satisfied with fostering environmental, social, and economic sustainability as the ultimate objective in business, education, community, or any other form of human activity. The growing evidence of overshoot and collapse of natural and social systems indicated the need to adopt strategic approaches that went beyond sustainability.

From the responses to the research questions, several key factors emerged to describe this style of leadership. Some of these may be found to be grounded in transforming or transformational leadership as described earlier by James MacGegor Burns (1978), particularly in his consideration of the importance of the development of moral values and trust within organizations. However, a clear distinction in this new form of leadership lay in that leaders were not basing their success on their charisma but on the driving factor of the importance of sustainability as an issue in itself. When people woke up to this imperative, there was a diminished need for leaders to persuade followers, and even less need to mandate policy or strategy. They had found that empowering others to connect to their personal sense of purpose and then to drive sustainability efforts considered meaningful for their own sake within their particular organization was the most effective strategy, as it tended to generate a more creative, innovative approach to regenerative practices. This reformulation of Burns' transforming leadership is defined here as purpose-driven leadership through the suspension of the ego and personal agendas in pursuit of a greater goal.

Organizational goals and objectives were then developed and coupled to assessment of performance linked to environmental, social, and economic benchmarks. This dynamic produced a strong balance in the commitment to individual and institutional goals, the permutation that Blake and Mouton (1964) considered the most effective in their work on management styles, which they called motivational/problem solving. It was also consistent with the entrepreneurial ethic as Tom Peters (1994) defined it, indicating that in this day and age, all personnel, including the janitor, are crucial to the successful operation of most organizations and must become personally committed to designing and implementing goals and objectives and measuring results, while driving for improvement and being accountable for maximizing the use of resources under their care. This belief in an organizational culture that sought to liberate people's highest levels of performance through empowerment showed a radical departure from hierarchical forms of authority. This recognition of the central importance of the contribution of every member of the organization was found to result in a powerful learning community that fostered the integration of "the intellectual, the emotional and the spiritual" (Harris et al., 2003).

Perhaps one of the clearest representations of the dynamic relationship between people's subjective reality and their behavior can be seen in Ken Wilber's (2001) All Quadrants, All Levels (AQAL). This was chosen as the blueprint over which the process of regenerative leadership was overlaid, as will be seen later. Grounded theory purists may voice concerns regarding the use of a preexisting framework to complement an emergent theory. To respond to this possible criticism, Wilber's conceptual map should be seen as a general organizing framework representing a synthesis of the human experience that served to provide a container for the leadership theory that emerged from the research. To revisit this framework briefly, the four quadrants in Figure 2.1 represent four distinct dimensions of the human experience. These correspond, on the left, to the interior/subjective and on the right to the exterior/objective dimensions of experience. The top two quadrants represent, on the left, the individual's stage of development with regard to personal values, assumptions, attitudes, patterns of thinking, worldview, and overall mindset. On the right, the quadrant represents the actions and behaviors in the external world that reflect that particular individual's mindset. The bottom quadrants mirror the upper quadrants, but in this case, they relate to the stage of development of the collective culture, values, behaviors, worldview, and overall mindset of an organization or a community, and these are translated on the right into strategies, systems, policies, regulations, and behaviors.

The findings emerging from the study can be laid over Wilber's framework to represent regenerative leadership and how this operates. For the following framework, however, the quadrants have been rotated 90 degrees, so that the interior side of the individual and collective subjective world has been placed on the bottom of the figure. The quadrants contain the concepts extracted from the leaders' responses, in some cases reformulated theoretically from further review of the literature.

In this model, following a continuous process represented by the infinity symbol, regenerative leaders have undertaken systematic inner work, as shown in Quadrant 1, to develop their mindset to the highest level of consciousness of which they are capable. As reported in the interviews conducted by the author, for some leaders, this process was initiated in a clearly identified point in time due to a life-changing event or epiphany; in others, the process began in early childhood and evolved incrementally over the years. In the most advanced leaders, this inner development may be described as resulting in an integral or systemic view of reality, where intellect, emotions, and the will to act have been aligned to serve a purpose that is considered to be of ontological significance. This worldview, which one leader in higher education described as a "butterfly mindset," promotes in the individual a more complete perspective of reality, since it brings with it the recognition that our actions have the potential to affect everything and everyone else. This world-centric perspective, as Wilber defines it (2000), fosters a global ethics that is translated into behaviors that reflect greater concern and compassion for the natural environment, for colleagues within an organization, and for fellow citizens within the local and the global community, as shown in the second quadrant. This is also reflected in leadership behaviors. Rather than acting on people's behaviors to effect change and elicit performance, leaders interact with others at the level of their values and purpose within an organization or community, as depicted in Quadrant 3. For purposes of this study, this has been defined here as purpose-driven transformational leadership. Through a process defined here as engagement of values and purpose, regenerative leaders at all levels of an organization indirectly transform the collective culture and consequently, the behaviors and strategies exhibited by the organization as a whole, as shown in Quadrant 4. This indirect process taken by regenerative leaders is indicated by the path taken by the infinity symbol. A leader is shown here as influencing the collective culture in order to awaken and

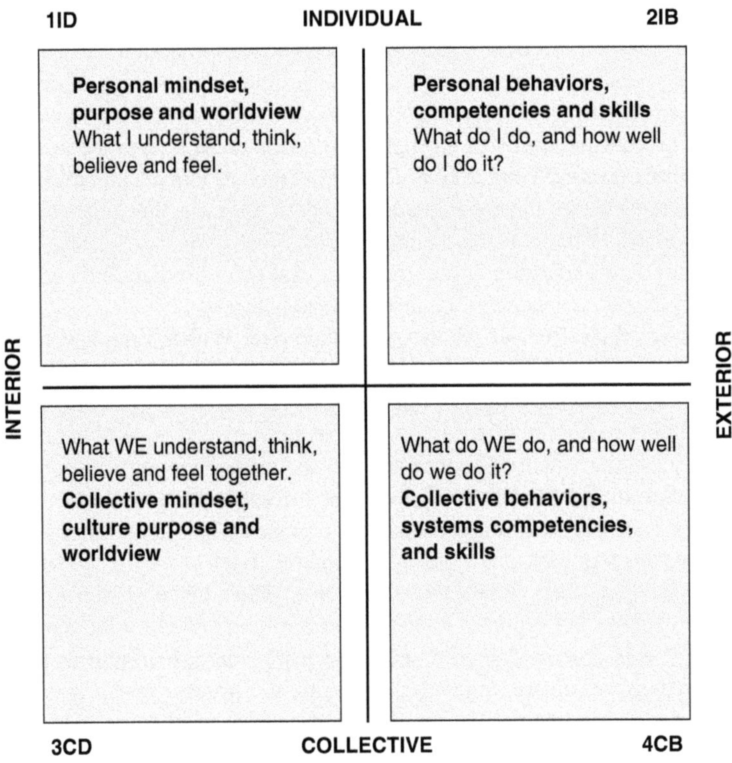

Figure 2.1 Integral theory.
Source: Adapted from Wilber (2001).

inspire a collective sense of purpose, which in this study relates to sustainability. This collective learning process is enabled through generative conversation. Though this is a behavior, it is intimately connected to the activation of a circular system or organizational process, where each individual stakeholder, internal and external, is integral to the achievement of the organization's purpose. Generative conversations act as a catalyst of a continual reflective feedback loop necessary for double-loop learning, which Argyris and Schön (1978) define as challenging the underlying assumptions that need to be corrected in order to produce successful change. The semicircular arrows surrounding the framework represent the circular organization or most advanced level of performance, that of the collective culture that can engage triple-loop learning, which Isaacs (2000) describes as the field of meaning that is generated through dialog, and which can lead to regenerative conversations. As little evidence of this higher level process emerged from the findings, this process is developed more extensively below.

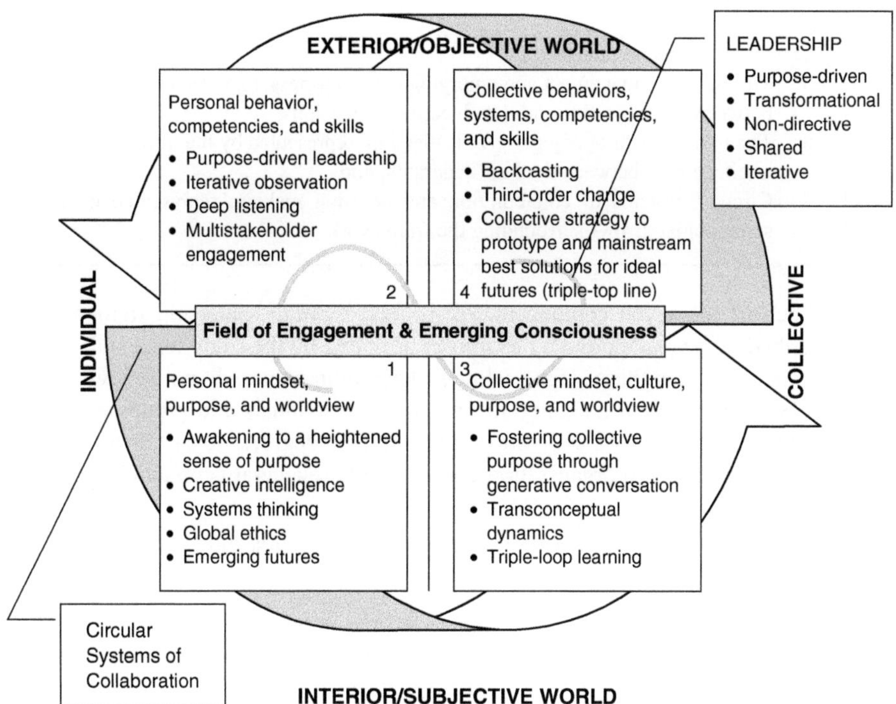

Figure 2.2 The regenerative leadership framework: an integral theory for transforming people and organizations from within.

As displayed in the framework in Figure 2.2, the following four-quadrant developmental process and the three resulting leadership factors were identified as integral to regenerative leadership when sustainability was explicitly referenced as the focus of attention:

Box 2.1 The four quadrants of individual and collective development, and the three leadership factors

The four quadrants of individual and collective development:

1 Facilitating access to the source of personal purpose and emerging self;
2 Connecting with others through keen observation and deep listening;
3 Eliciting collective purpose through generative conversation; and
4 Engaging in collective action to strategize and prototype the best possible solutions to emerging futures through third-order change and backcasting.

(*Continued*)

(*Continued*)

The three leadership factors:

5 The field of engagement and emerging consciousness, represented by the band between the subjective and the objective dimensions;

6 The indirect path of regenerative leadership, represented by the infinity symbol tracing a path between the four quadrants; and

7 Circular systems of collaboration and decision making, represented by the semicircular arrows surrounding the framework.

Each of the seven components of the regenerative leadership framework is described below, supported by examples provided by the study leaders. It should be understood that these stages, while sequential in nature, do not follow a linear process. They have a tendency to overlap as individuals and groups engage in the iterative process of evolving toward greater degrees of sustainability and, in the more advanced organizations, toward truly regenerative practices.

Quadrant 1: facilitating access to the source of personal purpose and emerging self

A majority of the study leaders emphasized the importance, for sustainability to be assured, of raising their level of awareness of the interconnectedness of natural and human systems, including their own place in the biosphere. This growing awareness was seen as liberating a personal sense of purpose and willing engagement in regenerative practices, which they sought to facilitate in others. The rationale supporting this conviction lay in the understanding that this would make it possible for people to engage more effectively in the complex dynamics that connect the natural, social, and economic systems within which they operate. As people become more aware of the types of interactions they sustain within their contexts, and how these can be positive or negative, they begin to attain a more integrated perspective or worldview. These levels of awareness and the worldview that they reflect, therefore, may be expressed as a continuum appropriate for sustainability leadership, measuring levels of engagement that go from fragmentation to integration, as shown in Figure 2.3.

These levels of engagement presented some clear properties and dimensions. The conclusion was that as levels of consciousness increased toward an integrated mindset and worldview, people's behaviors reflected more balanced choices, where universal needs and rights became equally important to those of the individual, thereby fostering a greater willingness to engage in sustainability issues. The evolution of people's individual sustainability could therefore be tracked in a progression that began with resistance at the most ignorant level, where the individual possessed a highly fragmented worldview and was stuck within a self-centered, short-term mindset. This was superseded when individuals showed some willingness to engage but still possessed a strong degree of skepticism as to the reality of unsustainable practices and their contribution to

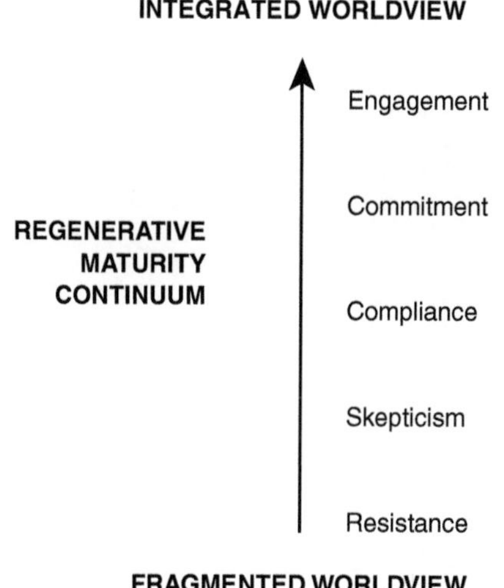

Figure 2.3 The regenerative maturity continuum: individual and organizational stages of moral maturity on the journey toward sustainability.

this situation. This could be due to their inability to consider the value of their real impact as individuals, or to a distrust of the evidence on issues of sustainability, as demonstrated by the dismissive attitude of some politicians toward the science of climate change (Brown, 2006; Gore, 2006).

At the next level, people engaged in sustainability efforts but mainly in compliance with external policy established by regulatory authorities at the level of local, state, federal, and international government, particularly when these threatened an organization's image or profitability. This also occurred when organizations came under increasing pressure from nongovernmental organizations and negative exposure in the media due to poor environmental management or unfair labor practices. This was followed by a commitment to sustainability, supported by the understanding of its importance, though this may not yet have been reflected in consistent personal or professional action. Finally, engagement reflected an integrated worldview, a global perspective that combined a high level of awareness with a willingness to modify decisions, choices, and behaviors that ensured sustainable and, in the best of cases, regenerative practices.

This increasing willingness to balance the common good with personal needs reflects a reduction of self-centeredness that may be expressed as a simple equation ($S = 1/e$), where sustainability (S) is inversely proportional to ego (e). If this relationship is legitimate, then regenerative practice may be viewed as the result of a highly developed personal ethics. This would make it possible for the continuum just described to be considered as a developmental model consisting of five stages, comparable to other models.

Table 2.1 Worldviews: a comparative table

Level of integration	*Regenerative mindset*	*Thought processes*	*Worldviews*	*Theory U*	*Hierarchy of human needs*	*Stages of moral development*
Level 5. Fully integrated	Engaged	Contextual/systemic	World centric	Mainstreaming Prototyping	Self-transcendence	Postconventional Universal ethical principles
				Crystallizing	Self-actualization	
Level 3–4. Partially integrated	Committed			Presencing		
					Self-esteem	Social contract orientation
				Sensing		
	Compliant	Analytical	Ethnocentric			Conventional
				Seeing	Belonging	Law and order morality Good boy/good girl attitude
Level 1–2. Fragmented	Skeptical Ignorant/			Downloading	Safety	Preconventional Obedience and punishment
	Resistant	Linear	Egocentric		Physiological	Self-interest
Worldview	Hardman	Capra	Wilber	Scharmer	Maslow	Kohlberg

Table 2.1 presents the findings on levels of engagement as a hierarchy, set against the developmental theories of five renowned thinkers in different fields, Ken Wilber (philosophy), Fritjof Capra (theoretical physics), Abraham Maslow (1943) and Lawrence Kohlberg (psychology), and Otto Scharmer (economics and management).

The highest level of consciousness identified here as engagement is reflected in Steve Seibert's comment on the need for people to "check their egos and their logos at the door," when working on large-scale sustainability projects. It is also clearly expressed in the words of Eve Williams, whose newfound passion for sustainable construction lay in having engaged in "something more important than me." Tony Cortese related sustainability to the need "to ensure that future generations and all of the species on earth can be sustained as a means to sustaining your organization." More recently, Cortese (2003) called this "the most serious moral and social challenge that humanity has ever faced." MaryBeth Burton also placed it within this greater context when she asserted that sustainability "comes from the awareness of how globally important this issue is. It supersedes any other issue. It's about human life on earth, the future of human life on earth."

Among the personal practices or inner work most conducive to awakening and deepening awareness and connecting to personal purpose, leaders reported that they set aside time for meditation and yoga (Coleman-Kammula), playing music (Laur, MacGregor, Thomashow), immersing themselves in natural environments (MacGregor, Singer, Thomashow), and engaging consciously in frugal or simple living (Coleman-Kammula, Burton). Chapter 6 provides meditation practices that I have found effective in the workplace when seeking to bring teams to higher levels of awareness and performance. While recent studies show that leaders have yet to reach the highest levels of consciousness required to move organizations toward sustainability and regenerative practice (McEwen & Schmidt, 2007; Rooke & Torbert, 2005), "we are beginning to understand the interplay of exteriors and interiors, and to recognize that development of interiors is a critical factor regarding large-scale and whole-systems change" (Schmidt, 2007, p. 27). As Schmidt affirms, it is only "amid wholeness – in contact with essence, pure consciousness experienced as presence – that we find the fundamental common ground of integral leadership and interior development" (p. 27).

Quadrant 2: connecting with others through keen observation and deep listening

Numerous leaders described a learning process connected with sustainability that involved suspending judgment after acknowledging that current practices in virtually all domains of human activity are unsustainable. The suspension of judgment pertains to the acceptance that traditional ways of doing things have brought us to the present globally unsustainable state of the economy, the environment, and society. It therefore becomes a precondition for sustainability, and even more so for regenerative practice, that we learn to bring to bear entirely different ontological, normative, and epistemological perspectives to reality. The leadership capacity to be "better able to listen to the whole than anyone else" (Scharmer, 2007, p. 20) involves engaging every aspect of human intelligence, mind, heart, and spirit in a profound disposition to perceive reality as it is, not as we are conditioned to see it. This involves the capacity to go beyond personal ego and a mechanistic mindset to activate a process of observation and listening to the most advanced practitioners with others, a practice that Scharmer defines as co-sensing and shadowing (2007).

Quadrant 3: eliciting collective purpose through generative conversation

Leadership for sustainability is exercised by engaging people in generative conversations focusing on sustainable development toward sustainability and beyond, to regenerative practice, as a central driving factor. This process is predicated on the genuine engagement of all internal and external stakeholders, and it is grounded in the quality of the conversations that are generated, in what Freeman (1984) defined as instrumental stakeholder theory. Recent studies have shown the positive correlation between stakeholder management through corporate social performance and financial performance (Ruf, Muralidhar, Brown, Janney, & Paul, 2001). Eschewing an authoritarian approach to change, effective sustainability is attained through the involvement of all players, within and without an organization, in the development of a collective culture grounded in the values of respect for the central importance of the individual's place in ensuring sustainable results. While on the surface this may not appear very different from current decision-making strategies applied in business, community, and education, the failure of these systems to materialize sustainable outcomes raises important questions regarding their effective implementation.

In the case of Coleman-Kammula's work in plastics, generative conversations took the form of workshops that brought together different industries, automobile, chemical, and beverages. The conversation centered around the transformation of waste streams into nutrients, by which the waste of one manufacture could become the raw material of another, thereby eliminating waste, reducing resource extraction, and the cost of inputs. In community, an example was provided by Steve Seibert's efforts to implement the goals of the Century Commission for a Sustainable Florida. In one particular case, the generative public conversation centered round a comprehensive strategy for preserving fresh water reserves in critical shortage areas throughout the state, while ensuring a fair distribution to all sectors of the population affected. The initial premise needed to ensure a successful outcome was that leaders, which included city officials, environmental representatives, and advocacy groups, must "check their ego and their logo at the door." The requirement that all involved had to divest themselves of their status as representatives of particular interests, so that they could be objective when considering the perspectives of others, regardless of their position, made it possible for a fair and successful water policy to be enacted through legislation, thereby ending what came to known as the "water wars." In education, this process was epitomized in the implementation process of the Curriculum for the Bioregion Initiative as described by Jean MacGregor at The Evergreen State University in Washington State. To the extensive listening and discussion process by means of which she and her colleagues engaged faculty in 52 (originally 32) colleges and universities in the state, they developed a comprehensive faculty and curriculum development program that ensured not only the design but also the delivery of an integrated sustainability-focused curriculum.

Quadrant 4: engaging in collective action to strategize optimal solutions to emerging futures

Once a collective culture for sustainability becomes integral to the status quo, it becomes possible for an organization to devise a cohesive strategy for sustainability. Unsustainable practices in organizations reflect a deep-seated ignorance of the inevitable long-term consequences of not considering environmental, social, and economic factors in all aspects of their business. At its worst, this can be conceptualized as a single bottom line (SBL) operation. For example, businesses which consider revenue generation and shareholder value, or greed in the definition of some, as their single priority would be classified as such, as the banking and automotive industries have recently demonstrated to such disastrous effect. Similarly, a nonprofit organization dedicated to feeding the poor using funding from philanthropy that disregarded environmental concerns and local empowerment, while doing so would also be considered an SBL operation. Educational institutions delivering fragmented curricula that ignored an integrative pedagogy promoting equity along with sound environmental and economic practices could also be classified as SBL operations.

The field of engagement and emerging consciousness

As the research evolved, there emerged a sense that there existed a dynamic interface between the internal and external worlds of the individual and the collective, shown in Figure 2.2 as the Field of Engagement and Emerging Consciousness. This interface appeared to act as the connecting and mediating space between the subjective realities of individuals and organizations and the behaviors they manifested in the objective world. As the study and work with organizations progressed, it became clearer that this indefinable space contained what could be defined as the seeds of regenerative practice, arguably the most important area of focus if regenerative leadership was to be understood and developed. In *Theory U*, Scharmer (2007) defines this space as a topsoil or "fieldgang," where this consciousness is nurtured to the point where it can emerge and give life to new behaviors entirely uncontaminated by previous patterns of thinking and doing. The metaphorical seeds alluded to here are defined as the potential for awakening a new mindset in the individual, to include a heightened sense of purpose, systems thinking, creative intelligence, a global ethics, and the ability to engage in working with ideal but unknown emerging futures. Similarly, in an organization, the seeds to be nurtured included transconceptual dynamics and triple-loop learning discussed below by establishing a culture grounded in generative conversation.

The indirect path of regenerative leadership

Connecting the four quadrants is the infinity symbol, chosen to represent the indirect, iterative process engaged by regenerative leaders in the achievement of sustainable practices at the individual and collective level. The regenerative leadership continuum, following this indirect path, is seen in the research and in the facilitation of organizational change processes as an iterative developmental process that acts less on the behaviors of others than on their values, assumptions, and beliefs, fostering a deep sense of empowerment and engagement that again calls to mind James MacGregor Burns' definition of transforming or transformational leadership (Burns, 1978). Regenerative leaders perceive themselves therefore as purpose driven and nondirective, seeking to coach others so that they may connect their own inner sense of purpose to their personal behaviors and to those of the organization or system where they work.

Circular systems of collaboration

Finally, the arrows surrounding the figure represent the heterarchical nature of regenerative leadership, labeled here as circular systems of collaboration. As organizations and systems become more interdependent, the distribution of power and decision making becomes increasingly diffuse, as collaboration across supply chains, stakeholders within and outside organizations become the norm rather than the exception in how they operate. Effective leadership across the boundaries of multiple systems, institutions, corporations, and communities requires leaders to develop the capacity to "check their egos and their logos at the door," as mentioned earlier. In high-performing organizations, all stakeholders are valued and included in the generative conversation that will lead to authentically regenerative practice.

Discussion

When fully enacted, the framework's developmental stages and leadership factors create a synergy that integrates the consciousness and actions of all individuals within a group. This synergy has the potential to harness individual and collective "minds, heart, and hands" (Scharmer, 2007) to bring to bear other faculties other than positivist rationality to creation and innovation. This process shows an evolution from the incremental and reflective forms of cognition that Schön (1983) described as single- and double-loop learning, to triple-loop learning, or awareness-in-action, which Starr and Torbert (2005) describe as a kind of "waking up, where you and the phenomenon become unusually present to one another, passing through our perceptual and conceptual filters with less distortion and more wonder than usual" (p. 3). This waking up is represented in the framework by the field of engagement and emerging consciousness. In this space, between the subjective and the objective realities of individuals and groups, lies the potential for creating a regenerative rather than a degenerative society. It is therefore the job of regenerative leaders to engage themselves and others in the inner work that leads to sustainable behaviors, rather than to attempt to control human behaviors. This shift in focus from the objective to the subjective world of values, assumptions, and beliefs gives rise to a coaching rather than a directive approach to leadership. In turn, this facilitates environments where risk taking and innovation become possible, defined here as third-order change, which Bartunek and Koch define as "a process in which schemata themselves become objects for continuous cognitive innovation and development" (1994, p. 25). They refer to the first two orders of change as within human cognitive capabilities. Third-order change, on the other hand, is a form of "transconceptual" experience, analogous to mystical rather than cognitive experience. Third-order change becomes viable when none of the current belief systems or schemata in an organization provides a satisfactory framework relevant to regenerative practice, and an entirely new schema, one that is disconnected from prior frames of reference, can be entertained. This requires the adoption of a multidimensional perspective of human personality that transcends the merely logical empirical approach to change leading to a collective process of inner development that can translate into organized collective behavior for regenerative practice and sustainability. Initially, this process can be enabled through the visioning strategy defined as backcasting. This involves collective envisioning of desirable futures and working backward to the present in order to map the intermediate steps that will make it possible for this future, and not others, to be achieved (Holmberg & Robèrt, 2000). It provides an opportunity for creating real lasting value for present and future generations, as it signals the possibility of acting with positive intentions across a wide spectrum of human concerns without the unintended consequences of strategies that rely on predicting the outcomes of goals established from the present.

This creative triple-loop learning process brings with it a number of challenges. It requires that we suspend all previous patterns of thinking to engage in a collective process of meaningful or mindful dialog (Isaacs, 2000). This type of work requires a "collective attention and learning," where the purpose of conversation is to "create a setting where conscious collective mindfulness can be maintained" (Romme & van Witteloostuijn, 1999, p. 240). This supports the more current trends that have substituted the process of building technical infrastructure to support knowledge capture, dissemination, and collaboration to building a human infrastructure based on dialog to create a shared field of meaning (Isaacs, 2000). This unleashes the collective potential for creating an organization capable of going beyond sustainability into regenerative practice. Herein lies the coming of age of sustainability.

Going beyond sustainability

Organizations committed to sustainable practices recognize the importance of addressing a triple bottom line balancing ecology, equity, and economics. Regenerative practice, however, does not end here, as working toward a triple bottom line may not necessarily be identified with restoring or regenerating surrounding natural and human habitats, which mounting evidence indicates as a growing need if we are to ensure a similar or better quality of life for future generations. In Florida, for example, the twenty-first century will require all businesses, communities, and citizens to establish a new consciousness and practice in the conservation of clean water. Beyond the triple bottom line, criteria for success enter the domain of regenerative practice and can be reported as the triple top line (TTL). According to Cuginotti et al. (2008), the TTL question *par excellence* is, "How can I grow prosperity, celebrate my community, and enhance the health of all species?" to which I have added "for all time." This and similar questions offer a natural lead-in to visioning strategies such as backcasting. This involves visualizing desirable futures and working backward toward the present in order to map the intermediate steps that will make it possible for this future, and not others, to be achieved (Holmberg & Robèrt, 2000; Robinson, 1990). This provides an opportunity for creating real lasting value for present and future generations, as it signals the possibility of acting with positive intentions across a wide spectrum of human concerns without the unintended consequences of strategies that rely on predicting the outcomes of goals established in the present (Merton, 1936). From a backcasting perspective, assessments of future scenarios "assume that the product or process exists in a sustainable society" (Holmberg & Robèrt, 2000, p. 295). Such practices introduce a new standard of product quality, performance, and success. Acting on these questions tends to build what McDonough and Braungart (2002) call a "design filter: a filter that is in the designer's head instead of at the ends of pipes" (p. 166).

This notion of regenerative practice was not easily identifiable in the organizations reviewed in the original study or in consulting and facilitation work. In business, Nike came closest to developing a regenerative strategy for the corporation. Beginning in 1997, it established its manufacturing strategy around the sustainability goals of "zero toxicity, zero waste, 100% closed loop manufacturing" by 2020. Using a backcasting approach, Nike then developed the goals and objectives most closely aligned with this end point. Examples of how this is being achieved may be seen in the push to develop products where synthetic and organic materials can be separated and recycled again and again, in a process known as upcycling (McDonough & Braungart, 2002). At a manufacturing plant in Europe, wastewater output is processed and redirected as input to begin a fresh cycle. Nike also went on to eradicate the unfair labor practices that had been standard practice until the end of the 1990s, shifting their corporate social responsibility policy to incorporate fair wages and improved working conditions. But not content with these achievements, the corporation also established a foundation to support young female athletes in the 40 poorest countries, as identified by the

United Nations. The outcome of these practices, while considered a high financial risk at the time, in effect led to increased revenue through stronger brand identification by consumers. Additional and very valuable learning emerges from this experience. To begin with, by leveraging the company's core business to do good, it has increased its direct positive social impact and recognition. This approach tends to be far more effective than deductible contributions made to charities, other foundations, or philanthropies. It has also generated greater internal stakeholder engagement, as the outcomes of the firm's philanthropic work are more visible and they are aligned with its own vision.

In community, the most salient example of a regenerative strategy was demonstrated by Nathan Burrell through the Honey Project, a microenterprise entirely run by high school students in Broward County, south Florida. Using high-tech skills, students have developed an Internet business importing honey from Ghana, Africa, and selling this organic product to a niche market in the United States. The proceeds from the sale of the honey are reinvested in developing the organic African beehives, and with the support of Citrix, Inc., the company has established a training center in the local community in Ghana. This comprehensive strategy can be viewed as an example of regenerative leadership. By means of education and training in business and technology, adolescents have learned the skills of developing a successful business with a social purpose, creating prosperity by empowering a disadvantaged community to develop a self-sustaining, environmentally sound local economy. Graduates from the program are supported in the development of their own businesses. Some of these have gone in the direction of profit-driven enterprises, whereas others have opted to develop new social businesses. Quite recently, the success of the initiative excited the interest of similar organizations in South Africa, and Mr Burrell and his students received an invitation to present their project at a conference in that country in April 2009. This opportunity will allow them to visit and work with the bee farmers, and from that contact and observation, the students will develop greater capacity to build new regenerative businesses. This project serves to demonstrate that regenerative community development can be promoted through the application of simple but creative ideas that generate revenue for all concerned, raising people's living standards while having a regenerative impact on the environment.

A good example of the integration of sustainability principles – economics, environment, equity – and education was provided by Dr Jaap Vos in his work with traditional farmers in the Netherlands. Though this initiative may not be considered truly regenerative, several aspects of the project are worthy of mentioning. To begin with, while teaching sustainable farming at the local university, Dr Vos encountered a strongly entrenched mindset in local farmers. Farmers believed that they needed to increase their crop yields every year in order to improve revenue. This was achieved by increasing the use of fertilizers and pesticides, which entailed more work and higher costs in equipment maintenance, use of fossil fuels, with the subsequent increase in greenhouse gas emissions and soil toxicity. Through a systematic process of engagement through conversation intended to generate trust and a willingness to modify their practices, Vos was able to persuade the farmers that it was possible to increase revenue with less work by eliminating the use of chemicals and turning to sophisticated organic practices. By lowering the overall costs involved in treating and maintaining soil, equipment, and storage space, the farmers were able to turn a greater profit at similar and even smaller yields, thereby breaking the cycle of artificial growth that was forcing farmers into ever more unsustainable practices. Given the drop in chemical runoff into the water table, these practices led to the improved health of local residents, increased recognition for the region's organic practices, and a subsequent increase in the demand and the value of their products.

The Regenerative Capacity Index

Further work has led to the piloting and development of the Regenerative Capacity Index (RCI), designed as a tool for the assessment of an organization's level of awareness of and ability to integrate the TTL in all its decision-making processes and systems. A sample of the RCI is included in Appendix 1, and the active assessment spreadsheet may be downloaded from http://regenerativeorganizations.com.

Chapter summary

This section provided a detailed description of the theoretical construct of the Regenerative Leadership Framework. This included an overview of its seven principal components listed in Box 2.1.

The next two chapters describe the actual developmental experiences of the dedicated leaders at all levels of their organizations in business, community, and education that gave shape to the regenerative leadership framework. Despite the diversity of their professions and of the size, nature, and importance of their organizations, the often surprising similarity of their perspective and approach to their work provides an insightful as well as a practical roadmap to leading for regeneration.

3 The inner journey

Check your ego and your logo at the door.

(Steve Seibert)

Introduction

Regenerative leaders are emerging, as will be seen here, from a wide range of backgrounds and experiences. This is one of the areas where, though they share common elements in their life stories, there is decidedly no single, compelling reason why they became attracted to engaging in sustainability work. Some of them speak of a clear turning point in their lives, an epiphany produced by influential events like the 1989 Exxon Valdez disaster or even as recently as Al Gore's "An Inconvenient Truth." In contrast, some speak not of a single event but of a number of smaller but significant instances at different moments in their lives, during their childhood, in adolescence, in college, and through their experiences in the workplace. Others recognize that they grew up with sustainability as a core value, as in the case of those born into a family that endured the Great Depression and continued to practice conservation long after survival needs were no longer a matter of daily concern. Yet others talk of growing up close to nature, a connection they lost over time as urban development encroached upon their natural environment, leaving them with a profound sense of having been deprived of the sense of freedom and independence provided by the outdoors. Others, with more than a little nostalgia, remember the short-lived environmental efforts of the late seventies sparked by the OPEC oil crisis and ensuing energy conservation efforts, later superseded by the appearance and rapid expansion of the "throw-away society."

However different their backgrounds, all of the regenerative leaders I have had the privilege to work with appear to share a common theme: *the commitment to sustainability through economic, environmental, and social regenerative practice begins as a very personal inner journey of awakening to a strong sense of purpose linked to a profound awareness of one's place in the natural world, and to the responsibility that comes with this knowledge*. The greatest driving force for sustainability, and what I have termed regenerative leadership in the most advanced of these leaders, is no longer the pursuit of any single bottom line, be it economic, environmental, or social, but the search for a purpose in life that integrates all of these perspectives into a meaningful whole. This chapter describes some of the more significant experiences I have collected of these leaders' personal journeys, and how these collectively have led to the development of the different components of the regenerative leadership framework.

Sustainability leaders in general are familiar with the history of the sustainability movement and of the most oft-repeated definition of sustainable development, as contained in the Report of the World Commission on Environment and Development to the United Nations (1987), entitled "Our Common Future." Better known as the Brundtland Commission Report, its second chapter states the following:

Box 3.1 Our common future (World Commission on Environment and Development, 1987, p. 54)

1 Sustainable development is a development that meets the needs of the present without compromising the ability of future generations to meet their own needs. It contains within it two key concepts:
   a The concept of "needs," in particular the essential needs of the world's poor, to which overriding priority should be given; and
   b The idea of limitations imposed by the state of technology and social organization on the environment's ability to meet present and future needs.

While they may be familiar with the conventional definitions of sustainability and sustainable development, from ongoing conversations and consulting with them, it is becoming clear that among these leaders, there is growing dissatisfaction with the currency of the terms to describe what they are attempting to achieve. From what they understand about the state of the planet, they believe that the term sustainability does not speak to the urgency of what needs to be done in business, community, education, or any other form of social organization, and that its widespread use and particularly misuse have devalued its power to act as a rallying cry for the changes that must be made. At least in part for this reason, the term regenerative leadership and practice has come to fill a much-needed gap in the definition of the change in perception and action that is required.

Of particular importance to corporations, universities, and communities, is the understanding in the most advanced Level 5 or world-centric leaders, as defined in the regenerative leadership framework, that lasting sustainability can only exist through the meaningful integration of all three concerns: environment, society, and economics. This is repeated time and again as the most central belief in the sustainability leader mindset across different professional fields. However, in each of these domains and at a lower level of leadership development, that of the ethnocentric Level 2, there exist certain preferences or inclinations which can lead to a double rather than a triple bottom line (TBL). For example, business leaders may emphasize issues related to the environment and how these can drive revenue generation, as acknowledged by Esty and Winston (2006). On the other hand, community leaders can tend to emphasize issues of poverty and marginalization, where environmental concerns are ignored. In fact, as has been seen again and again, in extreme cases, poverty trumps nature. These all point to a stage of evolution characterized in the regenerative leadership framework as a Level 2, or ethnocentric level of development. At this stage, it is still a challenge to convince sustainability advocates to suspend their sectorial agendas in favor of the bigger picture. Level 5 or postconventional, world-centric leaders in all domains, in contrast, express the need to go beyond sustainability into an expanded view that includes the notion of leadership for regenerative practice rather than mere sustainability.

These different emphases, and the higher level integration that can be achieved when environmental, social, and economic concerns are considered as equally important, are displayed in the Fractal Model of Sustainability in Figure 3.1. The tinted triangle in the center, connecting the three paired constructs of ecology/economics, equity/ecology, and equity/economics, represents the area of highest potential for regenerative practice and eventual sustainability. In this symbolically central area of engagement or heightened awareness, individuals and organizations no longer separate their core activity from the surrounding community or from the environment. All three dimensions are embedded as an integral aspect of the organization's identity and its mission.

The regenerative leadership journey

Sustainability comes from within

This notion of leaders who co-inspire others, and who by extension are themselves inspired, is at the heart of sustainability and regenerative practice. This was captured effectively by Jaap Vos, Director of the School of Urban and Regional Planning at Florida Atlantic University, when he spoke of the "third way" to achieve sustainability. This notion reiterated the importance of the inner work of leadership.

> There was a Dutch Minister of the Environment who said, if you look at sustainability or environmental regulation as a hoop, there are different ways of getting people to jump through the hoop. First way is by carrots, you hold a carrot, and they jump through it. The second way is by the stick, which makes perfect sense, they see the stick and they jump through it. But there's a third way, which is singing and dancing while holding tambourines. And I think that reflects what leadership is. It should be coming from within

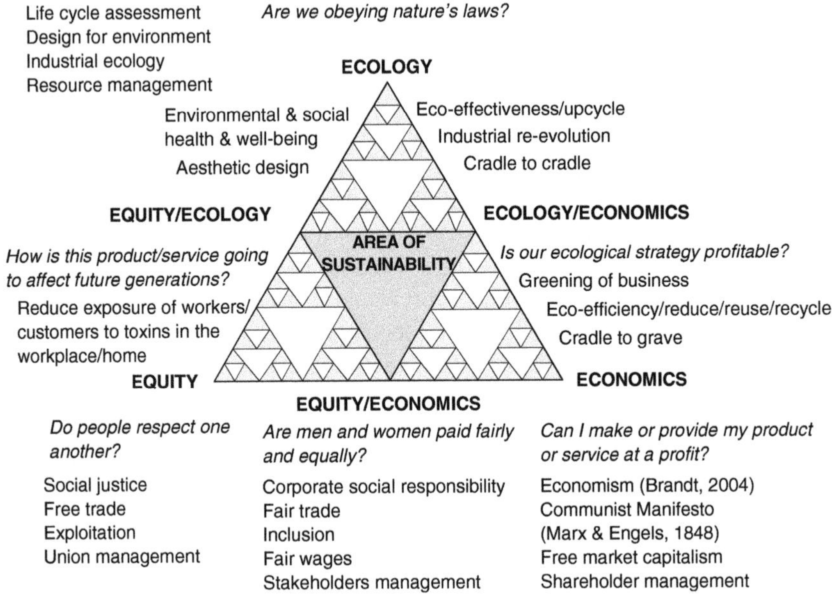

Figure 3.1 Fractal model of sustainability.

> people. And sustainable development should not come from the top, should not come from the bottom, it should come from within: From within the individual, the organization, the company. Otherwise you will also have to do enforcement. And it will always be a problem.

Vos' definition of leadership as coming "from within" resonated strongly with the reference of a number of the leaders in the three domains to the critical importance that leaders undertake what they called "inner work" and "inner change," which they defined as the development of a deeper awareness or consciousness of natural law and its implications for how individuals, organizations, and society must change in order to become sustainable. In the words of Joe Laur,

> I would say leadership for sustainability is first of all doing the inner work, within the individual, within the leader to surface their own mental models, particularly the ones that lead to unsustainable structures and behaviors. So we need to start from inner change.

There appeared to be a clear indication here that leadership for sustainability, and any effective kind of leadership that seeks to engage others in a collective purpose, starts with the leader's personal transformation, and to "walk the talk."

Anything less will not work. Joe Laur, Co-founder of the Sustainability Consortium of the Society for Organizational Learning, and co-author with Peter Senge and others of the recently published *The Necessary Revolution: How Individuals and Businesses are Working Together to Create a Sustainable World*, supported this view from a deeper perspective:

> So we need to start from inner change. Am I sustainable in my own lifestyle, am I sustainable in my impact on the planet, as Gandhi said, "we have to be the change we want to see in the world." The next thing is the willingness to risk, both inwardly and outwardly, and by that I mean to risk outwardly, by being able to put our opinions out there, our vision, our new points of view out there, even in difficult circumstances, even in reactive or retrenched organizations and systems, but at the same time to be open to influence from others, to be able to learn from others, and that we may not have the whole truth, and so to be a leader that has at least a semi-permeable membrane that allows exchange of good ideas and allows ourselves to be influenced. How do I hold true to my own beliefs, vision, and at the same time allow myself to be influenced by others, let that be a constantly evolving place.

Martin Melaver, CEO of one of the most sustainable real estate companies in Georgia in the United States, complemented Laur's words by linking the leader's personal values and beliefs, even a sense of struggle and vulnerability, to behaviors and how these can engage others by allowing their own values and beliefs, their sense of personal purpose, to gain full expression in the organizational context.

> Certainly some of the components [of leadership] have to do with walking the talk, being an evocation of those principles yourself; personally as well as professionally. It's not about breast-beating. It's just something, quietly kind of getting it, admitting that it's a struggle, acknowledging that it's a work in progress. So I think it's first and foremost about personalizing it, and being willing to expose one's vulnerabilities, not living up to fairly high ideals. There is a confessional piece to it, there's also an educative piece to it. But I think there's an advocacy that starts with self-modeling, an educational piece that has to do simply with transferring information and knowledge, and sharing of best practices and mistakes and those sorts of things.
>
> Beyond advocacy and education, it's really more about creating opportunities for others to realize that potential. I read a definition recently of leadership, that it is the capacity to get others to do to what you want them to do. And I would say actually on the contrary, it's getting them to do ultimately what they want to do.

In order to be sustainable, however, this freedom must be tempered by a higher level of values within a conceptual framework that promotes sustainability throughout an organization or society. Gregor Barnum, Director of Corporate

Consciousness at Seventh Generation, the green cleaning products industry leader, gave shape to this evolutionary model by asserting that:

> It's all about getting people out of old frameworks, in a sense building at a new level. So in that sense leadership is how an organization gets from the old white man hierarchical kind of framework into a holarchical kind of framework and build potential that allows for design at a whole different level. What you really begin to do is to think, Bucky (Buckminster Fuller) used to say this a lot, one of the last resources in the world is human potential, is human consciousness.

A holarchical system, as Arthur Koestler defined it, is a nested hierarchy of holons (Koestler, 1967). A holon is simultaneously a whole and a part of a living or social system. Koestler proposed that holons exist simultaneously as self-contained wholes in relation to their subordinate parts, and dependent parts when considered from the inverse direction.

This systemic awareness allows all members within an organization to operate from a qualitatively different level, where the old patterns of behavior that have led us to our current situation are no longer dominant in the stages of design, planning, and implementation. In *Theory U* (2007), Otto Scharmer has argued that decisions at the organizational level can ensure sustainability only if they consider "downstream, midstream, and upstream" processes within and across organizations (Scharmer, 2007, p. 77), which has meant that leaders have needed to embrace a qualitatively new management style. This is considerably different from the traditional command and control leadership style, or of management by objectives of the latter half of the twentieth century, as it tends toward a nonhierarchical, values-centered approach suitable for a more complex reality that demands continuous innovation and flexibility. Again, sustainability cannot be obtained within a single organization, a community, or nation, but results from global integration and interdependence. This need to go beyond the boundaries of organizations, to break out of the "silos" in education to ensure sustainability has contributed to the increasingly heterarchical nature of leadership, flattening hierarchies, and forcing leaders to learn the art of shared leadership within and across these holarchical boundaries.

Sustainability and human consciousness

A number of responses converged to support the notion that sustainability is inextricably linked to human behaviors, but that these are not necessarily the result of deliberate actions, but rather that they are rooted in the individual and collective level of consciousness from which we operate. Therefore, unsustainable social practices or environmental conditions such as climate change, short-term goal setting, depletion rather than preservation of natural resources, consumerism, among other effects, might best be conceptualized as symptoms of a low level of consciousness or human ignorance, what Ken Wilber calls egocentric (2000), and

Lawrence Kohlberg defines as the preconventional level of moral development (Kohlberg, Levine, & Hewer, 1983). At this level of understanding, the general response evoked in people is that of resistance or skepticism. On the other hand, higher levels of consciousness enable us progressively to recognize and comply with external regulations, then commit to, and ultimately engage in sustainable or regenerative practices. If this continuum is accepted as valid, then successful leadership for sustainability should be conceived not as an effort by one or many to modify external behaviors, but as a practice that seeks to enable individuals and groups to work on accessing deeper levels of consciousness. It is at these more profound levels that the individual's sense of purpose or meaning in life may be found (Frankl, 1984; Scharmer, 2007; Wilber, 2000). When successful, this process should lead to sustainability or regenerative practices as a matter of course, not as a response to external regulation or accountability. Quite simply, in this context, one just "can't not do it," as any other behavior would be an inconceivable violation of natural law.

A number of sustainability leaders emphasized the importance of this perspective of integrating consciousness with behaviors in a diversity of manners. In business, Coleman-Kammula, whose background of 27 years as senior researcher at Shell Oil led to the recent founding of Simply Sustain LLC, a successful sustainability consulting firm, expressed it as

> A way of being, which includes consuming. I think that can be at several levels. It starts with the self. We ourselves have first to realize our ways of being, and taking a stand on the way we live, I personally will take leadership and not over-consume, and not waste.

Taking this to a deeper level, Martin Melaver spoke of encouraging people to connect to a sense of personal purpose, to finding real meaning in their work. Linked to this internal dimension, he related sustainability efforts more to a developmental process that connected to action that was consistent with a search for personal actualization.

> It has to do with growth and maturation, personally as well as professionally, realizing one's highest potential, finding meaning and purpose. Really, it's couched more in a Maslow-like framework, hitting the higher end of that hierarchy of values. More colloquially, the following phrase is by an architect that is quoted in John Abrams' book, *The Company We Keep*, "Sustainability is doing what you are doing so that you can keep on doing what you're doing."

The ability to harness or engage people's personal sense of mission in order to drive sustainability would appear to run parallel to the capacity to connect to more profound levels of human consciousness, to bridge the external objective world to the internal subjective world of the individual. The leaders suggested numerous insights as to how engagement may be understood and accessed.

Speaking as an educational leader, Tony Cortese, founder of Second Nature, the top consultancy for higher education in the United States, and a founding board member of the Association for the Advancement of Sustainability in Higher Education (AASHE), cited Peter Senge's definition, "leadership is the ability to sustain people coming together to create a new reality." However, while this provided some understanding of what the process might be, it didn't explain how leaders were able to fully engage their colleagues and followers. Jean MacGregor, Director of the Curriculum for the Bioregion Initiative at the Washington Center for Improving the Quality of Undergraduate Education at The Evergreen State College, provided further thoughts as to how this may be achieved:

> Leadership is the ability and energy to inspire people to become engaged in work that is larger than what they think they can accomplish, and to motivate them to get involved, and in some cases to show them how to get started or to get involved. So it involves inspiration, motivation and actual teaching at times.

John Elkington, creator of the concept of the TBL in 1994, whose renowned work in global economics has shifted to social entrepreneurship in the past years, brought a number of concepts to bear in his definition of leadership for sustainability, when he asserted that

> Leaders are those who raise our sights, open out our time-scales, ensure we acknowledge the wider consequences of our existing and intended actions, and build critical mass for the economic, technological and social transitions that are now overdue.

Sustainability leadership as purpose driven

A second key notion in Jean MacGregor's statement related to the engagement of people in something that "is larger than what they think they can accomplish." Among other considerations, as many leaders asserted, sustainability involves a long-term view, an understanding that all sentient beings have rights equal to one's own, and the willingness to make decisions that consider the needs of future generations. In this context, inspiration does not result from leadership rhetoric, but from the capacity of leaders and followers to connect to something more important than themselves, something that will motivate the right actions even in adverse circumstances. MaryBeth Burton, former associate director of the Center for Urban and Environmental Solutions at Florida Atlantic University, was convinced that it "comes from the awareness of how globally important this issue is. It supersedes any other issue. It's about human life on earth, the future of human life on earth." Cortese supported this view by saying that

> Leadership for sustainability is really no different from leadership for other purposes, with the important exception that it is an extension of the need to

> ensure that future generations and all of the species on earth can be sustained as a means to sustaining your organization.

In *Bringing the Biosphere Home* (2001), Mitch Thomashow, President of Unity College, Maine, offered an even broader historical perspective when he spoke of the increasing prospects for what he called the sixth mega-extinction due to human impact on the natural environment. From the view of the experts in the field, therefore, the importance of the problem and of the need for appropriate leadership can hardly be overestimated.

Steve Seibert, from his experience with the Century Commission for a Sustainable Florida and his work in bringing sustainability to diverse communities at odds over critical issues such as clean water throughout the state, brought a fresh perspective on leadership, that of the value of suspending one's opinions, of becoming an active listener, and developing a sense of humility.

> It's difficult, then, to suddenly sublimate those opinions in an effort to be open to the variety of issues that make up the sustainability question. I went through this recently in Miami, just struggling to understand why this community is functioning so poorly. Having to listen to my political ideology being beaten around by advocates for that community, and realizing I just needed to shut up and listen. There is clearly a need to separate yourself from your ego. The whole conversation, by definition, is not about you.

Acquisition of new attributes

A number of leaders, when referring to this inner change that they believed to be central to effective sustainability leadership and to the implications this had for their personal and professional conduct, spoke of the need of putting one's principles to the test, despite resistance or possible consequences. This process, which several confessed created initial fear and anxiety, was perceived as leading to a powerful sense of empowerment and the willingness to take a personal stand. Joe Laur indicated that once the old and obsolete mental models had been revised, it became an imperative to demonstrate the

> Willingness to risk, both inwardly and outwardly, and by that I mean to risk outwardly by being able to put our opinions out there, our vision, our new points of view out there, even in difficult circumstances, even in reactive or retrenched organizations and systems.

At the same time, opening oneself to others in this way was not a one-way but a two-way process, which demanded that we

> Be open to influence from others, to be able to learn from others, and that we may not have the whole truth, and so to be a leader that has at least a semi-permeable membrane that allows exchange of good ideas and allows

> ourselves to be influenced. So there is a little bit of a tension. How do I hold true to my own beliefs, vision, and at the same time allow myself to be influenced by others, let that be a constantly evolving place.

Darcy Winslow, former business director at Nike and senior advisor to the Nike Foundation, spoke of acquired courage and of therefore "being comfortable going into the realm of the unknown and untried," and Seetha Coleman-Kammula referred to a similar experience, product of introspection, and a call to action:

> And as I thought about it more, I wanted to speak out about it fearlessly and to share my thoughts and my insides, and that's what leadership means to me. And to try and influence others' behavior, but that's not always guaranteed.

Eve Williams, LEED Projects Manager for the City of Tallahassee, Florida, from her community perspective expressed a similar view, adding a moral dimension to implementing sustainable construction standards in Tallahassee, Florida, that forced her to go beyond the limits that her otherwise easygoing nature would consider:

> I got there by pushing. We are not going to be told to do it, we are not going to have to implement a policy saying our buildings have got to be green or LEED certified, we are going to do it. We are going to serve as leaders for the community to say the city is doing it. I don't want us to have to mandate it. I want us to do it because it's the right thing to do.

A multiplicity of turning points

One of the most significant findings was that there were few similarities between leaders' first experiences and their resulting commitment to sustainability, both within and across the different contexts of business, education, and community. In effect, three broad categories were to emerge in this regard. Whereas some were able to single out a major event or experience that had brought about the change, others could identify two or three important turning points, while yet others spoke of a lifelong process, a gradual awakening to the value and importance of sustainability to their lives and to the lives of others.

Examples of leaders who had experienced some form of epiphany were Dr Daniel Meeroff, Environmental Scientist in the College of Engineering at Florida Atlantic University, who indicated that his choice of career was indelibly connected to the Exxon Valdez oil spill while he was still in high school.

> And this is about the same time that the Exxon Valdez disaster came, and I became very excited about this concept that they were bringing up in the news, about bioremediation and how microorganisms that are already there can be used to clean up a toxic spill for you instead of bringing in

> machines and making the situation worse. It was an elegant concept, sort of a natural attenuation approach, relying on natural processes. I did a two-year project on oil-eating microbes, and received an award for developing two methods that worked. That's what made me decide to become an environmental scientist.

A similar experience was reported by MaryBeth Burton. Though her educational background and experience in environmental studies went back over two decades, she identified a clear turning point, in her case at the time she saw the Al Gore film "An Inconvenient Truth," an experience that was powerfully reinforced when she attended a sustainability conference at the University of Florida.

> I see it as an awakening, there was really an almost "AHA!" moment. It started with "An Inconvenient Truth." I was unaware of the gravity of the situation, and that began it but that wasn't it, specifically. It actually was last year's Campus & Sustainability Conference at the University of Florida. I went, and I had an opportunity, I was staying on campus in a hotel room, and I was really, really impressed, and here I was at a conference and I was asked to bring my own badge holder, my own coffee mug, my own conference bag; we weren't given a bunch of crap. We composted our leftover lunch scraps. It sort of opened my eyes to everything that can be done, organizationally, and that for someone like myself to be promoting sustainability in the greater community, the first step is at home, both in my personal home, and my organizational home, to become more sustainable.

Among the leaders in the business world, Darcy Winslow identified her major turning point quickly and clearly. This had to do with the day she found out about the different chemical components of the Nike shoes and their effects on the environment:

> I will go back to April 14, 1997, which was literally the day that I changed course, and that was when Bill McDonough and Michael Braungart came in. At that time I was running our Advanced Research and Development Division for Footwear. It was made up of about ten different departments that focused on biomechanical research, advanced materials research, advanced engineering, design, product-testing, and so on. It was about at that same time that I was beginning to ask myself the question, "There's got to be more to life than just creating the next gadget on a shoe." And in come Bill and Michael and they showed us what was in the Air Pegasus, and I was like, "Oh, my God! There it is. Do we really understand the long-range implications of the investments we're making today as an Advanced R & D group?" If what we invest in today doesn't play out for two, to five, to ten years, are we really making the right decisions, asking the right questions, at the point of investment? And so that was the shift for me, and I've never turned back.

Seetha Coleman-Kammula, of Simply Sustain, told a story that was as much personal as it was professional, though the major turning point also came from a single, heartbreaking experience in India, the country of her ancestors, which served to give shape to feelings that had been brewing in her life:

> Several things came together. My own personal life, our own personal life, was life balance, was a search for balance, "this is not sustainable," we can't keep it up, we'd moved many, many times. Going to work on airplanes our bodies were getting tired. Our lives were feeling empty. We didn't have friends, we didn't belong anywhere and I was missing a lot of things out of my life. Our children had moved out of the house so there came a point when I said, "What am I doing?" And that I think was the first step.
>
> In terms of how it came about in the work I do, on my trips to India, increasingly so, how the whole of Indian society manages waste, particularly plastics, and the environment. In India nothing came in plastic packaging until about 5 or 10 years ago in the retail stores. And there is no solid waste management, and even Gandhi I think lamented Indian's lack of societal cleanliness and responsibility, you know, we just throw things away. It was just creating such a mess in the street, it was unbearable for me and I started to wonder, "What's happening? What can I do about it?"
>
> And that's really brought me into questioning. The other thing is the societal not just the environmental aspect in India. The poorest of the poor were often going through the heaps of rubbish on the street corners and picking out every morsel of plastic with their bare hands, going through pretty filthy and ugly mess, and that too turned my stomach. And I said "try and understand what is going on" and that led me to look at the physical aspects of plastics, what are good and what are not good. These are plastics I helped to create; I worked in the plastics area for Shell for more than 27 years. I didn't realize, of course, that at the time we developed all these products I was head of technology and head of business, and we sold them, it was a big "Aha!" to me one day I said, "You know, in all the time I did the research and developed and produced and sold these things, I never once asked myself the question, what happens to them at the end of their life?" Never did as researcher. If I had only asked that question I am not sure that we would have produced them with no technical solution at the end of life. And we wouldn't have designed them for non-recyclability.

Gregor Barnum, the Director of Corporate Consciousness at Seventh Generation, identified a particularly critical moment in his life when he realized how important environmental, social, and economic sustainability could be. In his particular case, this initial experience, sparked by moral revulsion, led to two further powerful phases in his life, the first of which had to do with his personal quest for a more satisfying philosophy of life, a quest that then led naturally to his current work with Seventh Generation:

Let me give you the personal part of this. My grandfather and his brother started a company called Rockwell International. It's now changed its name. And in 1984–1985 Rockwell had one of the worst, compared to the Exxon Valdez accident, one of the worst accidents in U.S. history as it goes in regard to environmental accidents. And I could see in the midst of this company that there wasn't a level of taking responsibility, there wasn't a level in which anybody in the company was going to rethink how they were doing business so that it was doing good rather than just making money.

And so at that point, from a sustainable or regenerative perspective, how do you look at the level of creating social justice while you make money, how do you look at this idea of really seeing what business is? Is it just the old Adam Smith coming through, is it just this thing of take hold of the stockholders and make them as much money as possible?

Or is it, given where we are, in the sense of building economies for people throughout the world, to hold people throughout the world? Is it a form that we have not yet conceptually taken on? And so, the quest at that point, and that was a turning point, was beginning to cue into people who had worked with Buckminster Fuller. Bucky had definitely the right idea, of how do you begin to design more with less, more and more efficiency into it, and at the same time to design for the well-being of all. And the next turning point was, working with 7th Generation, really beginning to see that when you take the Iroquois quote, which was the quote that we took the name from, is that how do you in every deliberation consider the impact of that deliberation seven generations down. And in that moment you've got to hold that. And so that becomes a way in which you begin to see, so that was a turning point.

In the context of sustainable community leaders, Dr Cecilia Campoverde, who was elected Social Worker of the Year for Palm Beach in 2007, and nominated for the same title for the state of Florida that same year, dismissed her prior work in Florida as less important than her current, far more ambitious social enterprise in a remote village in Guatemala:

I would say that it was really because of Hurricane Mitch, and what happened after that. Up to that point I had been a social worker and I thought I was a community organizer. I had started one, two, three agencies. But when I reflect on what I have done, those agencies were, for the most part, services agencies. Although in one of them we had a particular service, which is, because it still exists, mental health, nevertheless, I am sad to say, that most of the mental health services that are provided, and that we at the agency that I had also provide, were individual-oriented. Meaning, we worked for the individual to get strong, to cope, and that is not it. Now I am convinced that unless we mix, and we recognize obviously the impact or the involvement of the individual, but there are other factors that are perhaps much more important for that individual to be able to do something and to sustain her mental

> health than her willingness to just do it. And that is the environment; that is the employment factors; that is the economic solvency; that is the education that is capacity, the opportunities that a person has had to really be able to think critically. And if a person hasn't had that, all the good thoughts that she may have, or he may have, about getting what we call self-esteem is for naught.

Dr Campoverde's passion comes through strongly in her narrative:

> When we went to Guatemala because of Hurricane Mitch, and I saw a community that had been working so much, so diligently, in whatever they could, which was agriculture, which was to serve their masters at their masters' farms. And really they had not much by our standards, but they had a donkey, they had some pots, they had some chickens. And to them, that was all they had. And the whole thing was torn apart; they were left with nothing; literally, with nothing. I suppose some people during Katrina also were left in that way. It is a different experience. So here were these people, in an empty lot, with nothing. So somebody has to provide the resources so that that person who has shown to be a worker, and to have sustained their lives all along serving others, can either continue to serve others or, who knows, maybe start their own little bit of business. At that moment I realized, there is nothing that I can say to these people, self-esteem they have it, strength they have it, desire to live they have, desire to give their children the best, they have it. So what is it that they don't have? What we can give, the money, the opportunities, the wood for them to make a house; the money for them to start a little microenterprise. And at that moment, the whole thing fell into place. And now I am convinced. You have individual responsibility, but this is nothing without social responsibility.

At the other end of the spectrum, other leaders could identify no single moment in time when they became aware of the importance that sustainability had in their lives, but had become aware of it as a long process involving incremental change. Michael Singer, President of the Michael Singer Studio, a design studio that focuses on regenerative practices in major construction projects, recalled that

> It begins as a kid and recognizing that the most nourishing places for me were natural places, not human built. So I would seek solace, I would seek fun; I would seek spiritual connection in places that were natural, even though I grew up in an area that was suburban. I looked for those places, those sanctuaries. Then as I got older I began to recognize that I wanted to fill my life with places like that rather than the built realm. After college it took me about 15 years of work to allow myself to actually intervene in a place to really create a change.

> It wasn't until the mid-1980s that I made a piece that actually altered the way you experienced the place that forever changed that place. I felt I had gone through an initiation lasting years. When I finally did it I took a deep breath, and said, "Wow that's a step, that's a real change to anything I've ever done. I've actually allowed myself to intervene to change something forever, and I felt I had earned the ability to do that."

A similar case was made by Martin Melaver, who indicated that he had grown up in a family:

> With a strong orientation towards environmental and social issues, so I grew up with it, sort of the oxygen you breathe. So there was no transformative, catalytic moment, just part of what you get up and do every day. At a certain moment, you wake up and you realize that you are taking somewhat unusual steps. I think it comes from Gregory Bateson's famous notion of ratcheting up the temperature, of warming up water very slowly over time, small incremental steps every day.

Judy Walton, Executive Director of the AASHE, also spoke of an evolving awareness since childhood, as she recalled that

> I didn't experience an epiphany or a sudden change. It was really just a deepening of understanding. It started in second grade, when my teacher said, "If you had to carry in a bag all the waste that you threw out your whole life, it would be a very big bag."

Melaver also referred to increasing external pressures to relinquish those ideals as impractical or idealistic, and even laughable.

> What's interesting is what Warren Bennis (2003) says in *On Becoming a Leader*, that we should spend much of our adult lives unlearning the things that we have been taught. I think that the things that we are taught early on, not explicitly but implicitly, is that those values that we grew up with have been imbued with something impractical or idealistic, or they don't make any sense, or are laughable in some way. Learning to shed that armature of skepticism is a critical piece, but I don't think that's something that happens overnight. I think you just slowly kind of chip away at it. So what if someone calls me a tree hugger the next day, is that a bad thing?

Shifts in mindsets and behaviors

Similarly, to the diversity of responses regarding the turning points in their lives when they recognized that they became committed to sustainability, the leaders had a variety of memories that illustrated the shift that was produced in their mindset and how this related to sustainability or sustainable development. For some, it was part of a lifelong process without a clear beginning, whereas for others, there was a clear dividing line, an awakening, to a new perspective, where they felt drawn to becoming sustainable in their lives and their work. While some spoke of their own personal or professional mindset, others extended their responses to include a strong critique of Western society, most notably with regard to consumption patterns and their impact on sustainability. In numerical terms, 13 of the leaders had experienced defining moments in their lives that brought to a commitment to sustainability, education (5), business (4), and community (4). Eleven spoke of having always been aware or immersed in a sustainability-conscious environment, business (4), education (4), and community (3). For the majority, this had to do with the fact that they had grown up in close contact with nature in a family environment where conservation or political activism was part of their everyday lives.

From his experience in sustainable real estate, Martin Melaver asserted that for him,

> there are no grand moments, but there are a lot of little quiet moments every day. And with those quiet moments come shifts in mindset. I can remember early on being involved in real estate, feeling a certain unease driving through the Atlanta urban scape and for a long time trying to put my finger on that unease.

For Joe Laur, the shift in mindset related to a growing awareness of interdependent systems that forces us to acknowledge that sustainability does not end at can recycling, but has far-reaching implications for everything we undertake.

> I think the main change is becoming more acutely and more broadly aware of systems, and systemic functions and systemic impact, both for good and for ill, so realizing that simply recycling my soda cans, while admirable, is not really going to effect a systemic change. Realizing the need to root out what the systemic structures are, find leverage points, points of intervention that will have the largest impact on moving that system. Also, recognizing the non-linearity of systems, realizing that a flower doesn't gradually open over a period of two weeks. It's just sitting there getting ready and suddenly Poom! When the conditions are right there is a whole sea change in the system.

Along with some of the other leaders, Darcy Winslow related the mindset issue to both her work with Nike and her personal life. In her case, the shift was also more gradual than sudden.

> In 1997, as we began to embrace sustainability we included the simple question: Is it sustainable? At that time we were still relatively unsophisticated in the complexity of this undertaking and were naïve enough to just ask "Is it sustainable?" We quickly determined there wasn't a yes or no answer. It forced us to unpack that question. Fast forward to today, it has become embedded in

> our decision-making process that permeates the company from design, engineering, advanced research and development, transportation and manufacturing – to name a few critical areas – to a level that is far beyond the tipping point.

On the personal plane, she indicated that her sustainability mindset operated as a value system, guiding her decision making and her choices.

> It's become part of my value system, and determining where I will and won't work, and what jobs I will and won't do; it has to be at the foundation of whatever that job is. If it's not, it doesn't matter what the salary would be, I wouldn't do it. I have been a follower of sustainability for a long time before it was ever called sustainability. I have been in this for about 20 years. One thing that happened to me right after my M.S. is that to me it has become more of a cause and a broader thing than just a job.

For Seetha Coleman-Kammula, the shift in mindset had not been great, mainly because she and her husband historically had led a frugal existence. She was the first leader to bring up the concept of consumption as an issue of concern, which others would refer to later on. She also was the first to refer to a personal practice, yoga, and physical exercise in her case, as conducive to a deepening of her mindset.

> I think it's a physical set as well as a mindset. A big change is a lot more conscious. Yoga and physical fitness and practicing the breathing and reflection, more deepening I think, in terms of mindset. I can't say that there's been a great change in our consumption pattern; we have always been pretty frugal about that. So in terms of going from spending and eating a lot, to eating and spending less, I don't think that's happened. I don't think we really have had a great change in mindset.

Gregor Barnum, on the other hand, as cited in the Preface, affirmed that in his mind, the awakening process was more sudden. Though expressing some reluctance to use the comparison, he believed that the shift in mindset was similar to an instantaneous awakening or modification of one's consciousness. He related this shift to the presencing process Otto Scharmer outlined in his *Theory U* (2007), which in turn, Barnum asserted, acknowledged the contribution of philosophers and thinkers such as Buckminster Fuller, Goethe, and Hegel. From these, Barnum extracted the notion that much of the human mind is as yet untapped, and he laid part of the blame with education, particularly with current colleges of business, which he accused of continuing to teach programs inconsistent with the urgent need to address sustainability issues.

Eve Williams remembered what she and society were like at the time of her childhood and adolescence.

> When I was in school in the 70s and 80s, there were so many of us who were so energy conscious. The more we read about it, the more we talked about

> it, the more it tied in with me in the 80s, when I first started having my children. I started doing things like use cloth diapers. I intuitively knew that manufactured diaper would take a very long time to break down in the landfill and knew this couldn't be good. I reused everything I could so I wouldn't have to throw it away. I had read about a family of four out west that was able to conserve, reuse and compost so much of their garbage that they only had 4 bags of garbage in a year. I thought if they could do, then so could I. I made my own baby food, conserved water and stayed away from chemicals as much as I could. I owe it to the upbringing of my mom who use to (and still does) reuse, recycle, and collect rain water ever since I can remember. My mom came from the Depression era. She was always conserving everything.

Williams also argued for the need for a spiritual dimension to be brought back into the human experience in order to make sustainability possible. In herself, this has allowed her to become less self-centered, which in turn has brought about a new understanding of how her actions affect others.

> The inner self and the spiritual, it's got to come back into this to make us say this may not be the best thing for all of us, the whole world, to live in this way. This whole process has helped me to get outside myself, quit worrying so much about me and what's happening inside, more looking outward and how my actions are affecting everything around me. Now the changes I'm making I'm stopping every time I start, I look at everything I do and I think how is this going to affect something else. What kind of consequences is this going to have?

As a veteran social worker, Cecilia Campoverde confessed that she had become intolerant of society in general, of her own profession and academia in particular, which she accused of hypocrisy and of being "out of tune with reality." And this intolerance had led her to break with her past and to commit to a far larger undertaking, that of retiring from her work as a university professor to take up the challenge of living and working in community she co-founded in Guatemala.

> My mindset is at the point at which, in a very great way, and actually concerns me, I have become intolerant of society as a whole. I have become intolerant of my own profession. I have become intolerant of what I call hypocrisy. People thinking that they are doing things. When you really go deeper into what they are doing, they are doing nothing. I have become intolerant of academia. I am teaching research and I take my students through the methods of research so that we can have some basis for a conclusion. But in these research articles that we are reading, on a scale of 1–10 there may be 0.2 of the bases for saying what the authors are concluding, and yet most people, not knowing really the strictness of research, believe everything that

> is said, and we promote that, and I am getting a little bit tired of being part of this whole farce.
>
> And so this whole change of mindset that has happened to me has led me to want to, and I am doing it, to dedicate my whole life, including my finances, to something that I am doing, that I am seeing change, because I am trusting the people with whom I am working. And what I am doing is only opening the doors, putting the money available in there, purchasing a farm.

Jim Murley, Chair of the Florida Energy and Climate Commission and former Secretary of Community Affairs under Governor Lawton Chiles from 1994 to 1998, asserted that before his own mindset change, his training had provided him with a set of initial professional skills that "presented endpoints in terms of limitations: You shouldn't build any higher than this, or you need to minimize the impact of that." Once he had come to understand some of the implications of implementing sustainability initiatives, he realized that he needed to modify his way of thinking quite radically. In this new mindset, the traditional limitations of project viability and time scales had to be reconsidered, particularly as this approach involved future generations as part of the process.

> I had to start thinking about developing programs that operated on incentives and broader goal statements, even goal statements that didn't appear to be feasible, aspirational, they could probably fit in a framework for community building and redevelopment, because the new generations would have an opportunity to look at how to do this. So for a specific agenda, my mindset would have been thinking about the future in terms of from 2000 to 2010, updating your community plan in that ten-year decade, that census decade. Today, we are working on a 2060 plan, at a minimum, because we feel that if you don't think that far out you lose the ability to have a certain level of discussion, about issues evolving and adapting rather than being confined in a given time frame and being driven by the data.

From her work with refugees in the Balkans in the 1990s through a grassroots organization and later an American NGO, Rebecca Bardach confessed to a shift from a "general sense of commitment, and of idealism, believing in a capacity and obligation to try to create change and improve the world," to a pervasive sense of depression that had come over her as she came to realize how little of an impact she was able to make on the lives of people who were suffering during that terrible time. As she recounted:

> I was able to come to terms with the fact that the war had caused terrible suffering and could manage to not feel overwhelmed or depressed by it as long as I felt I was part of action that was addressing the issues in some way that was significant, even if incrementally so. While working with refugees in Hungary, where the challenges are very much about dealing with the day to day limbo of being a refugee, you could feel you were having an impact

> through short-term actions which temporary relieved some of the monotony, boredom, sense of purposelessness inherent to being a refugee; or through helping people reach their long-term goals of either return to Bosnia, family reunification, or resettlement to a third country. In Bosnia it was quite clear that the problems were so interconnected and extensive that you could only really have an impact, measure change, over decades not over days or months, or even a couple of years. It was also clear that any one change was contingent upon a series of other changes occurring, and that the power of the individual to affect change in a relatively short span of time was tremendously limited.

This affected her deeply, and it took her some time until she could come to terms with some of the tragic circumstances she encountered. She also referred to the importance of a short- as well as a long-term perspective for sustainability efforts to be effective.

> So my mindset now has turned to a balance between accepting, incorporating all those different mindsets, and approaches, being more accepting that it's about a very gradual process of working hard, always trying to be thoughtful of short term and long term, and just continue action and commitment with reflection combined.

In regard to his work as Executive Director of the Century Commission for a Sustainable Florida, Steve Seibert indicated that he used two questions to help people focus their collective mindsets.

> The first one was "how will this decision affect folks in the future if there's no immediate gratification?" The second builds on a personal predisposition for consensus building and collaboration and tying things and people together. I am a mediator by trade. My reputation is one of being a consensus builder. That's what I've always been. This effort in sustainability tends to draw out that kind of personality trait. It is all tied together. One question I asked fairly early in the century commission was "what is the Florida you fear in 2030?" That was one of the most productive conversations we had as a commission. Everyone had their own take, many of which were similar. People were going to be very concerned about environment degradation, transportation, affordable health, racial tension. As we started putting a list together, we clearly saw lines of connection between and among these different interests, these concerns. One of the board members said, "I get it, they're all tied together." That was a poignant moment for the commission. It is something I believe – that it's all tied together. My mindset is that it's all tied together. There is no separation, either between people or issues, when you're talking sustainability.

Seibert and his collaborators' discovery that "they're all tied together," referring to environment, transportation, affordable health, racial tension, was a significant finding that connected to Laur and Barnum's use of the concept of the interdependence of systems. In this framework, linear thinking characteristic of the modernist mindset is superseded by the awareness that reality is an integral whole. Seibert's question on Florida in 2030 also linked up to the numerous references to the long-term mindset necessary for sustainability.

In his case, Nathan Burrell, founder of The Honey Project, a high school student social entrepreneurship organization in Broward County, Florida, reported that his mindset changed radically after the crash of the dotcom boom. From the heady sense of excitement and unlimited possibilities that the technology bubble produced in him, he was obliged to rethink his life and work, which led him from the business of technology to social entrepreneurship, and to a renewed need to become self-reliant in order to ensure sustainability.

> After the bubble burst, after the shift, you realize that the limitation is within yourself if you're not planning to be sustainable. The change for me was recognizing that you have to look within yourself, you're talking about community development and building, you have to look within the community and the members of the community, and the people who are involved. The change in the mindset says that "We now have to be self-sufficient and reliant on self because without that you are limited in your potential. Only through sustainability is the potential unlimited."

John Elkington confessed that his mindset changes may be considered out of the ordinary, particularly when one considers his renown in the world of global economics. However, he indicated that these had come later in life, since he felt that his original viewpoint had remained virtually unchanged.

> No, I think it was hard-wired from an early age, at least on the ecological front. The social and economic pieces came later, but the mindset changes weren't exactly where you'd expect them to be. For example, I gave up economics at University in 1968 because it seemed to have very little to say about what was going on in the world – and what then needed to happen. I later had pretty much the same reaction to much of what passed for sociology and social psychology, though the areas addressed by all three disciplines have turned out to be crucial in the work I do.

MaryBeth Burton asserted that she had always held a sustainable mindset, and that this hadn't changed over time. However, in recent times, her normally positive outlook, in face of increasingly negative scientific evidence, was no longer quite so easily sustained. In her mind, this state of affairs, however, could work in favor of bringing people to work together in community.

> I try to stay focused on that positive opportunistic outlook, though there are times when it feels overwhelming for me, when you look at the science, and look at the impending doom of it. But I do think it's a great opportunity for

humanity to come together, for community to come together, for more people to wake up, like myself.

Dr Leonard Berry's sustainability mindset was honed through his experience with United States Agency for International Development (USAID) in the Tanzania of Julius Nyerere in the late 1960s. At the time and over a period of 2 years, USAID produced a six-page definition of sustainability that it was "eager to send out to the missions." Berry had some clear ideas as to how this affected how he thought about sustainability issues, though he was rather vague about his thinking prior to this time.

> So I think that out of that whole process over two or three years my mind became much more focused on not only what sustainability was but how you might begin to implement it in ways which dealt mostly with the natural resource base, the land, water and vegetation. But it's very hard to go back and say how I felt before that.

Another professor, Daniel Meeroff, had a clearer picture of his mindset prior to his own change.

> Just ignorance. I had never heard of the greenhouse effect or hydrocarbons before that time. It just opened my eyes to a whole new world. It opened my mind to chemistry, biology and the interactions with the human environment; to some of the things that we were doing in our everyday lives, for instance looking closely at products and reading what's on the back of packages. Finding out what those big, long words mean. Are they good for us? If they kill ants, what do they do to us? All these questions started coming up. That's what led me into this [environmental engineering] degree program. I wanted to know what these things were and their effects. I didn't know yet to change lifestyle choices and such.

Similarly to Len Berry, Jean MacGregor also underwent a profound change of mindset during her own experience conducting fieldwork in Africa. MacGregor offered an illustrative metaphor to describe the type of thinking that is characteristic of the person engaged in sustainability issues, that of the butterfly mindset, which she related to one of Ray Bradbury's short stories, *The Sound of Thunder*. She used these analogies to illustrate the interdependence of life, and the far-reaching effects that every one of our actions can have on our surrounding reality even to the furthest corners. In the Bradbury story, one of the time travelers unwittingly affects the distant past by stepping on a butterfly, an action that apparently leads to vast consequences for his own time when he returns.

> I think that my African odyssey got to my heart and my gut in ways that the book work and the graduate school work didn't, because the human-biosphere interface all became profoundly real; to be on the eastern edge of

the advancing Sahara; to be in a train station with 400 homeless lepers in the Sudan; to be in Kenya and talk to people about the tensions about the elections, even as we've read about them now, those tensions among ethnic groups were very real even back in the 70s. To be on the ground in the Kalahari and to become acquainted with the last communities of hunter-gatherers who had essentially occupied a place for, as far as people could tell, for tens of thousands of years, who were now being displaced by other people, pastoralists, who were now arriving in those places, who thought *they* had a perfect right to be there *also* because they'd been in southern Africa for three centuries. That sort of created those mind-and-heart paradigm shifts around the broad field of human ecology, so that every act in one's life, whether it's shelter, food or transportation, the purchase of a pad of paper, it all has a narrative that's highly interconnected.

MacGregor made reference also to Mitch Thomashow's *Bringing the Biosphere Home*, which she indicated called for what she believed should be the "kind of thinking that we should all aspire to, that is, a kind of biospheric thinking." During his interview, Mitch Thomashow himself indicated that in his case,

> It was not a transformation that was singular as much as that it was an emergent narrative. There are themes that have been in me ever since I was a child. At the age of 58 I can look back and say, "Oh, my gosh! When I was five years old I was thinking about certain things but of course there was no way that I could articulate them." So it's just sort of an emergent narrative throughout my work and my life, heavily influenced by other people and other writers, and changing contacts in American public life and global change that I've observed over the course of 58 years.

Tony Cortese brought virtue into his conceptualization of the sustainability mindset, and acknowledged the moral responsibility that comes with knowledge.

> I think that one of the most important solutions for me is to understand, just by virtue of living, and even by trying to live a virtuous life that I had an impact that is far beyond any negative impact than I had ever conceptualized. So it's a sense of understanding that now that I have knowledge that the way that I live has a negative impact on many other people of the world as well as lots of biological species, it leaves me with a different sense of responsibility. Now that I know what I know, I feel that I have an ethical duty to try to live my life in a way that will minimize the negative impact that I have by virtue of my life, and to help others to do the same.

Key priorities in the current agendas of regenerative leaders

Education and equity

From ongoing conversations and work with leaders professionally engaged in furthering regenerative practice, when asked to describe their personal agendas regarding sustainability, they indicated that they considered education as their greatest priority. As Michael Singer expressed it,

> Education has a primary role. It helps people question their beliefs. For example, consider the beauty of not having grass. It takes careful, creative approaches to education to help people realize the benefits, the beauty of this new vision, acceptance of the best practices. Education is about helping people learn different ways of looking at the world.

Joe Laur supported this perspective, describing education as critical for organizational and societal change. In his new role as vice president of content of Greenopolis, an online environmental resource funded by Waste Management, Laur stressed the importance of learning in dispelling people's blindness to sustainability issues.

> The first verb of our subtitle is learn. Learn, Act, Reward, Together. We really want to bring in educational institutions, K-12, secondary education, both to provide content and we also want to be a resource. We want to bring in Waste Management, which touches 10,000 schools, and 21,000,000 households. We really want to create this repository of knowledge, like a Google Earth crossed with the Library of Alexandria. And have a valuable resource for educators: Education and learning. People need to learn. People are not dumb but they are blind.

Laur considered that this learning must "to be done in community," which he believed to be "local as well as global." He also indicated that "nations have to get together as well as companies, and industries as well as neighborhoods." Greater levels of education have an important impact on communities, he asserted, particularly when they are directed at women. He also linked sustainability to poverty alleviation, which raised the issue of equity, the importance of which was shared also by a number of leaders. In Laur's case, he related the importance of education and poverty alleviation to a simple practical fact, that of the environmental devastation that occurs in situations of extreme poverty.

> The higher the level of education, I think in general, and empowerment and education of women particularly, economic and political empowerment education of women; birth rates drop, communities prosper, and so forth and so on. If you know your children are going to live to adulthood you don't have to have six or twelve, you can have two or four. I think sustainability is about

> alleviating poverty too, because if I can't feed my family I can't care about the planet. I am going to cut down the next tree, I'm going to take that next action, I'm going to do whatever it takes so that my kids will live for another day.

Darcy Winslow had a similar perspective, particularly after having transferred, at her own request, from Nike, Inc. to the Nike Foundation. Due to the fact that the mission of the foundation is "to support adolescent girls and poverty alleviation in the least developed countries in the world," she said that she had had occasion to come to understand "what it truly meant to integrate the social equity piece." She indicated that "it's been an unbelievable learning opportunity to understand the deep-seated issues around social inequities in the world and how we need to take action to create a different future." In practical terms, the work of the foundation consisted in

> Looking at these issues by sector; so whether you sit in government, the private sector, the public sector, as a donor, faith community, we need to take action and make investments to ensure that generationally we have a positive impact on peoples' lives, and in this case the 600 million girls in developing countries that are all but invisible.

This commitment to adolescent girls in emerging countries had become a clear priority for her because, as she had come to realize,

> Adolescent girls are one of the greatest investments we can make, not from a future consumer perspective, but how women enter the formal economy, and the opportunities and education they may or may not be given. If we invest on a global scale, the impact they will have on their family and their community can and will change the world. Right now I see a huge chasm at the highest level between the work of foundations, of businesses and sustainability, and therein lies the opportunity: How businesses begin to embrace long-term adaptation strategies. That's where I sit right now.

Seetha Coleman-Kammula also shared that equity and education were a priority within her own agenda. This new perspective had arisen from her initial interest in working to diminish the impact of plastics on the environment in her own country, India. In this effort, she had come into contact with extreme poverty and its effect on children, and how she may play a small part in making this situation better.

> In working with children in slums in India, education is so fundamental to getting them out of the slums, the schools exist without teachers, there are teachers with no schools, there are no toilets, the children just drop out, they don't make it, they go into child labor, so one of the things that really appeals to my heart, and I know this has no chemistry, no plastic

> component, just purely the emotional side of it, is we are starting to think about what we can do to change that, in a very small way perhaps, in the town where my mother lives, so I am going to go there next week. We are looking at mentoring programs to encourage children; we can't take up the vacuum of the lack of schools, that's really the government's job. What the government can't do and nobody can do is give them psychological support, and give them hope and encouragement, and information, and what else is possible, how life can be different, give them a different perspective on it. So we are thinking of just connecting information for them using university students to adopt them and mentor them.

Gregor Barnum's agenda also included a strong ethical perspective. When added to concerns for the environment and included as part of capacity building within an organization, he believed that this combination had the potential to evolve into a regenerative economy.

> First of all, building capability in everybody, and secondly, looking for more and more ways to evolve. The essence of the company is not just built on the environment but also on how we can have an impact, a social justice impact and an equity impact on the world. So we know what we are supposed to do on some level environmentally but we really want to find more and more ways to impact the social sphere. And then more and more we want to begin to find how do we impact the environment, how do you create regenerative systems, that are related to society and the earth so that you are delivering higher and higher levels of product that are feeding into a regenerative system, so that you are actually seeing an economy that evolves itself through regenerative ideas.

Eve Williams summed this perspective up simply but elegantly: "You see, the social issues, it's not just about equality; it's about the quality of life."

Expansion and acceleration

For others, their current priorities involved their search for ways to improve, either by increasing or decreasing the effect they had on the natural, social, and economic environment. Given a change she was about to make in the way she approached her work with the community in Guatemala, Cecilia Campoverde described this as "We are going to have to go macro." In her case, and due to the fact that she was about to retire and settle in the village in Guatemala she supported through her foundation, she was referring to the need to extend the project's international network of donors and volunteers to ensure continued support for the project until it became sustainable.

In the case of Rebecca Bardach and her work with refugees, this had more to do with the frustration of learning the job on her own, and of the importance of networking with others whose expertise could have provided her with much needed skills that would have allowed her to have a greater impact on the communities she worked with. She believed it was important to find a time and a place

> Where people have the chance to learn about, and think about and take a step back from what they are doing, and realize that there is a broader context within which they can think about these issues and connect with a broader network of the government, or international organizations or other immigrant groups, in order to improve what they are doing. Often I have been in situations where I have been asked or have fallen into being responsible for whatever I have worked on, and I have felt that I was reinventing the wheel, because there was no one to give me guidance. And I was aware there were lots of people out there who had done this, but I didn't have access to them. And so you were just fumbling along, in the dark, close to the ground trying to figure which way to go. And I have felt that if I could just have access to experienced people and expertise in that area it would just catapult me forward many steps, so that's how I see this. Many people are out there doing it, that I do believe that there are things that we can learn from each other and no one has all the answers but we can learn together that will move us forward and give us that broader perspective that will improve what we are doing. So that's what I am trying to create, and I believe that will be far more sustainable.

Debbie Koristz summarized this desire to improve one's impact on the world by referring to her perspective on her own contribution to sustainability.

> My biggest goal in life is really to leave this world a little bit better than I found it, in any way that I can. It's just such a big goal, and I am only one little person, but basically that's my driving force. Relative to sustainability, it's something that I need to work on every day, in order to really make it something sustainable, that is going to last. On a personal level, I would like to believe that we all want to do that, because even when we educate our kids, teaching them right from wrong, that's basically what we are trying to do. I think my existential goal is that, beyond the fact that I work within the Jewish community; I would like to think that in my own little, little way, even in my every day actions, hopefully I am trying to leave the world a little bit better than I found it.

Steve Seibert indicated that he could think of at least three important items that made up his sustainability agenda. One of these was personal, and related to how he sought to reduce his own impact on the environment and society. More broadly, he referred to some of the critical issues he believed the state of Florida currently faced or would face in the very near future if serious consideration were not given to them.

> The first is an understanding of what natural systems must be preserved, or conserved, to keep a certain quality of life and to build a sustainable state.

> That's a relatively complex discussion but it's one that we need to be having. One of my commissioners said, "If we're supposed to envision the future, we need to know what we can't touch first, we need to know what must be preserved." We've started to map these things, going through a process of very sophisticated GIS-based mapping exercises, bringing a number of GIS scientists across the state together to talk to each other about their layers of data. Getting them to talk about what they think, collectively, are the greatest priorities and putting them down on a map. Then, taking that map to people who own land and saying, "What do you think? Is this a communist overthrow of property rights or a fair conversation about the future of Florida?" This long-term natural element, to me, is really important. It leads to the second issue, which is the preservation of working lands. This is a very big question. I used to ask it when I would give a speech. I'd ask, "Do you believe we will have commercially viable agriculture in Florida in 50 years?" Often, the answer is "no." I find that scary as hell on about 19 different levels. The continuing viability of working agricultural and rural lands is essential to our future. You can only get there by total involvement with agricultural interests. You can't do it for them, but do it with them. The third issue that sits in my heart all the time is the loss of a hopeful next generation. It is the incarceration rates of young black men; the lack of education. It is the growing disparity in economy in many parts of Florida, and many parts of the world. It is the experience and the dream that I had and assumed everybody had and then reality told me that it's not true at all. This issue is about that people piece of all of this, the social piece of sustainability. If only half of your population has truly crafted a sustainable future and half hasn't, then you're not a sustainable community. I'm very, very concerned about this. It has cultural, racial, and historical aspects to it that we just have to talk about. This notion of two Floridas is very, very concerning to me. In sustainability conversations, people tend not to look seriously at the three legs. It goes back to this collaborative thing. The whole thing is we tend to fall into one of the camps. I tend to be more related to the growth management stuff because that's my background, but doesn't that have something to do with affordable housing and inner city redevelopment?

He concluded his description of his personal agenda by offering a short phrase that could be considered a *leitmotif* for the sustainability mindset. When referring to the mental attitude of the sustainability leader, he said, "My job, one of my passions, is to keep all these balls in the air."

From his experience in working with disadvantaged communities, Nathan Burrell concluded that he no longer believed in the effectiveness of programs, as these "come and go." "My hot button issue today," he asserted, is

> Really finding business models and areas where we can go in to provide sustainable economic development. We have no more interest in doing programs. I think some of the areas of need are outside the actual market system

> and the free enterprise system in those areas. So the hot button for me for that agenda is how we go in and jumpstart free and mixed market enterprises, and get the communities involved in the process in the prevailing market system of their area. Those are the hot button issues for me, in making sure that truly those areas are being addressed for poverty alleviation and sustainability. That's what gets me out of bed. I have traveled round the country and to several emerging nations, and doing community development, that is actually it. Programs come and go.

John Elkington held an agenda with a strong sense of paradox attached to it since he held two different though related perspectives. These were "the sense of being part of the biggest global movement of our time – and a concern that our civilization is in the process of going down the ecological tubes." Though he acknowledged that the global movement toward sustainability was very encouraging, his overall outlook was less than optimistic, particularly in that which related to the decimating long-term effect of disease on the human population.

> I suspect we will never get to 9–10 billion human inhabitants of the planet, because we are in the process of unwittingly building an incubator for pandemics that will apply a degree of demographic correction. Easy to say, but I have read enough about the history of the bubonic plague, the Spanish influence post-WWI and SARS to not look forward to this.

For MaryBeth Burton, her agenda was similarly connected to a social phenomenon. In this case, however, her concern related to a different type of disease, defined by some as the compulsion to shop or "affluenza." In developed countries, the accumulation of wealth that has made it possible for people to acquire possessions and to lead lifestyles that bear little relation to the satisfaction of real needs has led to the consumer society, which she considered unsustainable for a number of different reasons. In Burton's view,

> This is part of the awareness issue. And this has been bothering me for a long time and I wasn't aware of it consciously. It's the issue of consumption, and the issue of American culture and American society, telling all of us that for us to be or feel successful, we need a large house, a large car; we need the latest gadgets; we need manicures; iPhones. There was a part of me that was really troubled by it. Was I a part of it? Very much so, but now I feel that's another area of awakening and awareness that drives my sustainability. It is the realization that that lifestyle that so many of us are pursuing is not making us happy. We are making a dying; we're not making a living. We're spending more time at work, we are more stressed out; we're not living our lives. We are not spending time with friends and family, in nature, enjoying and experiencing all the beauty of life, which is the interactions with the land, and animals and plants, and people. We're losing that, and it's really no wonder that people are so miserable and stressed out. And

> I want to get off that. That's my personal motivation, to really jump off that treadmill. As part of the simple living movement, I am taking a magnifying lens to my life and identifying what is really important to me and not spending money or time on those things that are not really important to me. I'm spending conservatively so that I can accrue a nice nest egg to stop working for money. And that doesn't mean to stop working because I think that the primary motivator in my life is to continue to make the world a better place.

In response to this concern, Burton had become committed to what she called "living the simple life." This effort, however, was enormously challenging in isolation, which had led her to develop a growing network of like-minded people.

> Teamwork is especially important. Coming from the simple living mindset, we are clearly a minority in this country, people who are actively pursuing a simple life. The challenge is that you feel very disconnected from most people, especially now during the Christmas season. I don't go to malls; I don't look for the best buys. It's not my mindset. When so much of our culture and society is so focused on consumerism, it helps to find people in your world who are doing the same things as you in terms of sustainability. I am also on the board of Trash to Treasure, that's another manifestation of how I am trying to improve sustainability by reducing waste and consumption. But finding these people within the university and other networks to team with on specific initiatives and also to be social with, it helps to sustain the sustainability drive within me.

Len Berry's agenda emphasized the need for dissemination of the importance of sustainability issues. He considered that this was most effective when questions were addressed "from a topical sense, climate change in general, or water in Florida, and with as a broad and educational outreach as possible." He also considered it critical for environmental and social issues to be connected in people's minds and actions. In his opinion, this was achieved by

> Preaching the message to whoever wants to listen, talk to school kids, talk to public groups; but on demand, not on a soap box. I think it is very important to get the message out, I think we are collectively trying to do that in a variety of ways. The whole subset of climate change sustainability, if you use those titles you will come up with very similar sub-agendas to all of those. I think that the environment is so important that it should be a mode of learning that everybody should take. It should be a vocabulary, a literacy that everybody should take.
>
> And then, how do you relate environment and society? In my mind it's very straightforward. My hairdresser doesn't know where his water is coming from. And the relation between people and environment that was pretty straightforward in rural areas, and is pretty straightforward in rural areas, has to go through a different translation when we're dealing with city dwellers,

> and that each and every one of us needs to understand that the whole basis on which the globe operates is a natural basis and doesn't come out of a can. And the relation that exists is discordant. I would include that as one of the missions that we all need to have through the schools and the universities, but also through the community organizations, getting the simple message across.

To some extent, Daniel Meeroff shared MaryBeth Burton's view on the importance of awareness, on each individual's mental ability to make sustainable connections, which was where he focused his own personal agenda as an environmental engineer.

> I normally ask the question, "why can't we do something?" or "what are we doing to block something?" I'm always trying to find out why we aren't doing the simple things. If we don't do the simple things, we're just living the same way we were. It's not sustainable. We can make some changes, but what's preventing us from doing so? Usually, everywhere I've gone, it's not the desire to do it that is the problem. Everyone wants to do it. There's always something else that they can't get around. Sometimes it's lack of education, or lack of dollars but we can always find a way around it. Environmental Engineers are problem-solvers; I think that's why I became an engineer. If this road is blocked, we can go around and it won't take much effort to do that. And that's the way we do things. I work a lot with Dr Bloetscher, who's across the hall. We both went to the University of Miami, and one of our classmates, who was a very highly recruited student, his mantra was "if we can chlorinate the Caribbean, we can all swim in it," which is a highly ridiculous concept. Engineers look at things like that; they don't see the other parts of the reality. There is the physical reality and then there's everything else. And we impact all of that, no matter what we do. So, can't we find some way around some of these issues? That journey is what makes my job fun. Every time I find a solution to a problem that has been stopping this for a long time, that's how I get my joy from what I do.

Jaap Vos, on the other hand, indicated that for some time, he had begun to consider issues of equity from a very pragmatic perspective as an important part of his personal agenda. In his view, equity should not be considered just because this was the right thing to do, but because of the very real consequences that can arise from situations of inequity.

> Where I used to be a real environmental, sustainable development kind of person, I'm starting to look more and more at equity considerations. Because I feel there is more and more inequity, and more inequity leads to more and more instability and makes it continuously more difficult to find solutions. When we are sitting in this meeting and they are talking about getting the Deans to get involved in sustainability, I agree with the directive, as they are

> absolutely right. But the Deans have to deal with budget cuts, and if they have to choose between recycled paper and a faculty line, it's very simple, the educational component is more important. So I think you need to look at equity, you need to provide opportunities, and if these are not there …
>
> So it's not just the environmental component, people focus too much on the environmental component when they think of sustainability. The first time I read the Brundtland report I thought what a bunch of baloney. But I think equity is becoming increasingly important. What is missing from the three-legged stool of sustainability is a system of governance. Because this all has to happen within a system of governance, which also has to be sustainable. Part of that of course depends on what your area of expertise is. I'm interested in urban areas, in the built environment and how it relates to the natural environment. This doesn't mean that I am not interested in people. And if you are an environmental scientist this may not be a major consideration. It took me a long time to look at these equity considerations. Now I think that it's important. For me, that would be becoming increasingly important in my sustainability agenda.

Judy Walton's agenda also considered a shift in people's mindset as critical to sustainability. In her case, she spoke of the importance of increasing people's consciousness and broadening consensus with regard to sustainability issues.

> I think we need a really deep cultural transformation; a new way of thinking about the world. That to me is a tremendous challenge and I wonder whether inevitably it takes a crisis to happen or whether we can get there on a voluntary basis. I struggle with that, and my agenda, then, is to get as many people on board with this deep cultural shift and not simply tinkering at the margins. The other struggle I have is with the idea that it's good to get people partially on board, gradually becoming more aware, and assuming this will lead to deeper behavioral change. I'm all for that, and I don't discount their efforts, but I'm concerned that this can sometimes lead down a non-productive path. For example, buying green. If that leads people to consume more thinking it's environmentally benign, that's not a solution. Or take biofuels – look at the problems we face as we start mass-consuming corn and other crops for biofuels. That's not the answer we need. So my agenda personally is figuring out solutions that are leading in the right direction and not down a wrong path with all the best intentions. And that's not easy. I wish I had the answers, but I think it will ultimately involve a strong deliberative process, the leadership of government, and a change in the mindset of how we live our lives and how society is organized. It'll involve a tough, introspective look at the way we structure society, including our economy. It's ultimately about the survival of the human species in socially just and healthy ways. There are many ways that we could survive that wouldn't be so pleasant, or healthy or just.

Jean MacGregor described her own efforts at The Evergreen State College as her professional agenda to further what she called "the work of this century," and she then went on to outline the agenda she held for her own personal sustainability.

> Professionally, what is moving me most is learning how to best support these faculty communities to enable those individuals to sustain what we have started together. I'm in "Year Four" of what I hope will be at least a decade-long initiative. I'm in year one or two with these faculty learning communities. So what propels me right now, and has me excited when I wake up every morning, is how I can continue to enable, inspire, and motivate these communities of people to keep learning together, and to deepen their own commitments. Secondly, how do I help faculty engage with students and become leaders in the same way I described earlier, around motivating, inspiring and teaching students, when the knife edge between a fuller ecological understanding and a sense of community and agency, to make a difference on the one hand, and denial or despair on the other, is so prominent. It's the work of this century.
>
> In my personal life, with my spouse, we already have a pretty low carbon footprint, but how can we make it even lower? How do we do that? We do a lot of talking and thinking about that. That's my personal agenda, along with how to find those personal, reflective strategies for self-care so that we are not the problem that we are trying to solve, that I just described. I play the harp, and I try to put my hands on my harp every day, even it's just five minutes, because it's so uplifting. I have no aspiration to play concerts; I just love to play music. For myself. And I try to be out of doors in nature every single day, again even if it's just for a few minutes. And I'm fortunate enough to live very close to the college where there is also close access to wild nature, so this is personally restorative. So these are my contemplative moments, my kinds of meditation.

Tony Cortese's agenda contained three particularly important items, the first of which was global warming, which he considered critical if any of the rest were to have an opportunity of being attained.

> One is global warming; I think it is the greatest threat to us as a species and our life support systems. That is positively out of sync with all other life support systems. There is no way that we can solve all the other social, economic and health challenges that we face as a society, and we cannot create a peaceful and secure world unless we reverse that. The second one is that so many people here and around the world are having such difficulty in having a modicum of a decent quality of life. This means that I cannot sit back and say I've done some things with my life, maybe I can sit back and do some more reading and writing and commenting on the world. A third that is driving and is related to both of those, is the fundamental flaw in higher education that continues to reinforce

> that humans are separate from nature, that we are the pinnacle of creation, that we are the dominant species, that whatever we do in society is going to be sustainable and fine. The reason that I work with higher education is because here the mindset is reinforced that we believe that the only way to understand the world effectively is by taking all the pieces apart, and to compartmentalize knowledge and encourage specialization, as opposed to integrating our knowledge and thinking about whole systems solutions to everything. And that reinforces the idea that the problems we have are not a bunch of interdependent problems, but a large number of individual problems that are separate from each other. We have economic problems, political problems, social problems, population problems, national security problems, and they are viewed as competing and hierarchical, where one is more important than the other as opposed to being interdependent and systemic. And the third thing that drives me on a day to day basis is how the higher education system is failing us; how it's getting more expensive and how it's not helping to move society in the way that we all want it to move. The lack of holistic thinking results from that in every area of society. I believe, and many scientists believe, that one of the most important views about global warming is that this is the first "environmentalition." I think of global warming as a civilization and moral issue, as much as an environmental one. And one of the things that is very interesting about global warming is that this is the first time in the 40 years that I have been doing work that the scientists have been more worried than the general public or the policymakers. In virtually every other one it has been the other way round. For me, that is very worrisome.

Finally, Mitchell Thomashow of Unity College confessed to a sense of personal hypocrisy as a central item in his agenda. In spite of the efforts to foster sustainability in his work, he confessed that his lifestyle was less than sustainable, and that this caused him concern. However, he was also able to list some of the very worthwhile efforts he had developed to compensate for this failing.

> My life is still filled with hypocrisy. I like to travel places, I am a musician; I like synthesizers. My personal agenda, I'd probably like to be a little more circumspect in that regard. We are building the green president's residence, which is actually going up in a few weeks. It will be a zero carbon, solar home in rural Maine, 1900 sq. ft., where we will try to demonstrate that you can live well, entertain the public, in a small rural college. I think that is part of my personal sustainability agenda. Based on my prompting, we are a couple of weeks away from releasing a journal, "Hawk and Handsaw," reflecting on sustainability, it is really beautiful, excellent writing, coming out annually. And the idea of the journal is for people to talk about the contradictions and challenges inherent in trying to build a sustainable life. There's nothing really quite like that. Most publications are rather self-righteous. We are trying to cut through that. And it's hard to do well, and there are a lot of contradictions in doing this.

Discussion

Although the leaders' personal journeys to sustainability were dissimilar, occurring at different stages of their lives and for different reasons, their leadership mindsets at the time of the interviews demonstrated striking similarities. As will be seen from this discussion, some of the findings align with current theories of leadership, particularly James MacGregor Burns' definition of transforming leadership (Burns, 1978), Donald Schön's (1983) conceptualization of reflection-in-action, Senge's (1990) initial work on vision building, mental models, personal mastery, team building, and systems thinking, and Collins' (2001a) description of Level 5 leadership. However, other findings show a departure from these theories, and introduce fresh perspectives that give rise to new conceptualizations of what I have called regenerative leadership as appropriate for addressing change for sustainability.

A number of the leaders had reached the conclusion that sustainability, as a construct used to define and delimit their field, had become insufficient to describe the full scope of the work they did. Their sustainability efforts had gone beyond environmental actions such as reducing, reusing, recycling, or corporate philanthropy and equal opportunities in personnel recruitment and retention. Their personal and professional work had provided a more sophisticated understanding of the complexity and urgency of the problems associated with sustainability, which had led to a more integral response to environmental, social, and economic issues. As Tony Cortese expressed it, in a truly sustainable situation the three linked circles of environment, equity, and economics, as displayed in the Venn diagram with a central area of sustainability where the three overlap should be visualized as a single circle where all three dimensions are subsumed. The capacity to operate from this fully integrated perspective of natural and social systems would have the greatest potential for engaging in successful sustainability efforts. In the more successful cases reported by the leaders, their efforts had given rise to surprising and unanticipated positive consequences. These included a more robust bottom line through greater competitiveness and cost effectiveness, a restorative rather than a sustainable impact on the environment, and a renewal of social and economic structures due to the manner in which they engaged their supply chains and their communities.

As the findings revealed, numerous leaders considered that one of the most important aspects relative to making regenerative practice possible lay in deliberately increasing personal awareness through what Joe Laur called "inner work," the willingness "to surface and change one's mental models," particularly "the ones that lead to unsustainable structures and behaviors." This personal transformation was seen as a key to understanding the complexity of sustainability and of connecting this comprehension to a sense of personal purpose that Scharmer and colleagues defined as the often subconscious source, the blind spot, from which we operate (Scharmer et al., 2002). As Scharmer et al. asserted,

> We believe that an important blind spot in 20th-century philosophy, social science, and management science lies in *not seeing the full process of social*

> *reality formation*. We see *what* we do. We also form theories about *how* we do things. But we are usually unaware of the *place* from which we operate when we act.
>
> (p. 6)

In a conversation he held with Otto Scharmer regarding this internal consciousness development process, Master Huai-Chin Nan, a noted Chinese Taoist–Buddhist–Confucian scholar and teacher affirmed that

> What has been lacking in the 20th century is a central cultural [unifying] thought … We have not gotten into the center: What is human nature? Where does life come from? What is life for? Where does consciousness come from? No one can answer those questions today.
>
> (Cited in Scharmer et al., 2002, p. 7)

Scharmer et al. frame these questions within a conceptualization of leadership as appropriate to a shift in how we perceive reality. Arguing that the economic foundations of the world (of business) have been transformed from stable to dynamic patterns, "characterized by forming, configuring, locking in, and decaying of structures, the nature of leadership changes too. In this new environment, real power comes from recognizing the patterns of change," and by developing and deploying the capacity "to sense and seize emerging business opportunities" (Scharmer et al., 2002, p. 3). Scharmer (2007) formalized the process for illuminating our blind spots, which he asserts are "revealed in our theories and concepts in the form of deep epistemological and ontological assumptions" (p. 22), in a framework he called Theory U. In essence, Scharmer proposes a radical shift from linear thinking, based on the industrial age model of efficiency, growth, and consumption, to a systemic approach that suspends the use of traditional behaviors by integrating human thought, emotion, and will to stimulate a collective process of "co-sensing," "co-presencing," and "co-creating" entirely new solutions to current problems. This re-appraisal of the key role of the individual and collective subjective experience in the world of work has implications that Scharmer et al. express as follows:

> As we move from product- and service-driven stages of economic development to an era that is driven by an experience economy, the issue of developing a sound method for accessing experience will be of the utmost importance for leadership and strategy development.
>
> (pp. 6–7)

For the study leaders, the ability to develop a sustainable mindset, to "learn to tread lightly" on the planet, had involved what they reported was a highly personal process. This related to something beyond a limited positivist epistemology of practice or "technical-rationality," critiqued by Donald Schön (1983) in *The Reflective Practitioner*. Similarly to Schön's theory of reflection-in-action, the leaders highlighted the importance of engaging the visible world, the world of sensory experience, with the invisible world of subjective experience, in a dialectic process. This ongoing dynamic, which Rosch (1999) calls "primary knowing," reveals that mind and world are not separate but part of a unified whole. As she indicates,

> Since the subjective and objective aspects of experience arise together as different poles of the same act of cognition – are part of the same informational field – they are already joined at their inception. If the senses do not actually perceive the world, if they are instead participating parts of the mind-world whole, then a radical re-understanding of perception is necessary.
>
> (Rosch, 1999, p. 20)

Rosch's "radical re-understanding of perception" is central to making sense of reality as it is, not as we believe it to be, or as we are conditioned to see it. Gregor Barnum alluded explicitly to the importance of this awakening for a sustainability mindset to be attained. This process, however, is not viewed as an end in itself but as a purposeful means to an end, since it leads to the development of pertinent frameworks for sustainability. In Barnum's words, "the quest is how to get, using a very systems-oriented approach, a level of frameworks that actually creates well-being for all; well-being for the earth."

The leaders noted that by working on the interaction between the subjective and objective fields of attention, they were able to develop increasing sophistication of knowledge, understanding and skill in working with issues of sustainability. The contention here was that personal behaviors could only be as sustainable as the consciousness from which they originated, in that dynamic Schön called reflection-in-action (1983). Where regenerative leaders differ from Schön is that they consider that the accelerating speed with which natural and social environments are deteriorating precludes the luxury of testing out theories and learning from their mistakes, which Schön called reflection-on-action. This concept is further discussed in Chapter 4 in the organizational journey to regenerative practice.

From their different perspectives, all leaders spoke of the importance of checking "egos and logos at the door," of recognizing that leadership in the context of sustainability was most effective when it demonstrated the ability to listen actively, to engage in collaborative and generative conversations, and to empower others by considering all leaders' contributions as central to effective sustainability. In essence, if connecting to a personal purpose through inner work was essential to becoming effectively engaged in sustainability, this same emphasis needed to be integrated within the culture of an organization, and across related organizations. In the pursuit of authentically regenerative practice, therefore, a shared or collaborative leadership style was considered as possessing the greatest potential for success. This success was made most possible when all those engaged in the endeavor, whether leaders or followers, shared the goals of sustainability as a collective purpose. This relates to aspects of what Burns (1978) defined as transforming leadership, the premise of which is that,

> Whatever the separate interests persons might hold, they are presently or potentially united in the pursuit of "higher goals," the realization of which is tested by the achievement of significant change that represents the collective or pooled interests of leaders and followers.
>
> (Burns, 1978, pp. 425–426)

The impact of transformational leaders, though not devised with sustainability in mind when initially defined, is similarly directed at inner development. Bass indicates that leaders of this kind are capable of "raising colleagues, subordinates, followers, clients, or constituencies to a greater awareness about issues of consequence" (Bass, 1985, pp. 17–18). This heightening of awareness requires a leader with vision, self-confidence, and inner strength to argue successfully for what is right or good, not for what is popular or is acceptable according to the established wisdom of the time. The personal journeys of the leaders in this study strongly resonated with the developmental perspective of Avolio and Gibbons (1988) in their work on the life span construct of transformational leaders. In their study, they found that development entails

> the accumulation of both minor and major events across one's life span … which establishes a basic framework for interpreting future events and is the mechanism used to organize an individual's life experience into an integrated and interpretable whole.
>
> (p. 278)

However, at the time when Burns and Bass were proposing their leadership theories, successful transformational leadership was still at least partially associated with charisma. This was then an under-researched area which was debunked shortly afterwards in the context of the growing complexity and acceleration of change that undermined the stable nature of systems (Senge, 1990), and in light of the failure of innovations instituted by charismatic transformational leaders (Tichy & Devanna, 1990). This was ratified in the findings of Collins (2001a), whose research into high-performing companies revealed the greater effectiveness of self-effacing (Level 5) leaders who demonstrated relentless determination to ensure the success of their core business rather than their own. However, when questioned as to how these Level 5 leaders came to be, Collins admitted that,

> We would love to be able to give you a list of steps for getting to Level 5, but we have no solid research data that would support a credible list. We could speculate on what that inner box might hold, but it would mostly be just that, speculation.
>
> (Collins, 2001b, p. 76)

Then again, Collins' Level 5 leaders were not focusing on sustainability as a core value in their organizations, but were engaged in creating enormously successful companies in a diversity of industries.

In view of the responses of the study leaders, it could be argued that one significant difference between transformational leaders and their own experience lies in the contention that in pursuit of sustainability, all members of an organization are or should become leaders. The premise here is that sustainability is only attainable when everyone is fully engaged in creative change. However, their successful participation in the regenerative vision is not predicated on the persuasion exerted by a leader, whether transactional or transformational, but by the driving purpose to be found within themselves. Though positional power within a single organization cannot be eliminated entirely, the boundary separating leaders and followers becomes increasingly blurred as regenerative practices become embedded in its culture through the increasing level of engagement of all members. In the fluid interaction between organizations within networks in industry, education, and communities engaged in sustainability efforts, this differentiation between who leads and who follows becomes even more diffuse.

The goals of sustainability are common to us all by virtue of being human, sentient beings subject to the laws of nature. They do not exclude any individual or group by virtue of their race, gender, age, sexual orientation, socioeconomic status, religion, or any other categorization that may be devised to separate people by virtue of their difference. If human systems were aligned with natural law, in point of fact, there would be no need for these goals, as they would be an integral aspect of how we live, make things, and relate to others and the natural environment. If universal acceptance of these goals were the status quo, there would be no need for sustainability leaders, or for external regulation to ensure a less destructive impact on natural and social systems. People would lead lives within the limits set by the natural cycle, and natural resources would be preserved and renewed so that they could satisfy the needs of present and future generations.

However, whether deliberately or through ignorance, these goals and the values they represent of long-term global environmental, social, and economic sustainability do not underpin much of what we do as humans. Unwittingly, we have developed an entire social infrastructure based on the fallacious belief that we can continue to do things without consequences as we have since the beginning of the Industrial Revolution. Agro-industrial practices, resource extraction, manufacturing, and disposal processes, free market dynamics, consumption patterns, political, education, and other systems have become causal factors of unsustainability, and they are all man-made. Without the awakening, the inner work referred to before, regenerative leadership is impracticable and sustainability will continue to be at risk.

If human activity does not modify its current trend of increasing economic, social, and environmental entropy, sustainability goals will become less open to debate and negotiation. They will also come under increasing centralized, enforced regulation through taxation and penalization, and there will be less margin for leaders to offer trade-offs, or positive incentives to engage people in regenerative practices. If we are to avoid a descent into a destructively competitive global society in an increasingly resource-challenged, environmentally and socially constrained world, competition and the blame game will need to be replaced by a profound shift toward cooperation and community at the local and international level. In this context, efforts such as the only partially effective Conference of the Parties on Climate Change (see CoP 15 and 16, in Copenhagen and Cancun) must subsume sectorial agendas, ambitions, and aspirations to the common good. This is equally true of how corporations, industry, and communities must learn to operate. The journey to achieving this balance between organizational purposes and global imperatives falls within the domain of the evolution of organizations on their journey to sustainability and regenerative practice, the subject of the next chapter.

Chapter summary

As mentioned at the beginning of the chapter, the commitment to sustainability through economic, environmental, and social regenerative practice begins as a very personal inner journey of awakening to a strong sense of purpose linked to a profound awareness of one's place in the natural world, and to the responsibility that comes with this knowledge. Though the turning points and the journeys of regenerative leaders may have been quite different, there is a marked consistency in their collective mindsets. As displayed in the regenerative leadership framework (Figure 2.2), this inner journey evolves from a fragmented to an integrated worldview that expresses itself through surprisingly shared values:

Box 3.2 Quadrant 1. The regenerative leadership mindset

- Awakening to a heightened sense of purpose
- Nurturing creative intelligence unconditioned by previous assumptions
- Transitioning from linear to systems thinking
- Balancing self-centeredness and personal gain with a global ethics
- Developing the capacity to envision and enact desirable emerging futures.

In turn, a natural consequence of the development of these inner values is the emergence of consistent leadership behaviors, described in the framework as:

Box 3.3 Quadrant 2: The regenerative leadership behaviors

- Purpose-driven leadership where egos and logos are suspended
- Iterative observation of best practices
- Deep listening for authentic engagement and empowerment of others
- Multistakeholder engagement, both internal and external to the organization, in order to eliminate unanticipated consequences.

Emerging concerns in the regenerative leaders' most current agendas respond to the sense of urgency with which sustainability issues need to be addressed if we are to create a prosperous, healthy society before the situation goes "down the tubes,'' as John Elkington puts it. This has led them to place the following items front and center in their present work.

Box 3.4 Current agendas of regenerative leaders

- Education and equity: The first as a prerequisite for consciousness development at all levels of society, leading to a shift toward a more equitable, compassionate, mindful society capable of viewing poverty and conflict as issues that concern us all as responsible, ethical global citizens. Equity, however, should not be viewed solely as about doing the right thing, but also about understanding and anticipating the very practical consequences to even the most privileged of ignoring issues of global geopolitical instability due to environmental, sociopolitical, and economic events.
- Expansion and acceleration: The need to intensify sustainability efforts in view of the urgency of addressing complex, critical global problems before they overshoot our capacity to resolve them.

The following chapter reviews the strategies that regenerative leaders have found most successful, and the challenges they have faced, in taking their organizations toward ever greater degrees of sustainability and beyond.

4 Leading regeneration in the organization

We can no longer just think outside the box – we have to think outside the building.
(*R. Moss Kanter, 2010*, keynote address, International Leadership Association Conference, Boston, USA)

Complementing the developmental experiences of sustainability leaders presented and discussed in the previous chapter, it is crucial to understand how these leaders operate within their organizations in order to engage a collective strategy to sustainability and beyond. In the course of the past several years' work, a number of common conditions and strategies have emerged that leaders have found most effective in establishing sustainability as a key operating principle within their organization. While none of these may be considered as new to effective organizations, when applied consistently and systematically, they are seen to have a profound effect in shifting collective culture and behaviors toward higher performance in achieving sustainability goals.

Box 4.1 Conditions for the emergence of regenerative organizations

- Collective mindset development through multiple stakeholder engagement
- Regenerative leadership and the centrality of community
- Identification and activation of driving factors, and identification and elimination of challenges on the organizational journey to regenerative practice.

In this journey to regenerative practice, leaders at all levels face both significant challenges and compelling driving factors within and beyond their organizations, their industries, and their national boundaries.

Collective mindset development through multiple stakeholder involvement

One of the most significant commonalities to emerge among regenerative leaders and their organizations in business, education, and community is the manner in which they engage their personnel and their external stakeholders in reaching and implementing strategic decisions. To avoid the fallout of unanticipated consequences, these leaders understand the crucial importance of engaging multiple perspectives – and shifting mindsets – before initiating a strategy for sustainability. Multiple stakeholder engagement can take diverse forms, be it supply chain management in business and industry, charrettes, sustainability strategic planning workshops, town hall meetings for neighborhood regeneration, or cross-disciplinary integrative projects in education. In the complexity of the environments within which organizations currently operate, the deliberate inclusion of multiple stakeholders at the outset of any initiative, from a systemic rather than a linear perspective, is considered critical to this process, leading to what more recently has become known as collective impact. Kania and Kramer (2011) have found five conditions that together produce true alignment and lead to powerful results for collective impact:

Box 4.2 Collective impact (Kania & Kramer, 2011)

- A common agenda,
- Shared measurement systems,
- Mutually reinforcing activities,
- Continuous communication, and
- Backbone support organizations created from the collaborating organizations, capable of focusing people's attention and creating a sense of urgency, with the skill to apply pressure to stakeholders without overwhelming them, the competence to frame issues in a way that presents opportunities as well as difficulties, and the strength to mediate conflict among stakeholders.

In this context, top-down leadership is perceived as less effective than horizontal, collaborative leadership. Michael Singer summed it up by stating that:

> In order to understand how to generate change it is essential to involve many other people. We know from studying ecosystems that they're enormously complex. As soon as we take action a vast array of interactions and reactions is set in motion.

Without good judgment with regard to the best course of organizational action we should take at any one time, we are unable to perceive and avoid the unanticipated consequences of purposive social action, as Robert Merton (1936) defined them. This is particularly important over the long term, as many of our decisions will affect and already are affecting future generations. To best engage this complex web of cause and effect, regenerative leaders bring to the table as many of the internal and external stakeholders who can scan, scope out, and determine the most complete scenario *before* any action is initiated. Michael Singer described how he incorporated this notion of broad participation into his projects to the fullest extent possible:

> When I start to work on a project I also want to know something about the social dynamics of that place, so I'm going to invite an ethicist, to invite a social anthropologist, to invite a historian, a folklorist, I'm going to bring members of the community, perhaps a religious leader. I think leadership is recognizing that there are many points of view that help define a place. The actions, design, whatever you are doing in that place needs to be informed by multiple perspectives.

Michael's reference to "engaging" people through shared decision making revealed another major finding. Engagement occurs when we are able to connect the external objective world to our internal subjective world of experience, and thereby operate from a profound sense of personal purpose that is consistent with a regenerative perspective of life and work. At the organizational level, leaders understand that engagement has a critical role to play in the development of a shared culture for sustainability, where the notion of positional leader becomes weakened. Cecilia Campoverde, when recounting her experience of developing sustainability at the community level, expressed it in the following way:

> When we are working on this sustainability concept, it can only be possible when the leadership is very democratic. And by that I mean it doesn't really have a leader. All the members have a voice, and they have a rather equal voice, and I say rather, because there are times when we do have to make a decision, but that decision is always based, with a lot of respect, on all the ideas they have given. This happens to me all the time. I say to the community, "by the way, this is not my idea, this is what you have told me in the last two meetings."

From her work directing LEED construction projects for the city of Tallahassee, Eve Williams' take on this was unequivocal:

> For sustainability, shared leadership is a must. I think you get more buy-in from people. And I think you can get more ideas with more people. It's just that you have to assign tasks and then you will lead together. And you have to have meetings continually and make sure that everybody's done their part.

Speaking from his experience as Secretary of Community Affairs during Governor Lawton Chiles' term as governor of Florida, Jim Murley had a similarly strong notion of the importance of political leadership that fosters multi-stakeholder involvement.

> Leadership is the willingness to convene stakeholders, an unfortunate word, or representatives of these interests and be willing to give them equal time and an opportunity to be heard. Also, provide the necessary resources to enable everyone to play on a level playing field. Leadership is also, within an organization, wherever it may be on that continuum, enabling and

> empowering the people that are part of that organization to think about how sustainability fits their job, and taking the credit on their own sense of success and the organization's.

Jim Murley asserted that this concept of public involvement in sustainability matters has become standard practice in policy making, stating that, "The legislature acts rely on the foundation of consensus building and values."

Regenerative leadership and the centrality of community

Joe Laur extended the notion of the importance of the sense of purpose intrinsic to sustainability by referring to the complementary value of community, and how this allows us to connect to a more systemic and sociological view of reality. He indicated that an awareness of something beyond oneself enables us to

> Really connect with others, and to be able to begin to do this in community. Sustainability in the absence of community is meaningless, because at root sustainability is a systemic approach to environmental and social issues. It sees everything linked in a global system, and in local systems, all interconnected webs. So the ability to move in community, recognizing both the benefits and the constraints of that; I think that is also critical.

This notion of community reflects the South African concept of collective consciousness known as Ubuntu, which Archbishop Desmond Tutu defines in the following words: "In the end our purpose is social and communal harmony and well-being. Ubuntu does not say 'I think therefore I am.' It says rather 'I am human because I belong. I participate. I share.'" Singer brought a practical perspective to bear on this notion of community. From his experience in consulting work on issues of infrastructure such as waste management for the city of New York, he revealed how much a sustainable or regenerative mindset has changed how things are done even at the level of larger human systems.

> We are rethinking the way something as basic as a garbage facility or a waste facility actually becomes a benefit to its community. If you start from the very beginning saying that the city needs a new waste facility, citizens need to be involved, coming in and understanding what their role in it is, because they are actually the ones creating the need for that facility. And it builds from there, and then of course you begin to design or plan this facility for its full systems integration, its full potential, taking into account all aspects of the community, its social fabric, its economic fabric, its environmental fabric, its aesthetic fabric, etc.

As an integral part of the societal change toward a more sustainable or regenerative future, along with several other leaders, Singer considered that education played a key part in ensuring a sustainable community.

> Education has a primary role. The project is going to benefit the community. However there needs to be a process of informing the people of the importance of this facility and its potential in their lives. Sustainable practice or regenerative practice means we are going to take action. People need to know that when you take action you are going to practice sustainability. They need to understand what you are doing, how it is different and what role they play in it. Education embodies the ability to bring this message to a public that has assumed the worst about large infrastructure facilities, has been given the worst, and expects the worst.

Jaap Vos added a value judgment to the notion of community by referring to the importance of equity, and the negative social and environmental consequences of inequity.

> Where I used to be a real environmental, sustainable development kind of person, I'm starting to look more and more at equity considerations. Because I feel there is more and more inequity, and more inequity leads to more and more instability and makes it continuously more difficult to find solutions.

Added to issues of equity, particularly in community work, Campoverde highlighted the importance of a leader's respect for the capacity of individuals within a particular community, which required the leader to have "the humbleness, the wisdom, of recognizing that the people know what the problem is, the people know what the solutions are, the people know that 'we are going to solve this problem.'"

Rebecca Bardach's work with refugees in Eastern Europe and more recently in Africa and Central America ratified this inclusive leadership style.

> It's about inspiring and facilitating change, bringing your stakeholders onto the same page, and creating a process that enables people to see beyond their immediate short term self-interest and into the greater common interest. And so the real goal for leaders is to bring everyone on board to really be convinced of the power of that common agenda.

Also speaking from her work with displaced persons in Israel, Debbie Koristz emphasized that leaders must engage in relationship building in order to promote sustainable development.

> I think a leader is someone who can have a deep understanding of what's best for the general community or whoever the population is that we are talking about, and strives for that; but strives in a way that he or she is building relations with everyone else. You can't be a leader and just say this is what I want to do, and that's it. You have to really know what's best for the community, what's best for the future, and then strive to work in a cooperative way, in a collaborative way.

Steve Seibert of the Florida Century Commission added a political perspective to engagement of constituents and policymakers. Whereas he had seen a significant increase in public concern with regard to sustainability, he confessed that the most difficult task he faced was getting "the attention of other policymakers to address the future," which he called "the tyranny of the present crisis. It is almost impossible to get elected officials to put aside immediate concerns and constituencies and think about future concerns and constituencies." That said, he ratified the importance of widespread engagement for sustainability to have an opportunity, asserting that leadership for sustainability "is this willingness to tackle the future and the ability to get others to engage in it with you."

In education, while acknowledging the importance of bold leaders, Judy Walton of the Association for the Advancement of Sustainability in Higher Education (AASHE) strongly emphasized the value of multi-stakeholder involvement and leadership at all levels.

> I think most people envision a bold leader, a charismatic leader, but there are many other forms of leadership, and this includes people who are working in the so-called trenches every day to promote sustainability to a society that isn't thinking along those lines. People at any level can exhibit strong leadership skills for sustainability by bringing others along. We talk so much about leadership. But a good part of leadership is following the lead of others facilitating, and nurturing their capacities.

Mitch Thomashow, President of Unity College, Maine, referred to how others may be engaged in higher education in order to promote sustainability.

> My theory of leadership is that personally you have to promote innovation and reward folks who actually get things done. So, on a college campus you have to find the people who really understand the importance of these concepts and principles in order to give them every possibility of success. I think it's also important on a college campus, probably for most organizations, certainly a college campus, that you build a sustainability driven environmental infrastructure.

Identification and activation of drivers, and identification and elimination of challenges on the organizational journey to regenerative practice

In the three domains of business, community, and education, regenerative leaders supplied a diverse range of strategies that they had found most effective in moving their organizations toward greater degrees of sustainability and beyond. Some of these strategies related to the inner work, both individual and collective, that were mentioned previously as a finding. A number of them felt that this inner work was necessary to raising their own and others' understanding and awareness of sustainability. Other strategies referred to organizational policies and practices. Within the context of each strategy, the leaders identified factors that impeded or facilitated their effective implementation, identified here as challenges and drivers. Though conceptually a number of the findings appeared as common to all or most of the leaders, the domain-specific nature of the leaders' practical examples suggested that this section would most profitably be structured separately. At the end of the section, however, the strategies described are reviewed for their commonalities and differences across the three domains of business, education, and community.

Business

The most reiterated strategy identified by the leaders as a key aspect of sustainability leadership was the importance of implementing a "team process" in all projects, as indicated by Michael Singer, within a systems thinking framework.

> When a project comes into my business I immediately think of an index of professionals who I have had some experience with or who have been recommended by other people. I look at the project from a holistic point of view, again whole systems thinking. I want to know how many different systems are being affected by this project.

Singer connected team process and systems thinking to another critical finding, that of the importance of breaking down professional boundaries, which some referred to as "silos," and of overcoming resistance so that sustainability might become viable. He considered these boundaries to be among the most serious challenges to effective team building, and was of the opinion that these were the result of resistance originating from the insecurity people felt when they were asked to work outside of their area of expertise.

> The conventional model we have today is the separation between professional entities. The biggest challenge is getting folks to recognize that professional roles are interdependent. We need to overcome professional boundaries and resistances. Sometimes we can't, and this promotes failure. So one of the challenges is to develop a culture that accepts coming to the table, accepts permeable boundaries, professionals not feeling challenged by questions that may appear to be outside of one's professional realm.

Martin Melaver added a further dimension to the team process by relating it back to the issue of leadership, which for sustainability required allowing others to exercise leadership while creating an organizational culture that was sensitive to people's needs and values.

> One [strategy] would be shared leadership, clearly making the company a sensitive vessel for the expression of needs and values, and empowering

> folks to make decisions on the ground. As much as I would like to step into some of the details of managing the company, I try to restrain myself to a large degree to let others exercise their own leadership capacities and capabilities.

With regard to empowering others and the impact this can have on people's motivation and productivity, Melaver identified a challenge that the company had not yet overcome. While providing people with the opportunities to "exercise their own leadership" was of importance in driving sustainability, it could also become a liability when left unchecked, as it could lead to being consumed by the job. Melaver spoke of the need

> To ensure that work doesn't dominate all. That's probably what we most fail at as a company. When you get a bunch of charged, mission-driven, purposeful people engaged in work that seems meaningful, the tendency is to work longer hours and weekends, emailing at ridiculous hours, at early hours of the morning, it's crazy.

Personal lives and eventually productivity suffered in consequence. This effect was offset by "modeling," which Melaver admitted he did not do well, so that some sense of balance could be achieved.

> There have been times over the years when colleagues and board members have been worried because I seem to be some sort of innovation junkie, to put it in colloquial terms. Basically, you do one thing, and instead of repeating that thing, you are on to ratcheting up the expectations on the next project. I think a lot of what we are talking about has to do with balance on a global level. Part of that macro sensibility of balance has to do with basically going home at the end of the day, being with one's family, or doing something in the community, recognizing that the multiple facets of one's life all have to make sense in a coherent way. They can't be "siloed."

Though achieving this kind of balance was important, Melaver believed that fear of change was the biggest challenge to sustainability.

> This is what we all confront. I do, personally, certainly my colleagues at work, and regulatory officials. It's not just a simple sense of resistance, of comfort within the way things have always been done, but a fear that change appears to cause. If I am sitting here and I am fearful of some direction you want to go in, I am not likely to open up my basic, really my most fundamental fears to you. I don't care how close you and I are.

Melaver proposed that the best strategy to overcome the fear of change was through personal honesty and authenticity, which he indicated was a process that was continuous, difficult, but common to all.

> So dealing with fears is how you manage that. I think the strategy is authenticity, it's to make a personal change in your own life, it's to say, "not that I've been through that, or that I understand what you're going through," it's more, "I go through this every day." And I think if you're honest with yourself you do. So the strategy to deal with that major obstacle of fear is that I am not putting myself out there as any saint or anything close to it, I struggle with that stuff all the time, here's what I'm not good at, here's where I've found possible solutions.

Melaver identified three major drivers for sustainability. The first, defined in a previous finding, related to sustainability values, and the concomitant "sense of meaning and purpose," which he indicated extended to the company's shareholders.

> You've got shareholders as a major driver and the values of the shareholders. And the values are a critical piece of that. We are all on the same page of sustainability when it comes to this.

A second driver involved his colleagues' "sense of really being doing cutting edge stuff … there's a palpable sense of excitement, exhaustion but excitement, having to do with being pioneers." Finally, he asserted that "the market is a driver, is starting to become a driver." However, he was still not entirely convinced that this was a positive influence because he was skeptical of the values driving investments in sustainability at the time. As he said, though "there is in the last six to eight months a significant amount of institutional capital chasing this stuff, they're chasing it cosmetically."

Joe Laur supplied another dimension to the strategy of team building for sustainability. He referred to the value of conversation for sharing new knowledge and widespread participation, and described how this practice had become embedded in his own organization, the Sustainability Consortium of the Society for Organizational Learning (SOL), and in companies with which he and his colleagues had worked.

> We had regular meetings, regular conversations. I think this was the key business practice, important to hear all the voices in the firm. Whenever we had new knowledge, new ideas, put them out there, see what people thought, get other perspectives, and then look at the best policies to implement. That's something we shared with larger firms like Harley Davidson, where they too consider conversations as a key business practice, where you sit in circles and you talk about stuff, and you hear everybody's voice. And you work together, and it takes a little more time up front, but you get better results most times in the long run. So that's how we do it. So once we get a clear strategic direction we implement the policies.

Laur also spoke of actual practices, behaviors, and related policies that became an integral aspect of the organizational culture, which he defined as a process or journey in the constant search for greater sustainability. These practices related to issues of energy, purchasing, and travel, and how these could be improved through continuous review. The resulting policies also extended outwards to the company's supply chain, pointing the way toward a more systemic shift toward sustainability.

> Our small consulting firm that we ran for 14 years, we closed up shop this past year, it was quite easy, we owned and ran everything, we put in solar power that provided all the needs of the office, we looked at [carbon] offsets, we recycled everything, bought recycled as well as did recycling. So we constantly looked at our input, and put policies in place to change that. So that people who bought supplies for us were told to look for 100% recycled post-consumer products. As we learned, we tried to put that knowledge into place in our own small practice. With the other communities that we facilitated, such as the SOL Sustainability Consortium we took steps to offset carbon from meetings we were involved in, kept the meetings to two face-to-face meetings a year and did many workgroup teleconferences and so forth in between. So again, we tried to model moving toward, and I think it's always a case of moving toward greater and greater sustainability. I don't think there's a destination there, and it's important to reward progress and seek perfection, but you can't always demand it in the moment.

Laur also shared Singer and Melaver's consideration for the importance of breaking down professional boundaries for sustainability. However, he took this a step further, asserting that this boundary crossing had to occur not just within a company, but that "sharing the learning across organizational boundaries has been critical, which is why we started the SOL Sustainability Consortium to facilitate that kind of exchange." This process, however, is challenged, once again, by resistance from individuals, which is where he was convinced sustainability became a viable proposition.

> I would say one of the first challenges is linking sustainability work with what people have on their plates every day; whether you are working at the top level of the company getting the top leaders to understand that this is a strategic imperative, or at the low end of the survival spectrum.

Laur had also seen evidence of how sustainability can become a tremendous business opportunity. In the case of the oil industry, in 1995 a top oil executive told him, "as oil companies, we are in line to be the next tobacco industry, it's going to be us next." At the time, forward thinking companies like British Petroleum turned this situation to their own advantage by shifting their focus from oil to alternative energy sources, leading to marketing campaigns like BP's Beyond Petroleum, which lost credibility in the Gulf of Mexico oil spill disaster in 2010. Despite this setback and the very poor leadership that did little to help turn the situation around, this should not diminish the value of the efforts of those individuals within the organization who have changed their way of thinking and operating, and who are seeking to align their performance to concrete short- and long-term sustainability indicators. As Joe Laur asserted:

> It's not just an advertising campaign; it's really about how people in that company think. They began to develop hydrogen, solar, I think they're now the second, they were the largest, now they are the second largest oil company in the world working a lot with alternative fuels, natural gas, which of course is just a transition strategy, ultimately, but it's many, many times better than oil, and conservation. BP has developed a target neutral, carbon offset program, it has met its own reduction targets consistently ahead of schedule, and it has driven performance within the company, so it's been good for company performance. It's really aligning sustainability with what people are doing every day, and helping them see that, even though it may be long term on many days, not only for the most immediate needs, but that it's absolutely essential to the needs of the company.

And this is where he found the greatest challenge, in the inability of people to function within a long-term frame of reference, of creating what he called the appropriate "mindspace."

> It's helping people see that link, between the long-term necessary action and linking it to the short term day to day. Because we tend to focus on, we're driving our car and looking five feet ahead, and we fail to see that we are heading towards oblivion in the overall direction that we are going. And then linking it solidly to economic returns, so in the triple bottom line you have to take care of planet and people and you also have to prosper yourself, otherwise you aren't going to be around to do the other good work. So it's got to be linked like that, that's the biggest challenge, it's getting the mindspace, at least in Western culture.

In contrast, Laur raised one of the more frequently repeated drivers that offset people's inability to take a long-term perspective when engaging in sustainability: "Children." And in his work he indicated that he had encountered this driving factor not only in parents, but in a wider segment of concerned individuals.

> We've heard that link since the mid-1990s. People say, "You know, I've been going to work, and when I come home, my daughter says, 'what have you been doing about recycling, Dad, what are you doing about energy, Dad?'" There's always this undercurrent, even for people who don't have children, about the next generation, and passing something on, a legacy.

This concern pointed to another important driver, that of the kind of people that were needed to drive sustainability efforts, and how these could impact an entire society through organizational behaviors and education.

> Another driver is good quality people who can see the systemic long term and realize that if change isn't made, they don't have a future. So if Waste Management just continues taking garbage and burning it in holes somewhere, that industry doesn't have a future, ultimately, but if they take materials and convert them into new materials, and take materials and convert them into energy, and also take a position on educating millions of people that they touch on how to participate in that, that does have a future.

From a manufacturing perspective, Gregor Barnum addressed the development of a product line within a larger sustainable system as a strategy. He also identified the broader social implications of this approach.

> We are looking at more and more ways how we can create a whole product line that is really aligned with working with a system. I can't really jump into the proprietary aspects of that. I can give a little bit of an example. Apple has touched into it a little, of locking you into their system. I would say that Apple has not done a very good job of actually including the earth as one of their stakeholders. How do you create a system that allows for a higher level of interactivity with the customer? At the same time we want to create the idea that what we are doing is also creating a higher level of sustainability, regeneration, environmental impact, social impact. So that when anybody does something they see that they are actually doing something that is regenerative rather than wasteful.

Barnum went on to describe the Seventh Generation's product manufacturing process, which in essence involved doing more with less. As with previous leaders, this was also achieved through a continuous process of assessment and improvement.

> And then obviously with our present line of stuff, we have been working pretty dramatically with how to move more and more of the product doing less and less; changing packaging, adding more recyclable content, reducing our CO2 footprint, looking up and down our value-added chain, looking at every idea to reduce CO2. From my perspective, CO2 is only one of a number of things that you can cut back on. So, how do you begin to look at all the aspects from earth that we draw, from the palm oil, or the cotton, all the way to the other end when it gets dropped off somewhere? So that's been instituted more and more as the process internally.

In order to attain this systemic perspective of improvement, Barnum indicated that they focused on engaging internal and external stakeholders, while ensuring a more inclusive approach from senior management. As Director of Corporate Consciousness, it was his role to infuse a greater awareness of how to balance profitability and growth with the company's global and social impact.

> We are building people, building capacity, as I said before getting management to be more into the role of not being hierarchical and more holarchical, working more and more with the process of how you engage all the way down the value-added chain, each one of the different stakeholders, how do you work with that. And I think too, my role being Director of Corporate Consciousness, to deal with the so-called sustainability issues and whatever; it's really trying to find a way so that my position is somewhat absorbed into everybody there. How do you get them to realize that we have global and planetary and social metrics that we need to follow along with making money and growing?

The major challenge to this process toward sustainability, according to Barnum, is posed by the mental frameworks of people who have been successful in traditional ways, and that change can only be achieved by findings ways to move individuals to challenge the status quo.

> If you are going to move people out of where they are used to, in other words, the framework they've done business in, they've been successful before and this is how they've known how to do it, if you're trying to move people into sustainability/regenerative business kinds of process or every day activities, what you've got to realize is that you've got to find more and more ways to have people on their own challenge the frameworks that they're used to.

Finally, Barnum described two major drivers that the company had employed to offset this resistance. The first was a top-down push from the company's senior management, including CEO Jeffrey Hollander. The second was a conscious effort by middle management to involve all internal stakeholders in a periodic personal development process.

> We've been using Jeffrey Hollander, CEO of the company, who is a huge driving force and has been working with the management team at the highest level he can to keep getting and encouraging people to actually move in a different way. And so it's been coming a little from the top down. But also one of the things we have been doing is having a full day of so-called personal development which is really how do people begin to take on this idea of creating this thing that will make them more effective in their job. And so that's come down from each of the managers. Some of them actually require people to end up in this personal development day, which is actually once a month now.

Darcy Winslow described the team building process undertaken at Nike to move toward greater sustainability. The second referred to the sustainability goals emanated from the teams once the work had begun. Rather than strategies, Winslow referred to these as catalysts.

> There are two early catalysts. If we look at where we are today, and reflect back at the decisions, statements, and early partnerships that emerged, one was the creation of a group of about 100 internal champions, which we called Shambhala. This was an effort led by our Corporate Responsibility team, reaching out to different areas of the business, to introduce principles of sustainability and exposing these champions to external leaders and thinkers. The second catalyst happened around the same time and was informed by the work just mentioned. It was the creation of our 20-years sustainability goals: zero waste, zero toxics, and 100% closed loop. In Nike's case, this led to the creation of a small pioneering team dedicated to sustainable manufacturing processes, at the selection of materials, and the consequences this had on their supply chain.

The latter, she affirmed, consisted "of hundreds if not thousands of vendors, consequently we had to be very deliberate in whom we engaged in the conversation in order to have the greatest impact."

> Also around this time, we created a small team within the business that we called "Environmental Business Opportunities" and soon evolved to "Sustainable Business Strategies." This was a result of a conversation I had with Mark Parker and my boss, Jerry Karver, who was heading up Footwear and our contract manufacturing operations. I said, "If we're going to be serious about sustainability and really integrate sustainability into what we do, we've got to get it just out of CR [corporate responsibility] and into the business." And they basically said, "Great. Go figure it out." So that was when I started this team – with a blank sheet of paper and an org chart of one. The team that exists today is called "Considered" and their mantra is, "Consider your choices, consider your impact." They look at the design of the product, the materials we use, which we have termed environmentally preferred materials (EPMs), working through the supply chain with our materials suppliers. We began this effort intensely in the late '90s.

Sustainability consultants such as Roger Vardan and Seetha Coleman-Kammula supported the views of the previous leaders in several aspects. Vardan described two major strategies. To begin with, Vardan emphasized the critical importance of connecting strategy and sustainability in the senior management mindset, followed by product and policies innovation and development.

> One is primarily to change the mindset of some of the CEOs. I work with very high level people since I started my company, helping shape the mindset of the senior management in a company with strategic thinking about sustainability. I specialize in the nexus between strategy and sustainability ... to broaden the vision in a strategic sense with the very senior management. The other aspect of the strategy is to get into the deeper level of the organizations, into innovation for new product development or new service

> development, you need to factor these things in. The key thing is it is a two-pronged strategy – one is at the highest level of senior management, and the other is about new product and policies and how you innovate.

The challenge to sustainability, in his opinion, came therefore from the level of commitment of the senior management, which could be "quick to embrace and see the vision, but in some companies, small, medium and large, to get that vision implemented, to get it to percolate through the organization, that is not easy." However, when senior management is committed, it becomes easier to establish a sustainable process by recruiting "the right people to make it happen." This is complemented when time becomes an important variable, as he indicated by saying that

> We are pressed for time in this. I feel what Dr Martin Luther King said in a different context, about civil rights, it's a "fierce urgency of now." I believe that with what the world is facing there should be a tremendous sense of urgency toward sustainability issues. There is no time to waste. So if it starts at the top, then you don't waste a lot of time. If it's from the bottom up, even though it's well intentioned, it takes a lot of time before that's agreed upon. So the major driver is the push from an enlightened top. The guys really embrace the issue, and then positive developments will happen.

Meanwhile, Coleman-Kammula found that helping companies see the "economic benefit of the environment" is a first strategy she employed in her consulting work. This had an immediate effect on senior management engagement in this effort.

> One company has come up with an environmentally better product. They didn't have a way to see what good that did in terms of sustainability, either environmental or social. And in helping them see that, what has really helped them and us, is to make them see that the change they made impacted the whole supply chain, both their suppliers and their customers, so the whole system. So once we start to describe the whole system it becomes very attractive to them. One of the subjects certainly is helping people see how they are impacting the larger system.

Her particular success as a consultant, she indicated, came from "bringing together what's called value chain or supply chain workshop." This involved bringing together people from different companies "who are part of an overall system, but who have never been brought together in a room as part of a system."

> They didn't know whose waste they could use, who could use their waste. Using waste as food, and concepts like that. We brought 65 companies together, it was quite a big gathering; it was the first time they had been in a room together. They said, "Gee, we didn't know."

The process Coleman-Kammula described to foster sustainable efforts across companies resonated with some of the comments made by previous leaders regarding the importance of establishing productive conversations around sustainability issues. However, she went into greater detail with regard to how she approached her consulting work with multiple companies within an industry, which consisted of a

> One-day dialog on what sustainability means to them. So why they came together was not imposed, we weren't preaching to them saying this is what sustainability is. We said "We'd like to know how you are thinking about it, what are the pressures you are feeling, what are your needs, what are your customers' expectations, what are your own expectations, what do you think this is about, and do you want to talk about it? And do you want to hear from others?" And we created a little program; we brought in a couple of very powerful external speakers from another system. We brought in a pulp and paper person, the Chief Sustainability Officer of Time, Inc., who had worked with pulp and paper, and forestry, that supply chain system, so I said, "Let's see what we in plastics can learn from the paper guys." They were interested in that. So after the couple of speeches, we organized them in little round tables and put questions, really basic questions, "What does it mean to you? What do you think it means to your customers? Why are you worried? Do you want to change? Do you think there is a need to change? If so, what is the change?"
>
> So we were able to foster very simple conversations. We couldn't stop them from talking! At the end of the day, they were filling up flip charts, coming up with things they wanted to do. So, awakening their own curiosity and whatever they were feeling, getting their needs out, making everybody see that they aren't alone, that there are others asking the same things and they did not have all the answers. Giving examples of others who have done it and they become curious.
>
> And so the answer regarding the strategy is making them see the system they are part of, connecting them with others in the system, bringing them together in informal settings without preaching to them and making them discover it for themselves.

With regard to the challenges involved in this process, Coleman-Kammula indicated that as yet there were too few companies involved in this approach for it to have a significant impact. This was due in part to the fact that only a very few were changing because this was the right thing to do, and that a few others were doing it simply as a marketing strategy. There were those who resisted change, arguing that they were waiting for the "playing field to be leveled" by legislation. Additionally, similarly to Martin Melaver and Gregor Barnum's analysis, people resist change because it involves too much effort. Institutionally as well, when the reward systems in place are intended to keep "things the way they have been'' and encourage people to keep doing ''what they've been doing excellently, they become even more of a barrier to change than something else.''

What is different about sustainability, Coleman-Kammula asserts, is that:

> You want people to do something proactively and so this means changing the reward structures. So that when we do go and talk, we openly acknowledge this, we say, ''This is hard, and it's going to go in fits and starts, don't expect everybody to just move over from left to right just because we show them look at the amount of dollars you can save.'' It still means that people have to change what they are doing every day, the way they've been doing things before.

Coleman-Kammula's identification of drivers of sustainability was somehow ironic, as it contrasted with similar comments made by Martin Melaver, but in his case he had used similar terms as challenges rather than drivers. However, Coleman-Kammula made sense of these drivers by placing them in a clear political and economic context. Unfortunately, she affirmed, these negative emotions were still more conducive to sustainability than commitment and engagement.

> Fear and greed. Regulations have been changing and have really helped. What I've been seeing in the plastics world is that there are these plastics bans. We work a lot with industry associations, American Plastics Council, and so on. I think they were in denial for a long time. And then all these cities have come and established bans on plastic bags, and now they are afraid. So I'd say that in that case I think it's been fear of legislation which has escalated for plastics in the last two years.
>
> The other big driver is lack of legislation. It's funny to see that happening. There is a large number of companies that we work with, proactively lobbying in Washington for carbon regulation to regulate carbon emissions because some of these people have already invested money in reducing carbon emissions, and they want to get the financial reward for having done it already, it's called the U.S. Cap. So at a very pure and fundamental level, it's greed and fear. Commitment and engagement are still not drivers. What gets them off their bottoms to do something about it is when they see some money or when they are pushed to do it. They don't do it because it's the right thing to do. We are two or three years away from that.

However, there was still an aspect of greed which must be considered an obstacle to sustainability. Coleman-Kammula affirmed that businesses that respond to shareholders are still operating under traditional business principles where quarterly dividends and the bottom line are core priorities. Shifting shareholder value to environmental or social value, she indicated, was part of a ''bigger conversation.''

> Fundamentally, I'm now talking about business, business works within the very artificial rules of shareholder value, and as long as that doesn't change,

> business isn't going to change. On one hand, CEOs are held accountable for how many dividends you pay and if you've shown growth, and I think that business is going to find it very hard to change. And so really the bigger conversation that needs to happen is changing shareholder value for environmental value, and societal value, so the rules of governance have to change, and that's a much bigger thing.

Community

Similarly to the importance given to team process by business leaders, the group of leaders committed to sustainability within the domain of community also highlighted the value of teams and the strategies that were most effective in driving sustainability efforts. However, their perspective varied significantly. To begin with, the kinds of teams or groups to be found within sustainable community efforts were more diverse, and the leaders interviewed in the study belonged mostly to governmental or nongovernmental organizations (NGOs), and therefore their initiatives were not driven by profit, but rather toward community building. In addition, while some of the leaders interviewed led teams of highly skilled professionals or worked with communities within socially developed contexts such as the United States or Europe, others were more involved in efforts within marginalized communities in Central America or displaced persons in the Balkans. In the latter cases, rather than business organizations seeking to integrate environmental and social concerns with their bottom line, these were groups of individuals coming together to satisfy basic needs. The departure point of the initiatives was therefore also quite different, as these individuals' educational level tended to be more diverse than that of business professionals. This required considerable groundwork by individuals and external agencies before sustainable local initiatives could be established successfully. In some of these cases, the challenges came close to impeding the successful implementation of sustainable development initiatives.

From her position as a founder and coordinator of a community effort in Guatemala, Cecilia Campoverde had considerable experience in the process of community building. To begin with, she identified three principal constituents within her community: that of the people of the community itself or internal stakeholders, that of the donors or external stakeholders, mostly in the United States, and herself, given her background and experience in both countries, as the moderator between the two. She focused her attention mostly on the evolution toward sustainability of the local community, which she described as a process made possible by a conscious strategy intended to transform the collective culture from one of mistrust and passivity to active engagement and self-sufficiency. When she first began working with this community in El Triunfo, the local community in Guatemala displaced by Hurricane Mitch in 1998, she found that the people there

> Had been promised so many things, and so they didn't trust anybody. So they just wanted things to be given to them, and when they saw that the mission of

> the project was not to give but to provide the mechanism for them to do whatever they wanted to do, they didn't like that very much.

While trying to establish a microfinance program to support the development of microenterprises within the community, Campoverde found initial greater acceptance among the women, "who trusted perhaps in trying to raise some chickens. But when the men saw that growth in the women, they began to complain and say, 'Hey, I want to be part of that, whatever you are doing.'"

With the passage of time, this process led to the development of a rotating system of loans to support the development of small business initiatives, among which were pig and chicken farming, brickmaking, bicycle repair, ice-cream vending, and vegetable gardening and commercialization at the local markets. At the time of the interview, the return rate of these loans stood at 98 percent. Part of the success of the initiative resulted from the informal town hall type meetings that Campoverde held outside her home, to which all residents were welcome.

> When I go there, we hold meetings at least twice a week, and we hold them informally, right in front of the house where I am. About 15 or 20 people come to each meeting. And we just sit there, and have a cup of chocolate. They just come if they want to, there is no obligation. They know that I am always there. In the house where I live, the building itself is conducive to having people sitting outside. You have your own space. And of course the kids can play; they make a bonfire, while we are over here. And they now feel that they have the support, that they have the guidance. I hold meetings with them, not at paying time, which is the first and fifteenth of every month, but at any other time. So it's a constant kind of reminding, to actually teach them how to learn that process. And they are growing that way. It saves them face, and that gives them more strength and greater sustainability to the program.

Campoverde outlined the benefits that the use of microloans had had on the attitude of the local residents toward work and the conduct of their lives. Whereas relief aid provided by external agencies had fostered passivity in the recipients and minimal productivity toward self-sufficiency, the microfinance program sustained by the community meetings had brought about a profound shift in people's attitudes. On the one hand, the individuals who took out the loans began to develop the confidence needed to create their own enterprises, and to seek out further challenges when they had their first taste of success. On the other, the community meetings provided a forum for sharing experiences that became both an invaluable learning environment and a way of bringing people together.

> Another thing is that by having these meetings, they see each other more, and they learn, not exactly what the problems of the other people are, or what they are going through, but it kind of builds up a link, and they don't

> speak out too openly yet, but it links them a little bit more. Everybody knows everybody. We are not talking about a million people in a city. Nevertheless, you get to know each other better and to support each other better. I think that has been very good.

Campoverde also highlighted another important impact of this approach on the potential for the community to engage in truly sustainable development. Whereas initially the elected community council, which had consisted of women at its inception, had tended to be extremely dependent on her for guidance, as time progressed the council's decision-making style had taken a very different approach.

> At the beginning of all of this, I called them often, just like when I am there and I have meetings. So, the women in charge of this project, they said, "What do you think we should do about this project?" They would say to me, "We want to ask you, what do you think that we should do?" at the beginning. I haven't heard that for a long time. I still remember the first time that they called me to tell me what they had done, to inform me about a decision they had made. That drives me, because I know that there is hope. I know that you just give them an opportunity, open the door, trust them, and give some guidance at the same time; they are going to do what they need to do.

While working with the New York-based American Jewish Joint Distribution Committee, Rebecca Bardach was engaged to work with the United Nations High Commission for Refugees (UNHCR) in Jerusalem. Once there, Bardach discovered that the commission's main office in Geneva provided "practically zero budgetary or professional support to that office, which was officially an Honorary Consulate." She also found that there was "no governmental system in place, there was no legislation, there were no policies." Dealing with refugees entering Israel under these circumstances was extremely challenging. She realized then that "even though I didn't know what all the answers were, I could see that the way things were happening was not the best way to do it." From that initial understanding, she began to work at developing a comprehensive system at several different levels.

> So the question was how we could work with the government to build the policies that they needed so that it would become their system, how to work with UNHCR in Geneva as the head institution that was supposed to be interacting more with the issue here, and how we instituted policies and procedures within the organization that were really fair, that went really deep into people's issues, and their cases and their claims, which I felt was not really happening at the time.
>
> So it was an ongoing process, working at all those levels, really changing the way we did the work internally, creating fair, deep and standardized

> approaches and procedures, and then working with the government and Geneva to really establish a different approach that was going to involve a long-term commitment with resources and people and training, etc.
>
> The most effective strategies, first and foremost, were to understand where that party came from, and what their concerns were. In order to get them over to your way of thinking, you absolutely had to understand and be sympathetic to what their perspective was. In that way you could begin to persuade them, to influence them to make any sort of change or begin to adopt some of the approaches that you thought were better for whatever reason. And then, once you had really listened and understood, it was about not imposing and saying this was the only way or the best way. It was about the longer process of education and convincing them why this approach was in their best interest, showing them from an internal to an external process, so that they would come to their own realization that they were tapping into their self-interest, so that when you talked about it they saw it. It was not that you had told them but that you had presented it in such a way that they came to that conclusion by themselves. And that is definitely the best way that I have found to bring people on board to the perspective that is most sustainable or the best approach and to getting that implemented, working towards those changes.

Though the social realities she addressed in her work were substantively different to those prevalent in Campoverde's efforts in Guatemala, a strong similarity was evident in how both leaders sought to build a sustainable community from the bottom-up. In addition, Bardach's understanding of the importance of building from within the community also met with a similar challenge, that of people's strong initial dependence on external agents.

> First of all, as much as I believe that you can create systems that operate well on their own, they are still very people-dependent, on the quality and commitment of the individuals who run that system, be it top, middle or low level, which is harder to control.

To ensure sustainability in such a complex political context required the establishment of appropriate systems, particularly in the long term, as the initial leaders were replaced by new ones, with potentially different values and capacities.

> It is easier to create a system; it is much harder to ensure that all the people in it are going to do things at their best. And so you need to create a system that can function very well even if mediocre people are operating it, and that no matter what you do, people who are either bad at what they do, or have bad intentions, might do damage to the system. No system can protect you from people who are going to do wrong within that system, whatever the context. And I really believe in the potential for systems and policies to bring a lot of added value. People alone can't make the changes, but systems and

policies alone can't either. You really need that combination. And that's very hard to control. It's hard to find, and it's hard to ensure on a long-term basis.

In Bardach's opinion, this balance between internal capacity building and regulatory policies and procedures appeared to be a key to establishing a sustainable new situation for the refugees with whom she worked. However, no matter how clear and thorough policies and procedures might be, the greatest driving factor for success remained with the quality of the individuals within the community itself.

> I would say, really tapping into the existing goodwill and commitment, or cultivating it. But generally, when you have everybody wanting the same thing but going at it from different perspectives, the most successful approach is to bring all of those energies, that will, resources of whatever kind, capacity, commitment, when you can bring them all to work together, and not at odds, that is your biggest driver.

In order to achieve this result, Bardach had found that the best approach was in the manner in which both the external agents and the communities worked together.

> You achieve this alignment through a lot of hard work around understanding perspectives, bringing them on board, having them begin to understand why we have a shared and common agenda, having them work out and create a context which enables them to figure out together what we have in common and how we are going to work together on these issues and hammering it out. And that might be through broadly coordinated efforts to meetings, or a lot of individual things, going through long processes, education, persuasion, showing, etc. I feel there is no formula, and it's messy, but it's all about a process of getting people on board, and developing a common vision.

In her own work with refugees, Debbie Koristz argued for a similar strategy to building sustainability within a community-building initiative, stressing the importance of collaboration and good relationships, an approach she also applied with her colleagues.

> One of the things that I really try to do is to work in a really collaborative way. To work either with other colleagues or other agencies that help me in the effort that I am trying to do, and because if you have a goal, a very big objective, it's not easy to do on your own, and it may not even be right to do it on your own. That's one of the strategies that I try to implement a lot, to build relationships with other colleagues, to work in a collaborative way, and every time that I have done that I have been much more successful in implementing the objectives and in making the projects much more sustainable.

Koristz also emphasized the importance of flexibility as a conscious strategy for ensuring program sustainability, due to the fact that these could evolve in directions unanticipated at the outset.

> Being flexible definitely; when I see a project or program, and it's almost like a creative process, it starts out with something you write down as a draft or outline. It grows and develops; sometimes it changes and looks very different in the end to what you started with in the beginning. So I think flexibility is something else I try to use as a strategy, or a tool.

These variables, internal capacities, collaboration, policies and procedures, and flexibility, could only function successfully and sustainably when placed in the appropriate context, Koristz asserted.

> They are important in the context of where you are working. If you are aiming for something sustainable, you don't work in a vacuum, you work in a structure and within a community that has greater goals than just my personal projects. It's very important to make sure that whatever I am doing, whatever I am working on, is within the ideology of the organization or within the beliefs or the values of the organization. So I think in order to do that you really need to understand those values or the greater picture, or where you are working, and collaboration is definitely part of that, in order to understand that.

All these different factors build up to what Koristz called another strategy or tool, that of "strategic thinking and having a strategic plan. And usually this isn't something you can do by yourself, most of the time it requires working collaboratively with others involved."

Koristz identified two major challenges to sustainability in her work. The first related to the inner workings of the organization she worked for, and concerned the loss of creativity through repetition, and how this affected her.

> The biggest one is sometimes coming up with new and creative ways to reach your goals. The organization that I'm with has been in this business for so long, we talk every day about how you build community, how you reach people, how you do outreach, how you build identity. It's almost like we've been there and done that. It's kind of coming up with new and interesting ways to reach sustainability, to ensure the continuity of whatever I am working on. I think that's a major challenge for me personally.

A second challenge had to do with her work with individual leaders within her organization and the communities her organization supported, and how the different interests and opinions needed to be balanced in order to determine the best solutions for the community.

> And in working with leaders, many times I find myself working with people who are considered leaders in their own professional capacity. How do you

> lead a leader? How do you manage interests and conflicts? You have groups of people who are used to being a leader, and they have their own interests, their own opinions, how do you balance all that within what you want to do and within what you think is best for the community.

To offset these challenges, Koristz reiterated the importance of flexibility, to which she added persistence.

> I think for me it's still flexibility. That's one of the most helpful things. I think the capacity to go back and start from scratch. The ability to say this is not working, so let's try something else, and completely throw out an idea and start from scratch. I think sometimes, as a professional, we are very connected to our projects, and we want to see them through, sometimes they don't work, so we have to know when to give something up, or change it around. So I guess what I want to say is flexibility and persistence. Not giving up, just being persistent.

However, all of the strategies, the challenges, and drivers of individual projects took on real meaning within a much larger context or perspective, the sustainability of the Jewish people.

> And really, aside from just having the goals of the specific project or what you are working on, is having really greater existential goals, of what you want to accomplish through this program, and always keeping those in mind. Because the project or program can always change, but you need to make sure that whatever you are working on is really contributing to that major, major objective which is usually something much greater, something that's beyond the inner workings of the program. It's really about what you want to achieve through the program, where do I see the community going in ten years, do I think that this program is going to help with that. It's like having a vision, if I can be so esoteric. An existential goal is the continuity of the Jewish people, and from that a whole number of objectives derive, whether they are related to identity or social services.
>
> And from that, my ideal or belief, speaking specifically to the work that I do, as Jews we all are responsible one for the other, and whatever happens in one part of the world, even if I am here in the U.S., in my nice little house in Boca, I should still care about that. So that for me is an existential goal, and every program that we work on and that I strive for, is really with that last goal in mind.

In his work with the Century Commission for a Sustainable Florida, Steve Seibert highlighted the importance of "getting the organization to agree to rely on objective information" as a first strategy to help focus a team. He also emphasized some of the key values that supported a collaborative approach.

> Getting the organization to agree to rely upon objective information, data. You can be quite at odds, but if you can get everybody to agree on objective criteria upon which to rely, that is a strategy. If everyone agrees to that, then you can start looking at the data. When the conversation is about that rather than other, less productive things, you start to move. It sounds really trite, but the strategy has got to be openness and honesty and civility. It has to be inclusive. All of those things must exist. People have got to believe that, if there is an agenda, it is on the table. Personally, and as a group, that nobody is hiding anything.

Seibert's reference to inclusiveness as one of the values for effective collaboration echoed the concepts offered by the previous leaders. In addition to values of honesty and civility, he asserted the importance of personal humility as a critical attitude for successful implementation of sustainability initiatives. In his work with diverse groups convened to resolve sustainability issues throughout the state, he sought to reach the point at which,

> Somewhere along the line, the group as a whole strives to reduce both their egos and their logos. I borrowed this from a colleague of mine; he talked about walking into the emergency operations center during a hurricane. He said, "Steve, this is the only place in state government where you check your ego and your logo at the door." I thought this was wonderful. Early in the game, I told this story to our commissioners at our second meeting. I said, "Is this a commission where we can check our egos and our logos? Frankly, I'm significantly less concerned about your ego."

Seibert illustrated his concern with the issue of logos and how these can interfere with sustainability efforts.

> When groups of people gather in these kinds of commissions, or councils, they are often chosen because they represent home builders or county commissioners or the environmental community. So everybody proudly walks in with their logo on their shirt. You know, "I'm here as a big city mayor." The discussion of sustainability will be thinking boldly about new ways of governing that might be quite offensive to the larger group of city mayors.
>
> So, can you think independently? How do you move a group toward more sustainability? Have an open conversation about who you represent and whether you're capable of walking away from that identification. They did not agree to do it. But we talked about it, and that's okay. To me, that was fine.

To offset this problem, Seibert found an effective strategy in sharing his own story with community leaders in the state. By sharing some of his own struggles with issues of sustainability, he found that he was able to disarm some of their ideological and political defensiveness, which he ascribed in part to the fact that people are more apt to show their ignorance if they feel they are not alone in this.

> Early on in the game, and I don't do this as much as I used to, but I should do it more, I would send out personal emails to the commissioners. I'd take them down my own personal journey. I would let them know what I was struggling with. I would admit not exactly knowing where we were going but also let them know how I was intending to help them work through it. I think a little bit of humility is a helpful mindset and strategy for moving a group when you don't know where you're going, or when you don't have a clear path.

Concurrent with this notion of opening oneself up and showing humility in face of a complex problem such as sustainability, Seibert believed that one of the greatest challenges in implementing successful sustainability efforts related to trust. In his view, a lack of confidence in the process or the leader had a significantly inhibiting effect on people's willingness to participate and offer their ideas.

> A challenge to moving an organization towards sustainability is not having enough trust in the process or the leader to express yourself openly. You have to trust the integrity of the process and of the leader, and their openness to hear a variety of viewpoints. If you don't have this, people clam up. When they clam up they will either come at you later from the side and try to trash the process or, more importantly, you won't get the benefit of their perspective during the process.

At the outset, Seibert and his team faced another challenge, "getting people to think this was worth spending their time and energy on. This future stuff. Vision thing." However, he found that the inherent goodness of people allowed this to occur and was a powerful driver of sustainability, as Koristz and Bardach affirmed before. In Seibert's case, he also discovered that this goodness was nonpartisan, and that it considered both present and future generations.

> The drivers of sustainability have been, for instance, the inherent goodness of the people in the process; this fundamental concern about family, neighbor, and planet. It's there. You see it in the liberal and in the conservative. You just see it. When you can find it, you have to recognize it and then jump on it and note the connection. It's really exciting when it happens. There is much more common ground than people think, not just in the issues of today but in the issues of the future. Everyone talks about doing this for their children and grandchildren.

At this time, Seibert added, this concern for the future generations had to be followed by concrete actions if they were to receive a better planet than the one we received. So talking about doing things for their children and grandchildren was good, but there was more to be done, particularly if Americans were to fulfill the destiny established by their predecessors.

> You have to go a little further: if you don't do it for your children and grandchildren, you're leaving them in a worse position than you are in. And that's just damned immoral. And un-American. Maybe not so much today, but that was the purpose of the John Adams quote. What society has left their children worse off than they were? The "not on your watch" thing. I think it's important to go to that next level of saying, "we're not kidding." This is about whether, when you're long gone, people will refer to this as a very bad time in American history. Sustainability really is an ethic and a behavior. Those are the positive parts that move you forward, when you start to talk in those terms rather than saying, "let's focus on climate change." Nothing wrong with that, but you take on some baggage sometimes when the motivation is drawn down to a political issue – or what can be perceived as a political issue – rather than trying to keep that vision going.

In the context of her own work in Tallahassee as a project manager for the city's green building agenda, Eve Williams took this commitment to action somewhat differently, by becoming more outspoken and confident in her behaviors toward others. This had led her to place action ahead of policy, indicating that she was no longer willing to wait for state legislation to mandate green building codes that she considered should not be delayed further. Her outspokenness echoed sustainability business consultant Seetha Coleman-Kammula's comment on how she had learned to be fearless when she spoke about sustainability. As Eve Williams put it:

> And I have to speak up. I get in people's face. I don't do it in a rude way. But now I am very boisterous. Wherever I am at I will start talking about it. I told everybody at the office I want them to copy double sided. Not even copying double sided, they can do it electronically. From now on we are buying no more pens; we are going to buy cartridges to reuse the housing. We have all become less conscious; we throw that whole pen way. I got there by pushing. So now we are implementing it in a bigger level, my office is going to develop green standards for all our buildings. And we are going to do it. We are not going to wait to be told to do it, we are not going have to implement a policy saying our buildings have got to be green or LEED certified [Leadership in Energy and Environmental Design], we are going to do it, we are going to serve as leaders for the community to say the city is doing it. I don't want us to have to mandate it, I want us to do it, one because it's the right thing to do, and two it is actually more economically feasible to do.

Williams observed that people had begun to acknowledge this different attitude, which she ascribed to a shift in her environmental consciousness.

When I talk about it people say "You have so much energy about this." I like this and I got fired up when I went to the USGBC [United States Green Building Council] last year, because there was so much energy and enthusiasm. Why? Because everybody is passionate about it. You are energy efficient, or perhaps not yet, but environmentally conscious, inside and outside.

In Nathan Burrell's context of working with communities through applied technology, the first important sustainability strategy implemented by his member-based organization, the Minority e-Commerce Association (MECA), came soon after the crash of the dotcom industry in 2000.

We thought that we would have an opportunity from a policy and an organization standpoint to oversee the changes, and be a part of implementing changes and to really be an overarching organization with technologists, community members, and those that are involved to oversee the direction that the technology and community development was going.

The first policy we had to change after the dotcom bubble burst was the fact that we weren't sustainable, and that ours wasn't a sustainable model. So the first policy we changed, number one, was that we became a service-based organization. So, we went from being an organization that sits on the balcony overlooking the horizon, to literally getting on the ground and getting involved in the community, in the development of programs. That was the first policy change for us.

This change in the organization's policy was complemented by an expansion in its governance, which served to provide greater accountability, which he considered

Important for sustainability. The constant testing and measuring, and putting board members in place, and putting an oversight committee in place that could keep you focused in the direction you were going. And the process of sustainability I think is exactly that, is looking deep inside yourself, asking the hard questions of yourself as a leader and an organization.

Similarly to Debbie Koristz, he considered flexibility to be another critical strategy for sustainability.

Two, you have to be willing to change, and keep being flexible enough to be relevant and to be able to move in the new direction. And three, be able to test and measure what kind of impact you are having in these areas, and to see if these new policies are moving forward. So you have to implement these processes in moving towards sustainability.

This did not mean that there were not important challenges to be faced. The first of these related to redefining a clear personal identity and that of the organization with regard to the real work to be done for sustainability to be achieved.

> Right off the bat, I really believe that you go through a phase that you think who you are or what you want to be. The real challenge is really trying to redefine yourself, and find your space, your actual niche that fits in and makes you relevant. And for us it was technology as a tool for economic development of the community. Not trying to be everything to everyone, but to be specialized, and to hold to that.

Within this clarifying process, Burrell identified what he considered to be a key challenge to sustainable social entrepreneurs, that of becoming involved in too many projects at the same time rather than concentrating efforts on a specific and relevant number of tasks.

> So the challenge to moving towards that sustainability agenda, is trying to be everything to everyone, and spreading yourself too thin. And I think that's where you really have to come back, because if you do that, you're not going to be sustainable. You have to stick to what is relevant to you, what is it that you bring to the table, and not being pulled in so many directions which is so easy to do.

Part of this challenge occurs from what Burrell then went on to define as a driving factor of sustainability. He referred to this as the coming together of a community's powerful need to evolve and develop with the social entrepreneur's strong commitment to respond to that desire.

> I think the tremendous need, not only that you have a desire, but a commitment to the sustainability of life, it's almost like breathing. If I take that analogy, it's very funny, when you start a business, and you do community development, you have this tremendous desire to breathe and to see grow the vision and the agenda that you put forth. And what accompanies that is the need for people to use some of the services or the programs that you are developing and taking to the area. So, you have this tremendous desire to do and to produce, and the communities have a tremendous need for what you are doing, so it goes hand in hand. So, for us it was tremendous desire and the ability to go into those areas and communities and do what they needed.

Another sustainability driver, Burrell found, lay in how he had modified his own personal style of engagement with others. In the process of redefining himself in his work with disadvantaged communities, he discovered the value of working at the grassroots level rather than from a distance, a notion similarly expressed by other leaders like Seibert, Koristz, Bardach, and Campoverde. This personal involvement allows for a far deeper understanding of the issues at stake, and for greater sustainability to be infused into a project.

> I think I engage people a little differently now. Because we are talking about sustainability, the last thing you want is the bottle rocket approach. I think my conversation becomes a little more at a micro level, than you do at a macro level. So now my conversation has come more down to the ground, because if I know what's happening on the ground with leaders or others involved, then you are able to back into a sustainable plan and to move those agendas forward. So, it's almost really kind of an organic, from the bottom up approach, instead of from the top down. So those are the kinds of conversations that I have now. Very bottom of the pyramid driven because those are the areas that have a tremendous need, and that's where you can fit in and move towards sustainability.

For John Elkington of Volans Ventures, a shift toward sustainability often begins when an organization is impacted by an important destabilizing social issue, which he described metaphorically. He indicated that one of his strategies involved taking advantage of this situation in order to begin the change process toward sustainability.

> Very often it needs a whack around the corporate head with a societal equivalent of a 2-by-4 to get companies' attention, which is another way of saying that often we introduce our strategic ideas (including the TBL [triple bottom line]) into destabilized organizations, where the old certainties have been challenged in some way.

Elkington added that more recently his organization's strategy had shifted from developed to emerging economies, though the focus of the work was largely the same.

> Whereas we once focused on the business case for action in developed countries, and on reporting on stakeholder engagement, we now increasingly focus on the same things in emerging economies – and, in other parts of the world, on business models, disruptive innovation and scalable entrepreneurial solutions to sustainability challenges.

Education

MaryBeth Burton, at the Florida Atlantic University (FAU) Center for Urban and Environmental Solutions (CUES), also was convinced that change toward sustainability came from personal involvement at the ground level. In her work at the university, she highlighted the crucial importance of networking among key stakeholders as sustainability implementation strategy. She offered a brief anecdote on recycling to illustrate her point.

> I think much of any organizational progress comes from the people, at this point. One of the first things that I did personally was to investigate recycling practices at the campus where I was working, in Ft. Lauderdale. It was very clear to everyone that it wasn't happening. So that was one of the first places I turned, and I found a great champion and partner in Reid Morgan, who is the facilities manager of the Broward campuses. I went to Reid and it became very clear to me that he was a strong proponent of all things sustainable, but that he was in the business of running buildings, and was understaffed. He didn't really have a champion to get the word out, to make the connections between the necessary vendors, all those kind of other steps that are needed to take place for implementation of a new program. But he was very supportive. And we are fortunate in the city of Ft. Lauderdale that they have a full time recycling coordinator who has actually developed a program to incentivize businesses like FAU to recycle. They can piggy back onto the city's contract, and the city provides the recycling bins for free. So you have the city's contract, which is also much cheaper than having to go out on your own and getting bids. So you contract with their provider, but the city provides the recycling carts. You just pay for pickup of the carts.

In the same vein, Burton indicated that the opposite was also true. The principal challenge to attaining sustainability lies with people, particularly those in key positions, who resist changing their way of thinking, and in this manner break the interdependence among diverse stakeholders needed to move sustainability forward.

> There are still those who are very resistant to change. I've seen it here, within the university. I think one of our biggest challenges is in one of our departments. We have someone who is our liaison between the vendor and the university, who doesn't want to participate in sustainability initiatives, an FAU person. She has served as a gatekeeper. I don't know that I have been all that successful in changing the mindset of those extremely resistant people. And I haven't really met this person so I am not sure exactly what it is about it that bothers her so much, whether it's just someone questioning what she's doing and she doesn't appreciate that. I think that's more it than the issue of sustainability. In the times that I have contacted her via email I get this sense that it's more "this is my job, I have the authority to deal with this, and you should just stay out of it."

Burton believed that this engagement in sustainability, though not part of her job description, constituted "my moral responsibility," and that the major issue was "lack of collaboration." When there was collaboration, the sense of personal frustration she sometimes felt at confronting this complex challenge on her own, was alleviated significantly.

> On the flip side of that though, I have found some great partners, across departments, across campuses, across schools, I am working with Broward

> Community College, and now Palm Beach Community College, I am going to start working with them, to partner on some issues. Because we are so vulnerable, I think it helps to band together to get the strength from being part of a larger group, knowing that this isn't a personal uphill battle that you're facing alone, that there are others that are willing to face it with you.

For Dr Len Berry at the FAU Center for Environmental Studies (CES), a deliberate sustainability strategy was to engage multiple stakeholders at the outset of a project, a practice that numerous other leaders considered as one of the most effective in business and community. In his case, Berry highlighted the importance of bringing together representatives of three specific constituencies, academia, government, and business, which he considered brought specific added value to a project.

> What we've tried to do in CES, in the organization, when tackling a topic or a meeting or a subject, as a deliberate strategy to involve the academic community, the business community and the government community. At our first meeting in 1995 we were looking at our ecological systems in Florida and in how we should be able to maintain them. So why does getting those together mean anything about sustainability? Well it allows you to combine the philosophy of academia with the practical world of government policy and business practice, and what we have done with a number of those topics, not all of them, is to follow up the initiative with a long-term process of working with small groups of people.

Dr Berry supported this perspective by recounting a case where he was involved in working with Florida ranchers in an effort to support them in a shift toward profitable but sustainable farming.

> The best example from that meeting was that we began to work with a working group of ranchers and some people from the center and some people from government and we were looking at the whole theme of how, when you have private lands or when you have public lands, how you can make them profitable though environmentally sound. And so we encouraged some of the ranchers to look into ecotourism, for example, which meant they had to preserve part of their farming land as natural habitat and many of them were doing that, so it really was a case of using a process of long-term interaction and education where you are leading people from a viewpoint that says one I'm in this to make money but I also want to do a good job to saying that if I do this job in these different ways then we're creating a long-term sustainable enterprise.

Berry had encountered several challenges in his work. The first related to the short-term view prevalent in policymakers, who were resistant to the fact that sustainable results rarely materialized within a 4-year time frame. A second challenge, which also had been raised by other leaders, related to the unwillingness of people to engage in projects outside their specific area of expertise, due to the discomfort this provoked.

> And that's true of the USAID SANREM [United States Agency for International Development Sustainable Agriculture and Natural Resource Management] project too. We found that when they set up activities in Latin America and the Philippines and in Africa; different groups managed each of those activities, and though they were all supposed to be sustainable resource management, what you found was that there was a tendency to want to follow their expertise. And so one group was focusing much more on water issues, one group focused on soil issues.

This fragmented approach was offset, Berry had found, by the less discipline-bound perspective of "the anthropologists, who had a broad-based viewpoint. They were much more like Geographers; they were looking at people's resource base from a broader perspective." As he indicated, "The problem is therefore getting away from the disciplinary nature of most of our training and feeling comfortable with that, you get away from it but you don't always feel comfortable with because you're out on a limb."

Berry identified two further challenges to sustainability. One related to the lack of green collar jobs outside of academia, though he acknowledged this had improved in recent times.

> And the other problem with dealing with sustainability until pretty recently is that there aren't many jobs, so that you find that people involved in activities that cover this range of things are in careers in departments at universities; they are in careers and finding ways in which they can get rewarded and recognized for what they are doing has being tough. It's gotten easier now but to me it's still not easy.

Finally, Berry identified funding, or the lack thereof, as a challenge for sustainability efforts, an obstacle that he linked to the short-term perspective of policymakers.

> I think funding is always a challenge. As I've worked internationally and here in Florida I think that people who allocate money for tasks don't usually allocate it with the label of looking at sustainable outcomes, at least until recently. Therefore, there are a lot of things that you try to do in the name of sustainability have to be couched in other terms, because the funding is not there. There are two issues, one is that the funding doesn't target sustainability, and the second is that it doesn't usually recognize the time periods that you need to deal with, the latter being more important than the first.

With regard to facilitators, Dr Berry identified a diverse range of drivers of sustainability. The first of these related to a particular quality of leadership, that of the capacity to adopt a long-term perspective in contrast to the short-term view of the policymakers he had referred to previously. This particular quality entailed

> The recognition among the more thoughtful in the business that we are using resources in a way that is not sustainable. So one of the drivers is the few people with a longer vision of trends in resource use. That goes from the use of ground water from western U.S. to Yemen. We are using ground water at an unsustainable rate. How do we change that and the use of soil and vegetation resources at unsustainable rates?

Berry also identified as drivers both global and local issues of a practical and even critical nature. In this regard, Berry was categorical: Sustainability "is a practical issue," not a philosophical one, in spite of the fact that much of the conversation on the topic leaned toward this area. He strongly believes that global problems such as population growth and affluence, or local issues like land and water use in Florida, are very real problems that demand pragmatic rather than philosophical solutions. Berry identified a further driver in the growing global awareness of sustainability issues fostered by international conferences on the topic.

> Stockholm in 1972 was the first world environmental conference which again was a response to a perceived crisis. If you go back further, to post World War II, you have the formation of many new countries with the dissolution of the Soviet Union. Today we have more than 200 countries. Those are all managers of resources. We have found that many resources are transnational. And so we've got the '72 conference, the '92 conference, and the 2002 Sustainability Conference. You have a growing global interchange of opinion with some of the people who were not part of the discourse now being involved, the developing countries. So you've got not only a local awareness, but a growing global awareness.

Finally, Berry suggested an even more universal factor that he considered had contributed to shifting people's understanding of the planet as an integrated whole.

> Another driver, and this is hard to prove, but I think is the use since 1962 of images of Earth from space, which created in people's minds, whether they are literate or not, an image of the globe as one whole thing. And I think as we identify much more with the globe as a whole, I think that we are getting a better sense of the problems and that we have to deal at a global level.

For Professor Daniel Meeroff, the first strategy to promote sustainability lay in leadership by example, even in very simple matters, and the fact that people often would like to do something for the environment but lacked the knowledge to do so. Providing simple sustainability strategies, therefore, gave people opportunities to do something significant with the reinforcing sense of satisfaction that accompanied the action. It also enabled people to share their accomplishments with others.

> For instance, it's just like going to the secretary and saying, "Look, this product number you've been buying for 100 years is 100% virgin paper, and it's \$2.50 a roll. Look at this one, it's \$2.49 a roll and it's 50% recycled. Let's buy one and see what it looks like." And after that, she just switches over to that number. It's as simple as that; kind of little things that you can do. Just realizing that, at least here, Office Depot has a green website. You can type in "paper," and you'll get 600 choices from which you can select the cheapest option. But if you go to the green website, you can get all the green choices available. The same for Home Depot and so on.
>
> So if you do something that works, and then you touch 10 different people, hopefully they'll implement it at home. I talk about what I'm doing in my house, and now I see people trying to do the same thing in their new houses. It's not like you should be doing this because if you're not doing it, you're bad. I'm doing it because it's easy to do and it's good for the environment. It also makes me feel better. Other people see that it makes me feel better, and they say, "Wow, I should be doing that."

The satisfaction that came from these small changes, and the effect this had on people's willingness to communicate and share their findings with others was a powerful factor in moving sustainability forward. Meeroff compared this effect to that of a religious belief, and how in a similar manner sustainability was disseminated by word of mouth.

> So I think it has to go person to person. I keep coming back to this religious analogy, but I'm sure that's how religion began too. Somebody had to walk around with a book, saying these are the teachings, and someone else took it to someone else. There was no Internet back then! It's just kind of being a resource that makes that barrier a lot shorter for people to jump over. Because they want to jump; they're just afraid that it's too tall.

In his professional work as a consultant and engineer, Dr Meeroff also indicated that he applied the strategy of multistakeholder involvement favored by other leaders, "Bringing everyone together at the table from the beginning of the project and defining a sustainability goal with sufficient importance assigned to it as to guide the design and implementation and selection of alternatives."

Meeroff also had found that there was a widespread belief, a "pervasive feeling: that it's too difficult and it can't be done." However, he indicated that convincing people is not difficult, particularly when there are economic benefits attached.

> Even this Florida Green Lodging certification (as an example), you go to the hotel and say you're going to save money in all these areas. It's going to turn out to be big savings later on and you're going to get promoted. And

it's someone else saying, "I will do all the work for you, I've got this checklist and I'm going to go around here showing you everything you can do to save money on all kinds of stuff."

Dr Meeroff strongly believed in the value of education as a major driving factor of sustainability. Though people felt the urge to do something for the environment, the complexity of the issue required more than simply implementing isolated actions. The challenge of sustainability lay in that it needed to be addressed from a systemic rather than a linear perspective, and this was difficult for many.

> People want to do things; they just don't know what or how to do them. It's complicated, because like I said earlier, everything we do has a consequence and a trade-off. There's nothing that's 100% green. We just found out that carbon dioxide is a pollutant, so you're polluting right now just by breathing. How do we get around that mindset? There's a lot of external pressure and it's not a linear approach. It's not like, if I do this, I'm saving that. It's, what else are you doing that makes a difference too.

Similarly to Daniel Meeroff, Professor Jaap Vos also affirmed that education was a key strategy for sustainability: "The common thread in everything I have done in my career has been education. The strategy was always education and awareness." However, he was convinced that education by itself was insufficient, asserting that "it only works if you are able to imagine yourself in somebody else's footsteps." This prompted him to engage in environmentally related practical work, initially in the Netherlands, adopting a perspective Len Berry had recommended in his own interview. He realized in the process that this approach shifted the nature of the relationship he established with the people he worked with, in this case farmers.

> The first that I learned when I was teaching in an environmental college was to understand how a farm worked. I needed to understand what their concerns were, what their daily worries were. And when I understood that and I could talk in their language, and understand what they were concerned about and translate the problem, and the issues that I saw they had to deal with on a daily basis. That changed the whole discussion.

A second major strategy for sustainability, Vos explained, came from his discovery that the farmers with whom he worked were concerned solely with increasing their farms' yields. As he pointed out, he was able to shift the farmers' obsession with increased production once he was able to demonstrate that their profit margins could be increased with less investment and labor while preserving the quality of their soil and the environment.

> The turning point in teaching agricultural students about environmental issues was that I realized that they were interested in increasing yields. That's the only thing that farmers were always taught. And when I realized

> that increasing yields is not the same as increasing the bottom line I became effective. It's about making money. Who cares that you have 5 thousand bushels, if you made more money last year. And when we got them to talk about the bottom line all of a sudden they could talk to environmentalists because now they realized that "if I don't spray pesticides I don't waste time in going out, I don't spend money on gasoline, I don't spend money on pesticides. I am actually saving money. When I look at input and my output, I am now making more money, and I work less."

This pointed out two driving factors. The first was the search for increased revenues. The second was that this willingness in the Dutch farmers to change their farming methods was attained by applying a bottom-up rather than a top-down approach, working from the practical realities and the mindset of the people themselves. As will be recalled, both strategies were indicated as important by a number of the leaders in all domains. Vos indicated:

> So those kinds of things I think are very important, and that's what I think I like about sustainable development, the idea that you don't come at it from a top-down kind of approach, you need to look at them by understanding them in how they work.

For Vos, there were two principal challenges to sustainability. The first was "Ignorance; the inability of people to look beyond appearances." The second had to with trust and how this obstructed the ability of leaders to work with minority communities.

> What I mean by that, I work a lot in minority communities, and in a minority community I cannot do anything until people trust me. And it's the same with environmental issues and sustainability; you have to wait until people realize that you are on their side. So it's always a barrier if you deal with people who are so close-minded that they can't even give you the time of life to get to that point or they realize that you are not their enemy. Sometimes it's a barrier that people think that they already know it. And I think that's often a barrier. And they are not willing to look critically at what they do themselves.

According to Vos, a more systemic challenge had to do with the political context within which organizations operated. Whereas in Europe, governments tended to be consistent in how change was implemented, providing a strong degree of certainty within which long-term planning was made possible. However, a very different climate prevailed in the United States. This supported Len Berry's view with regard to the short-term vision of policymakers with whom he had worked in Florida.

> In the U.S. what I see as a real barrier is an ever changing direction. In Europe, we are used to progress that is extremely slow, in incremental

> changes, but we never look back. But in the U.S. you have swings. And as long as you have swings you don't make progress. Companies will not make changes in these field processes until they know what direction they are going in. The most important thing for a company is certainty. You see that in things like planning. The most important thing for a developer is not cost, it's certainty, it's making sure. A developer works in a pipeline. The pipeline needs to move. If you stop the pipeline somewhere the developer is losing money. It's not the cost. It's the certainty that the process can go on. If you have continued progress, like you have in the Netherlands the company can predict what is going to happen. They know that they are serious about enforcement. They know that they had better start doing something about it or they are going to get stuck. Here [in the U.S.], if you can stick it out for four years, the whole policy climate might change. So I think that the big barrier is this. There has to be continuous funding, there has to be progress, and if you can't create certainty it's not going to work.

On the other hand, Dr Vos singled out several driving factors of sustainability, such as influential individuals, Florida Governor Charlie Crist among them, and also publications, important incidents, international conferences, and even industry.

> In my history, the Brundtland commission [1987] was a great driver. I was studying environmental science at the time, and the publication of that report caused such an uproar in the Netherlands. Everybody was interested in environmental issues. There were so many conferences. As a student, you could go to a conference almost every day.
>
> And even since then I have never seen anything like it. From one day to the next, agriculture started talking about sustainability. The Churches started talking about it. An alarming but at the same time a hopeful book; the same as the reports of the Club of Rome. So publications can make a major impact. Certain people can make an impact. Sometimes it's an individual. A year ago we didn't care about climate change in Florida. But since Governor Crist paid attention to it now suddenly it's a hot issue and everybody pays attention to it. So individuals can really be drivers, but they can only be instigators, they can't really drive the process forward very well, they can get it on the agenda so that everybody pays attention to it but then that's where it stops, that's where the challenge is of sustainability.

Vos summarized the most important influences as

> Publications, people, major incidents. One of my professors said one of the best things that can happen is an oil spill. A major oil spill. And he was right. And oil is spilled in daily regular leaking operations. And an oil spill gets people's attention, and outrage. But it makes a big difference. The reality is that oil is leaking every single day much more than these oil spills. But it can

be a turning point, an agenda setting issue, it can raise awareness, but if it's not followed up, it's going to fall apart.

And the interesting thing in the Netherlands was that sustainability was driven by industry. It was private industry that drove environmental policy to extremely strict regulations. They wanted certainty. They saw it was coming. And they wanted to know from government "What are you going to do, when are we going to have these rules in place?" So that they could make their business plans accordingly. And it worked, because if you look at all these high efficiency light bulbs, they're from the Netherlands. Those companies realized, "We are willing to do this, but government needs to set the regulations so that we can get rid of these competitors who are not doing it right."

Vos referred to these drivers as a "combination of the bottom line and ethics," where the bottom line had provided the initial stimulus for change, with the hope that values would follow.

It had nothing with ethics; it had to do with resources becoming scarce, and expensive. There is a niche market, we can be the first in that market, and if in the process the government sets up the regulations we can get rid of some of the competition. The values may have to come later. And of course there were people who had the right values, and had a different opinion about it, but it worked because there were economic opportunities. Economics can be a major driver, you don't need to have a cultural change, a change in the way people feel, if there are economic incentives to do this.

However, he did believe that some people had made the change based on values before weighing its economic advantage. Vos referred once again to his image of the balance between the use of sticks and carrots or regulation as opposed to people dancing with tambourines, a figure of speech he used to indicate the "change coming from within." As a concrete expression of this balance, in the Netherlands the government had provided a grace period allowing for change for its own sake. However, at the same time, it established a clear set of expectations and an implementation schedule, after which period regulations would be strictly enforced, to the point where violators of environmental policies could even serve prison sentences.

One of the things with this whole idea with sticks and carrots and tambourines, the way it worked in the Netherlands was, we start with the carrots and then after the carrots we will have people that will be jumping happily. There will have been people who jumped before that with the tambourine in their hand. And after that we will start with the stick; but we will give them five years. And in that process we hope that ultimately we will get to the tambourines, and we won't need the stick any more. It's a really interesting kind of approach. And it only worked because the stick had become really

> real. There was ten years of policy when that stick became real, and people got fines, and went to jail. It makes it much easier if there is clear and very strict enforcement.

Judy Walton, Executive Director of the AASHE, indicated that as part of its overall strategy, the association was developing its own sustainability plan "to codify many of the organizational practices that we're already engaged in. This includes the way staff organize ourselves according to sustainability principles – valuing diversity, participation, and equity, and thinking for the long-term."

> Our organization's mission is to advance sustainability on college campuses and in all of higher education, so we definitely have to walk the talk in our own practices and programs.
>
> Unlike many organizations that have to strategize to get employees on board with sustainability, our staff are already fully on board, and actively seeking ways that AASHE can become even more sustainable. Our latest idea is to take the STARS rating system developed for campuses and see how well we can apply it to our own organization, how well we would score.

STARS (Sustainability Tracking, Assessment & Rating System) is a self-assessment rating system for colleges and universities, under development by AASHE at the time of the interview. STARS addresses one of the greatest challenges to sustainability at colleges and universities: that of the "silo" effect, which Barlett and Chase (2004) refer to in *Sustainability on campus: Stories and strategies for change*, arguably the best compilation of sustainability efforts in higher education published to date: "Sustainability is a particular challenge in our society when most structures are set up so hierarchically, with silos of knowledge and responsibility that prevent people from seeing the big picture and thinking in terms of the whole."

Jean MacGregor, Senior Scholar and Project Director of the "Curriculum for the Bioregion" at The Washington Center for Improving the Quality of Undergraduate Education at The Evergreen State College, offered highly targeted strategies for sustainability. Acknowledging with her colleagues that Evergreen had a "very strong environmental and social conscience" since its founding years in the 1970s, they also realized that much of the sustainability under way was "quite fragmented, it's not well organized, and we have a very, very large group of colleagues to educate in the faculty, staff and student body." This led to the creation of a task force to develop a master plan for sustainability as an initial strategy, supported by a consultation process involving active listening with hundreds of stakeholders on campus, and a review of the university documentation of any and all sustainability practices. This was followed by a retreat at which time the task force prepared the master sustainability plan.

> So we did a series of Summer Institutes for faculty, staff and students over a period of years, and a couple of years ago, maybe three now, the president

decided that it was time to do a new strategic plan and a new campus master plan. So we took it as our work, to make sure that sustainability was very prominent in those two exercises to the degree that we asked the president and the provost to create a Sustainability Task Force to actually write the sustainability portion of the college's master plan. They agreed and we created a task force of about 15 people.

But the process, the story that stands out for me, is that as we decided that in order to strike a set of goals and benchmarks on the wall according to the strategic plan's template, we needed to undertake a listening process on the campus, to assess the degree to which our colleagues understood sustainability and to explore what kinds of ideas they had looking out to the future. And we engaged several hundred people in that listening process. I believe that it helped get the work quite energetically down the road and it actually resulted in tremendous buy-in on the part of many campus leaders including our president. This was simply a good old tried and true "sensing interview" strategy that most community organizers would recognize.

MacGregor went on to describe her Curriculum for the Bioregion Initiative as perhaps the most longstanding and "scaled-up" strategy for sustainability reform in higher education in the United States. Given its value in the context of the study, this passage from the interview is transcribed almost in its entirety.

The Curriculum for the Bioregion initiative is a project that involves 32 colleges and universities in the Puget Sound bioregion. We have involved 19 community colleges, 5 public four-year universities, 7 four-year private universities, and one tribal college. The unit in which Curriculum for the Bioregion lives is the Washington Center for Undergraduate Education, a public service center of The Evergreen State College, The Washington Center has been a resource to all of these campuses for over 20 years, so we began our work with the momentum and credibility of many years of other statewide reform projects. Many faculty and campuses associate the Washington Center with the learning communities approach, that of linking classes together during a given academic term to increase student engagement, build community, and connections among disciplines and ideas. They also associate us with diversity work, and with math reform work, focusing on fostering academic success for under-represented students. So the Curriculum for the Bioregion initiative represented a new institutional initiative that these campus could join. They are not required to, of course, but with every single opportunity that we can put forward related to this initiative, we invite faculty to get involved if they would like to, for very low registration fees or for free.

We are creating communities of faculty within the disciplines that we call "faculty learning communities" to inquire together and work together over an academic year, actually to invent integrative assignments that teach a big idea, a cornerstone concept in the discipline, but they also nest it in a sustainability concept or a sustainability public issue. This approach is based in the assumption that faculty members need to start right where they are, with the courses they regularly teach, with the disciplinary concepts they work to get across, day after day.

My goal for the next few years is to reach the fifteen disciplines in whose introductory courses there are the highest student enrollments. They are pretty much the highest enrollment classes in any state: Freshman writing, math, intro biology and chemistry, psychology, political science, geography, history, philosophy, economics, anthropology, etc. The idea is to introduce interesting, indeed *exciting* sustainability concepts and topics as a *norm* across all kinds of classes in undergraduate education. Now I'm very aware that environmental science is another avenue, and of course the introductory environmental science class is a point of opportunity because many, many students take that, not necessarily because they plan to major in that field, but they are just taking it as their science distribution requirement. We are working with that community as well.

And then, we are also discovering that many of the involved faculty, because they have got into this sustainability work, they are starting to join or lead their campus sustainability task forces or starting sustainability-across-the-curriculum projects on their campuses. So they are beginning to emerge as leaders. We are also undertaking some additional reinforcing and community-strengthening strategies (such as other conferences, workshops, and field learning experiences on pressing regional issues) but mainly the faculty learning community piece is the heart of our strategy. It is about face-to-face community-building and curriculum-building. It's also about asking faculty to be much more intentional about their design of learning experiences, and more importantly, their design of assignments. In the end, the intentional curriculum creation is very important, but just as important is the faculty formation.

To give that group of faculty a little help we provide them with the time and space to work collaboratively. We also provide some resources, and this list of sustainability learning outcomes is one of them. If you look at the Brundtland definition of sustainability, it could encompass everything but the kitchen sink. We wanted to clarify and hone down what sustainability learning outcomes might look like. So, at our inaugural conference in 2006, a conference of about 120 people, we said "Okay, you might encounter your undergraduate students in only one class, and that might be the last economics class, sociology class, chemistry class, that your students might take. To be sure, it's often an introductory class, but it *also* might be the *terminal experience* the students have in your discipline. So if you could only teach one concept about sustainability and you could be assured that they could walk away really understanding that one concept, what would it be, in your discipline?"

So we asked them to brainstorm not only concepts, but skills and habits of mind. And of course, with this large group of faculty, we got 300 bright

> ideas! So a group of eight of us (drawn from as many disciplines) went on retreat for two days, and we boiled the big list down to these three pages. So that's where this came from. It's not the be-all and the end-all list of sustainability learning outcomes, but it's a prompt to get people thinking about what this field includes.

From her engagement in this work, MacGregor identified several clear factors that she considered were driving forces for sustainability at her campus and in the region more broadly, the first of which was the "institution's heritage of values and its culture of commitment to environmental care and social justice." The second driver, she affirmed, was the growing awareness of sustainability as a source of real concern, which she described as "the wider consciousness about global warming, peak oil, deteriorating ecosystems, and environmental justice issues." MacGregor affirmed that this awareness had led to a greater willingness by people to engage in sustainability issues.

> The opportunity is we are now living in a media swirl that's helping people to be "very, very worried," as Time Magazine put it. It's past time to be very, very worried. It is time to be very, very *active* with our students, being co-learners with them. I've discovered that there are people out there just waiting to be asked, to get engaged in this sustainability work. And so that's the opportunity that we've got right this minute.

Finally, she highlighted the progressive mindset of people in the Pacific Northwest itself, which she considered to be another significant factor in driving sustainability.

> The other thing driving this forward is that we are in Washington, a state with not only longstanding leadership in environmental matters, but also a long heritage of populist values, where public processes are highly valued and consensus decision making is actually a pillar of good governance. So the listening processes that we chose resonated with what people value and care about and enabled them to join in.

In contrast, MacGregor identified several challenges to sustainability. This related mainly to the fragmented way in which people lead their lives, a condition she associated not only with higher education professionals, but with society as a whole. This fragmentation leads to people's inability to connect at a significant level, to focus deeply on complex issues, and to a troubling superficiality of thinking.

> These have to do with the times we live in. People live in a world of fragmented information and endless, mind-numbing multi-tasking. There is very little time for deep focus and reflection and the hard work of making hard choices. I believe that the pace of modern life and overwhelming information

> fragmentation, this living-in-a-rushed state holds back our work. It translates to people with an inability to show up for every single committee meeting, to the degree that we have to work out times to have 5 and 6-hour retreats rather than 90-minute, rushed committee meetings, and it also translates to a kind of superficiality of thinking and lack of sustained reflection. I think this is not only a troubling feature of higher education today; it is a troubling aspect of our society.

MacGregor expanded on this notion by delving more deeply into the consequences of the highly demanding environment within which faculty currently operated.

> What's getting in the way, as a challenge, is faculty members in today's media-saturated and information-saturated world and in the generally frenetic pace of today's academy are almost at the breaking point of being stretched in too many directions, with too many expectations on them, most especially I see this in young faculty members in their tenure track path. I think it's highly unfair. So much is being asked of them, they seem to have little time for their personal lives and no time for reflection. As a result they are either distracted or frantically busy. So how do you get distracted people to slow down and pay attention to things, or even to follow through in a project as modest as the one I am describing? It's really challenging my community organizing skills as never before.

Dr Anthony Cortese, founder of Second Nature, an organization dedicated to supporting colleges and universities in their commitment to sustainability, considered that the most effective strategies began from an understanding of where people's awareness lay. If we are unaware of the impact we have on our surroundings we are less likely to act sustainably.

> First of all, awareness of the consequences of our actions. One of the problems is that the negative impacts that we might have are largely invisible to us. Because they are invisible, they don't count. If we don't see value we don't measure it, and if we don't measure it, we don't manage it. One of the things is to make people aware of the consequences of their actions. It has to start with awareness. If you are not aware of the consequences of your actions, then you won't be aware of different possibilities of action, and then you won't be motivated to take action.

Once this awareness was achieved, then it became possible to develop what he called a vision for sustainability, followed by an implementation strategy supported by clear incentives and accountability.

> Once you get awareness, then you need to develop a vision of how to create a different and better reality for your institution that is based on eliminating

> negative unintended consequences. And so the next place is a vision following that is developing a set of strategies to get people in your institution to buy into that vision, and to help establish a system of incentives for people to embrace that vision and turn it into a series of plans and policies.
>
> The incentives would be a means of rewarding people within the institution for buying into the vision and the values, and helping to establish a reward and accountability structure so that people in the institution who buy into the vision will be personally rewarded for taking the institution in that different direction.

Cortese outlined the following phase of the strategy by describing the process by which it became possible to engage the broader university community, and establish appropriate policy for successful implementation.

> So once you establish the vision and goals among your senior leadership in any institution, then there has to be a next level, of bringing in as many people as possible in your institution to essentially own the vision and to have them work with the senior leadership to establish the policies, programs, and actions for the implementation of the vision, including means of measuring, accounting and reward.

This process, in Cortese's experience, is not always smooth. He associated two key driving factors to sustainability, communication and recognition, the lack of which tended to act as a serious obstacle to its implementation.

> One of the most important, I have a little saying. I believe that communication is to sustainability as location is to real estate. It's about communication because it's about people coming together to understand each other in different sectors and responsibilities within an institution, and the interactions with society will take those people to understand a different way of doing things.
>
> It's also about ways to recognize and celebrate all the things that people are doing that are moving in the direction of sustainability. And one of the things that you find in many institutions and it is probably worse in higher education than in most other institutions; and I've been in government and worked extensively with industry and higher education. And one of the things in higher education that we do very poorly is pat people on the back to tell them that they are doing well. The primary subculture of faculty is tenure and promotion, and facilities, and summer off so that you can get a supplement. And very little attention is paid to rewarding people who are faculty, staff, and in operations who are contributing to the well-being of the community, and one of the attributes of well-being is sustainability.

In addition to these, Cortese identified four further barriers to sustainability. These echoed previous references to the effects of the demands placed on people at this challenging time, on a fragmented understanding of the full scope of the notion of sustainability, on a misconception of the negative costs associated with sustainability efforts, and on the unwillingness of people to expose themselves by undertaking a change of behavior before a supportive culture had been established.

> The first is that people think that sustainability is such an unachievable goal, and a belief that it's requiring us to change everything by tomorrow. So there is a resistance to change that occurs because people feel that they are overwhelmed in their daily and institutional lives, and asking them to do something different means that we will have to do something new on top of everything else that we are doing. So the resistance to change that comes from the inertia of everyday life and everyday institutional thrust is huge.

A second issue is that many people think of sustainability as primarily about environmentalism, and not about the need to create a different reality for the purposes of being successful, from a health, social, economic as well as an environmental standpoint. So the people who think that it's largely about environmentalism think that it is meant to attack all the existing power structures in society. I think that this misunderstanding is another source of resistance.

> A third one is that many people don't understand the large-scale dilemma that we have, and so they think that sustainability is something that involves a trade-off between protecting the environment and everything else. The idea is that we will do this when we can afford to do it and we will do as much as we can afford.
>
> And then the final one, which is important for any kind of change, as social-psychologists tell us, if you want to get people to change, some people aren't willing to be the first person to do it. There have to have been others who have done it and been successful. So being able to show examples of how they can get there. Their issue is that it has to be in their self-interest.

Cortese acknowledged the seriousness of these challenges. However, he went on to identify several factors that he had encountered in his work that he considered powerful driving forces for sustainability. The first two of these related to moral values and economic constraints, which he summarized by suggesting the phrase, "to live by treading lightly," which echoed Jean MacGregor's reference to the "butterfly mindset" of those engaged in sustainability.

> Well, I think there are moral drivers. People say it's not right. There are a billion people in the world who don't have basic sanitation. There are different and better ways of doing things that can save resources; that can allow us to have a good quality of life, to live life by treading lightly. That fits with a fairly deep cultural philosophy for most people. We shouldn't waste resources; it's bad to waste resources. There is a big concern about leaving the earth so that future generations can have a decent quality of life. I believe

> that the economic constraints for people to run their business in a successful way are a major driver for industry and government.

Cortese also considered that the "entrepreneurial spirit" in the United States constituted a third driver for sustainability, particularly in the competitive spirit that drove people to seek creative solutions to difficult problems. He referred to entrepreneurialism not only as a characteristic in business, but as a growing phenomenon in the nonprofit sector.

> In the U.S. there is a very entrepreneurial spirit that says that we were able to get to the moon, so we should be able to create a sustainable world. And I think that the competitive spirit is a very strong motivator, because I don't believe we would be developing all these alternative technologies and ways of doing things that people are working on if it weren't for that sort of drive that we can make a difference. I think that's a huge one that has driven a lot of people in business.
>
> I think if you look at the growth of NGOs (nongovernmental organizations), and why do we need NGOs? We need them when there is market failure or when the government isn't stepping in to help solve the problem. An important signal that we are living unsustainably is the fact of the number of NGOS, nonprofits, which are at around 2 million, and growing at an exponential rate. It's like global warming is the starkest symptom that humans are living out of sync with our life support systems. I am fond of saying that Second Nature should not have to be in existence. If the American Council on Education, which is the 800 pound gorilla in higher education, were doing its job, it would be looking ahead and asking what are all the challenges that we face in society and how should higher education be organizing itself to meet those challenges. And because it is not doing this, we had to create Second Nature.

Dr Mitchell Thomashow, President of Unity College, Maine, described the strategy that had been implemented at the university. Within an overarching commitment to sustainability and a master planning process, the university welcomed a diversity of approaches to the issue.

> We're building sustainability initiatives. So everyone comes at it differently. For example, the officer of residential life and the people in the finance office. Some people take it more seriously than others. The role of the sustainability coordinator is to make sure that all this gets done. At the President's level, we have signed the President's Climate Commitment, we discuss buying carbon offsets, we engage in long-term natural planning.
>
> I try to build consensus around that, so we have engaged in a master planning process. Even at a college like ours, it's incredible how traditional people are, and you constantly have to remind them. People are creatures of habit and routine, especially faculty.

Thomashow highlighted his own role as a leader in this process, which was "to provide people with the bigger picture." He found this to be a personal leadership challenge, which he considered involved the ability "to balance urgency and patience, the sense that we must get this done quickly versus the fact that we can't get it all done now." He also identified two specific challenges to sustainability, which he defined as falling into two categories: "One is fiscal, and the other is organizational-psychological."

> First of all, it is the role of leadership to explain to people that given the kind of economics that we practice, cost-accounting is delusional. We need to implement cost-accounting that has to do with the ecological system, and that is very hard to do. It is delusional because it has nothing to do with the ecological reality.
>
> The second challenge is organizational-psychological. There's always a lot of inertia in an organization that doesn't help people understand that there is an entirely different way in which we can conduct business.

On the other hand, Thomashow identified a significant shift in the current environment in higher education, far more supportive of sustainability initiatives, which he described as a powerful driver of sustainability. Though prevalent as a matter of course at Unity College, he was pleased to see that universities were beginning to compete for students using sustainability as a marketing strategy.

> Because we are an environmental college, it is implicit that we have responsibility to move this forward. There is a kind of arms race going on way right now, in a good way, in that many colleges are competing. The atmosphere in higher education today is extraordinarily competitive. And what is happening right now is that colleges are competing using sustainability to attract students. I think this is the best thing I've seen in all the years I've been in this field. There are all these colleges doing these very neat things about sustainability. I've never seen anything like it. In order to stake out our marketing edge, we have to do that too. But none of that matters if people don't believe it. That's really the most important thing.

Discussion

With the collapse of communism in 1989, there has been a profound change in the global environment within which organizations and societies operate. Along with the rise of capitalism as the dominant economic paradigm of recent times, the rapid evolution of technology has led to the globalization of economics, trade, and knowledge sharing in a way that has flattened the world (Friedman, 2005, 2008). Indicators provided by the International Geosphere-Biosphere Programme (2007) show just how quickly human systems, particularly in the past 60 years, have accelerated patterns of foreign direct investment, urban population growth, water usage, greenhouse gas emissions, paper consumption, among others. The implications of the impact of this acceleration on the stability and sustainability of natural and social systems are still not widely understood (AtKisson, 2008; Costanza et al., 2007). As reported by the leaders in this study, however, those organizations and communities that have acknowledged the importance of these indicators and how they pertain to their well-being have initiated a profound shift in their systems of governance, management of internal and external stakeholders, operation of their facilities, and the manner in which they engage their immediate and the broader community.

Several findings in this section on effective strategies for sustainability were common to a majority of the leaders. Principal among these was the need to involve multiple stakeholders at the outset of any sustainability initiative in order to ensure the most effective result. This was true for sustainable businesses, which are showing a shift toward stakeholder rather than shareholder management, thereby freeing up internal creativity and potential, establishing a systemic sustainability-oriented relationship with the company's supply chain and customer base, and engaging the wider community in issues of social and environmental justice. For community leaders, this was described as a collaborative decision-making process harnessing the talents of local residents in a bottom-up approach to building sustainable communities. In education, engagement of faculty, staff, and students across departments and colleges was seen as the key to sustainability, and diverse strategies described processes conducive to overcoming the "silo" effect prevalent in hierarchically organized educational institutions.

Effective multiple stakeholder involvement and organizational behaviors consistent with the principles of sustainability were seen to derive from a prior condition: Enabling all leaders to connect a personal sense of engaging in a higher purpose with the goals of the organization, the core aspect of which was the alignment to the sustainability principles of ecology, equity, and economics. Positional leaders therefore focused less on directing behaviors than on creating a working environment that enabled the development of a high level of engagement in social relationships and creative collective approaches that incorporated sustainability into every policy, process, and behavior within the organization, and in its dealings with external stakeholders. Trust and transparency were seen as keys to establishing this shared culture, one of whose major goals was the wholehearted engagement of all members of the organization. As mentioned before, engagement has been conceptualized here as people's capacity to connect the external objective world to the internal subjective world of experience in a dynamic process that increases personal and collective consciousness. This interactive process between the invisible and visible dimensions may be visualized as an increasingly fertile layer or topsoil of consciousness from which creativity and innovation can emerge. This allows stakeholders to identify and address emerging opportunities and challenges more quickly and to prototype solutions that are more likely to break from unsustainable past practices. At the organizational level, leaders saw that engagement had a critical role to play in the development of a shared culture, a collective mindset for sustainability, and that this was more effective in embedding sustainability than external incentives, regulations, or mandates. This process was enacted through active listening and generative conversations, thereby distributing the participatory role in decision making among all stakeholders. Scharmer et al. (2002) describe a process of distributed leadership based on what they called "three levels of emergence":

1 The behavioral level of social reality;
2 The level of emerging patterns of relationships; and
3 The deep tacit level, or "source" – what we call the blind spot – the place from which a system operates.

(p. 7)

At the first level of emergence, conversation generates little more than a repetition of habitual thinking patterns and points of view, and the ability to create and innovate is lost. At the second level of emergence, conversations lead to the discovery of new connections and emerging patterns evolve and are recognized. At the third level of emergence, which Scharmer calls the blind spot or the deep tacit level, conversations "would evolve in the mode of deep flow, presence, and collective co-generation" (p. 7).

For a number of the study leaders, getting beyond the first level of emergence presented one of the greatest challenges they had faced when seeking to foster a collective mindset for sustainability. Several factors were offered to account for this. One of the most repeated related to people's resistance to engaging in interactions that required them to operate outside of their area of expertise and to admit to ignorance of how to resolve problems linked to sustainability. In meetings where this resistance was prevalent, the people involved were more likely to adopt inflexible positions, defending old ideas that did little to contribute to productive discussion and decision making. The more reticent were reluctant to expose themselves to possible ridicule if they offered new ideas that did not fit the status quo.

The most successful leaders reported instances of situations within the organization where the second level of emergence came into operation. One example from each of the domains of business, community, and education is summarized here to illustrate how the process was initiated. In some cases, this was provoked by external consultants or change agents that created a tipping point within the organization. Such was the case with Nike and the work the corporation undertook with environmental architect Bill McDonough and chemist Michael Braungart in 1997, which brought about a sea change in the company's vision and goals in regard to issues of the environment and corporate social responsibility. In the past 10 years, Nike has made significant progress in achieving their goals of "zero toxicity, zero waste, and 100% closed manufacturing loop." This initial iterative reflective process, added to negative press regarding its social practices, led the corporation to make important changes to its labor relations, eliminating sweatshops, and expanding its foundation dedicated to supporting young female athletes in emerging countries.

Similar results were reported by Cecilia Campoverde, through her engagement of the local residents in the community she founded in Guatemala. By applying a grassroots approach that required people's direct involvement in building and governing their community, Campoverde found that the local residents, displaced by Hurricane Mitch in 1998, which had destroyed their homes and their livelihood, changed from being passive recipients of external aid to a vibrant, self-confident community that sought creative ways to develop and grow. By empowering them through microloans leading to the development of small businesses, the involvement of children and adults in the construction of the elementary school and housing, and by holding town hall meetings where all voices were welcomed, Campoverde was able to demonstrate that sustainability does indeed "come from within," as Jaap Vos expressed it. This was consistent with the findings of Seelos and Mair (2005a), Paul Hawken (2007), and John Elkington and Paula Hartigan (2008), whose research into social entrepreneurship has provided a clearer understanding of how impoverished communities, through strategically provided support such as microfinance, education, and training, can be empowered to take over their own destinies and change their lives.

In education, a similar emergence of the ability to detect new patterns characteristic of the second level of emergence was apparent in the response of Jean MacGregor, who laid the groundwork for highly productive conversations to take place through the Curriculum for the Bioregion Initiative. She and her faculty colleagues were able to do this by engaging people in something "larger than what they think they can accomplish," and by reformulating courses in ways that enlarged and stretched their disciplinary understandings and ways of designing teaching and learning environments. In this context, leaders and followers were inspired to connect to something more important than themselves, something that, ideally, would motivate the right actions even in adverse circumstances.

Though all leaders reported significant gains in the establishment of better practices regarding environmental and social issues, and in the case of companies, how they had sustained a viable bottom line in the process, none of the leaders was able to offer examples of the third level of emergence, which Scharmer et al. (2002) called the "mode of deep flow, presence, and collective co-generation." Chapter 6 offers some insights and techniques on the use of contemplative practices to achieve this higher state that may be found to be of value.

A complementary finding to this third level of emergence was the consensus among the leaders that sustainability was only attainable by adopting a long-term perspective, considering future generations as genuine stakeholders in decision-making processes. This raised an important consideration regarding how to design organizational strategies that addressed uncertain and even unknown futures, and how to develop the ability to predict the most desirable outcomes of decisions taken before new challenges and opportunities had begun to take shape. As Jim Murley argued, planning at the present time could no longer consider 5 or even 10-year scenarios. Consistent with this mindset, one of the publications on the future of Florida for which he was responsible, called *Southeast Florida 2060*, presented "a bold effort to create a long-term vision and strategy for a sustainable Southeast Florida" (Center for Urban & Environmental Solutions, 2008, p. 1).

Envisioning desirable futures so far in advance places enormous demands on the individual and collective capacity to create and innovate. Avoiding unanticipated consequences of a potentially exponential nature calls for a highly sophisticated approach to strategic planning. From a review of available research and increasing experience in the field, three approaches emerge as most effective. The first is the use of dynamic systems modeling to data using specifically designed algorithms to forecast possible trends and scenarios (Meadows, Meadows, Randers, & Behrens, 1972; Meadows et al., 2004). Theoretically, from this type of analysis, it is possible to predict probable outcomes should particular trends and conditions such as population growth, resource depletion, unemployment, continue to increase exponentially. It also requires a profound awareness of how systems operate and interconnect, and the implications of this for organizational structures. Extrapolating from his work on neural networks computing and the World Wide Web, Barabasi (2003) asserted that

> If we accept that everything is connected to everything else, then efforts to foster sustainability cannot be organized only by means of a hierarchy. It is central to the success of any initiative to welcome and promote self-organizing, heterarchical or panarchic initiatives.
>
> (p. 47)

Panarchy is defined by Sewell and Salter (1995) as an "inclusive, universal system of governance in which all may participate meaningfully" or more simply, "The rule of all by all for all" (p. 373). In this model, all leaders must be engaged in order to limit the possible negative outcomes of long-term forecasting.

A second approach involves groups in co-creating desirable futures (Scharmer, 2007), through a collective consciousness development process Sharmer and his colleagues (Senge, Scharmer, Jaworski, & Flowers, 2004) have described as presencing. This is a blending of the words "presence" and "sensing," and refers to the ability to sense and bring into the present one's highest future potential – as an individual and as a group. This makes it possible to design desirable new futures unconditioned by past or current solutions to problems. Complementing this process, a third approach consists in the use of the visioning technique of backcasting (Cuginotti et al., 2008), which makes it possible to design strategic plans in reverse chronological order, avoiding the unanticipated consequences inherent in planning from present scenarios.

Strategies such as these have implications for organizational structures and authority. Internal processes must adapt and change in response to highly fluid new environments, complex external pressures, and the imperatives of sustainability. One of these changes, acknowledged by Peter Drucker almost 15 years ago, is the tendency to modify the traditional organizational structure based on rank and power to a structure, in what he calls the emerging organization, based on mutual understanding and responsibility (Drucker, 1995). This increasingly fluid environment has undermined the traditional status quo of the relationship between leaders and followers, as highlighted by Day in his contextual focus on leadership and leader development, where he proposes that "Both individual and relational lenses are important concerns" (Day, 2001, p. 583). The implications of the findings on the developmental experiences of leaders and organizations in their respective journeys to sustainability are discussed in the conclusions and recommendations in the following section.

Chapter summary

As described here, leaders seeking to integrate the triple top line as a core value in their organizational strategy have found the following conditions to be a strong predictor of success.

Box 4.3 Conditions for the emergence of regenerative organizations

- Collective mindset development through multiple stakeholder engagement
- Regenerative leadership and the centrality of community
- Identification and activation of driving factors, and identification and elimination of challenges on the organizational journey to regenerative practice.

As their experience has shown, sustainable development and regenerative practice are enabled far more when leaders focus attention on the deeply held values and sense of purpose of individual personnel that go to make up the organizational culture rather than on their behaviors. When aligned to sustainability principles, this capacity to engage people at the personal level has led to the establishment of generative conversation and decision-making processes far more likely to eliminate unanticipated consequences. Herein lies the potential for engaging triple-loop learning or suspension of all previously held assumptions in order to generate radically new solutions to problems and challenges, defined here as third-order change. In this re-evolution of decision making, by dissolving internal and external boundaries, organizations can become capable of the approach to change necessary to emerge as locally and globally regenerative. The next chapter describes a number of case studies in the field that serve to bring the accounts contained above into an even more pragmatic perspective.

5 In the field

In this chapter, ongoing research and process consulting work reveal how sustainability leaders are becoming more effective while creating greater financial, social, and environmental value in their organizations, by embedding rather than eluding the core principles of environmental, social, economic, and even educational sustainability in their organizations. The case studies, and the personal and organizational strategies reported here are intended to highlight conscious, deliberate behaviors intended to connect oneself and others to a driving sense of purpose that decreases and supersedes the need for hierarchical leadership and management, and leads instead to spontaneous engagement of people's efforts in a common endeavor. A number of the implications and applications of these findings are developed here.

Purpose-driven leadership

As CEO of Melaver, Inc., a leading sustainability-focused real estate corporation in Georgia, the United States, Martin Melaver exemplifies the corporate leader who is engaged in sustainability and beyond in every aspect of the firm's business. This drive came at an early age as he was beginning his career as a real estate developer. He recalls driving through downtown Atlanta, seeing the tall, imposing office towers with the names of leading corporations on their sides. Observing these, he noted in himself a ''certain overweening ambition or desire to have the company's name on the side of a building, and the anxiety of somehow not measuring up to these clearly powerful, successful and wealthy real estate companies'' (personal communication, November 11, 2008). Martin went on to remember that this sense of

> anxiety for success, and performance, and ego, had more to do with fearfulness than with following in the same track. But it takes a while for you to, one, put your finger on that unease, two, really get your hands around what the source of it is and three, make adjustments consciously and rationally. But there have been a lot of those moments in the last fifteen years. Now this doesn't bother me at all anymore. I view myself as a very typical, standard, person. Not exceptional.

> It has to do with growth and maturation, personally as well as professionally, realizing one's highest potential, finding meaning and purpose. Really, it's couched more in a Maslow-like framework, hitting the higher end of that hierarchy of values. Certainly some of the components have to do with walking the talk, being an evocation of those principles yourself; personally as well as professionally. It's not about breast-beating. It's just something, quietly kind of getting it, admitting that it's a struggle, acknowledging that it's a work in progress. So I think it's first and foremost about personalizing it, and being willing to expose one's vulnerabilities, not living up to fairly high ideals. There is a confessional piece to it, there's also an educative piece to it. But I think there's an advocacy that starts with self-modeling, an educational piece that has to do simply with transferring information and knowledge, and sharing of best practices and mistakes and those sorts of things. And then I think, beyond advocacy and education, it's really more about creating opportunities for others to realize that potential. I read a definition recently of leadership, that it is the capacity to get others to do to what you want them to do. And I would say actually on the contrary, it's getting them to do ultimately what they want to do.
>
> When you get a bunch of charged, mission-driven, purposeful people engaged in work that seems meaningful, the tendency is to work longer hours and weekends, emailing at ridiculous hours, at early hours of the morning, it's crazy.

A consequence of this connection to a purpose that was "more important than me" has the effect of generating a stronger sense of humility in those involved in the effort, a sense that is increased when people come to greater understanding of the magnitude of the undertaking. This brings with it the understanding that individual efforts are ineffective unless they are an integral part of a concerted strategy shared by many, and connected to the broader community. Given the underlying sense of urgency that accompanies the central topic of the book, it also causes people to be more willing to confront others with their convictions, to become more outspoken and fearless, and to seek by all possible means to persuade others to modify their attitudes and behaviors in face of this larger mission. All possible means, however, should be qualified, since there is consensus among sustainability leaders that it is essential that a good balance be reached in the tone they use when communicating issues of sustainability if they want to guarantee the most productive response. Some call this the 80-20 ratio. From experience, they have found that overemphasizing the catastrophic outcomes of not responding to the challenges of sustainability (80 percent probability that our efforts will not work) has the effect of depressing and disengaging listeners. A similar reaction obtains when the serious nature of the situation is downplayed and people's good natures are appealed to in unconvincing ways (80 percent probability that someone will come up with the solution). In this scenario, people are not effectively mobilized to change ingrained attitudes and behaviors.

Integrated worldview and global ethics

With regard to the level of moral development or maturity of regenerative leaders, it is becoming clearer that a majority has evolved well beyond a self-centered or even an ethnocentric mindset. This has led them to attain a more integrated worldview as well as a global ethics, or a Level 5 in the regenerative leadership development continuum. The values emerging from this planetary ethics relate to what Jean MacGregor in higher education calls the "butterfly mindset," which she defines as the ability to acknowledge that every decision and every choice we make has the potential to affect everyone and everything else, no matter how distant. This pervasive sense of the interconnectedness of all living and nonliving things asks many of these leaders to balance personal needs with the common good, and to seek ways not only to minimize their impact on the "biosphere," but to have a restorative or regenerative impact whenever possible.

Multiple stakeholder engagement in practice: doing business unusual by getting (absolutely) everyone to the table

Over the course of the 27 years she worked for Shell Oil in the United States, one of Dr Seetha Coleman-Kammula's primary assignments was the creation, development, and commercialization of plastics. During this time, she often traveled to India, her home country. Witnessing the progressive and alarming accumulation of plastic waste over the years, she told me the following story about how she and her husband decided to initiate change in the corporate world by starting up their sustainability consulting company.

> In India nothing came in plastic packaging until about 10 years ago in the retail stores, and there is no solid waste management there. We simply throw things away. The appearance of plastics created such a mess in the streets that it was unbearable for me, which was the turning point that brought me into questioning my work. These were plastics I had helped to create at Shell as head of technology and head of business. When we developed all these products we sold them with no concern for consequences. It was a big "Aha!" for me one day when I realized that in all the time I did the research, developed, produced and sold these things, I never once had asked myself the question, what happens to them at the end of their life? If I had only asked that question I am not sure that we would have produced them with no technical solution at the end of life. And we wouldn't have designed them for nonrecyclability. The way they are made you can't recycle these plastics economically because you can't take them apart. With some foresight, we could have designed them for recycling. And that huge realization has now become the central theme of our research, our work, and our consulting company. When we talk to companies today we say "If you just work backward from end of life to beginning of life, or if you think of a

next life for these things, you will design them so that you can give them not only a next life but a higher next life." This opened up a new and wonderful challenge, as we developed a way that we could talk about it in a very positive way to the industry.

We launched our consulting company by bringing together 65 companies for a supply chain workshop. In working for sustainable results, one of the topics certainly is helping people see how they are impacting the larger system. It was quite a big gathering, and it was the first time they had been in a room together. It was very engaging for them and very engaging for us.

Our greatest success so far has been in the development of the value chain or supply chain workshop. This brings together people who use the same product, in this case a certain plastic, who are part of an overall system but who have never been brought together in a room as part of a system. In this case, they weren't even aware they were part of a system, or even how big the system was. They didn't know whose waste they could use, or who could use their waste; using waste as food, and concepts like that. The carpet manufacturers were sitting next to the bottle manufacturers, who were sitting next to the bucket manufacturers, and they didn't realize that they were all using the same plastics. And what was really powerful and very satisfying was bringing these companies together to create that social change, and that social change became the foundation for environmental change.

The first challenge was getting them to agree to come together. I had an intuitive sense that sustainability was becoming a big issue for them, and nobody was doing much then, it was 2007. We charged very little for that first meeting, $400.00 for a one-day dialog on what sustainability means to them. And we made a point of not preaching to them saying this is what sustainability is. We said "We'd like to know how you are thinking about it, what are the pressures you are feeling, what are your needs, what are your customers' expectations, what are your own expectations, what do you think this is about, do you want to talk about it, and do you want to hear from others?"

So we created a program. We brought in a couple of very powerful speakers from the paper industry, a different system. We brought in the Chief Sustainability Officer of Time, Inc., who'd worked in the pulp and paper industry and the forestry supply chain system, so I said, "Let's see what we in plastics can learn from the paper guys." They were very interested in that. So after a couple of speeches we organized them in little round tables and set really basic questions:

- What does sustainability mean to you? What do you think it means to your customers?
- Why are you worried?
- Do you want to change?
- Do you think there is a need to change? If so, what is the change?

> In this way we created some very simple conversations and we couldn't stop them from talking. At the end of the day, they were filling up flip charts, coming up with things they wanted to do. Clearly, the process had awakened their own curiosity and brought out whatever they were feeling, allowing them to get their needs out into the open. This made everybody see that they weren't alone, that they did not have all the answers but that there were others asking the same questions. They were ripe for this, for one reason or another.
>
> They were ripe because they had been sensitized through media coverage and other things, and they were curious. Is this a buzz word that is going to go away, like the environmentalism of the 90s? Is it going to come and go like a flash in the pan, or is it here to stay? Slowly but surely the conversation is moving to, "Gee, this is going to make money," and the more I stand up and say, "There is a lot of money to be saved, not just environmentally, but your own bottom line, because everything we have done comes from a legacy of abundance." In all the design and manufacturing process, there is still so much room to reduce the amount of materials we are using, to cut down on carbon emissions and energy consumption. All of that equals money, and the only way you are going to find the money is by collaborating with the supply chain. You won't find it within the boundaries of your own company.
>
> Providing examples of others who have gone through the process awakens people's curiosity and interest. The strategy is making them see the system they are part of, connecting them with others in the system, bringing them together in informal settings without preaching to them, and getting them to discover for themselves.

The strategy of informally convening multiple stakeholders, even competitors, within an industry to discuss ways to approach and resolve sustainability issues is fast becoming standard practice throughout the corporate world. Quite recently, Peter Senge reported on a similar project conducted with Starbucks' entire supply chain. In this case, the engagement of their stakeholders is intended to replace all nonrecyclable materials from their product line (Senge, 2010). Identified in the regenerative leadership framework as circular systems of collaboration, this practice serves to identify common issues of concern leading to the design of integrated solutions across organizational boundaries. These solutions often lead to environmental, social, and economic benefits previously ignored. As an example, in 2010, a consortium of over a hundred apparel manufacturers such as Nike, Target, Patagonia, Levi's, and JC Penney developed the Sustainable Apparel Coalition, an industry-wide index to measure the environmental impact of apparel products (see Environmental Leader, 2011). This coalition is especially interesting as it crosses multiple boundaries through the involvement of nonprofit organizations as well as governmental agencies such as the Environmental Protection Agency (EPA). Aside from the sustainability reporting value of the audit, the potential increase in revenue, improved branding, and legitimacy in the

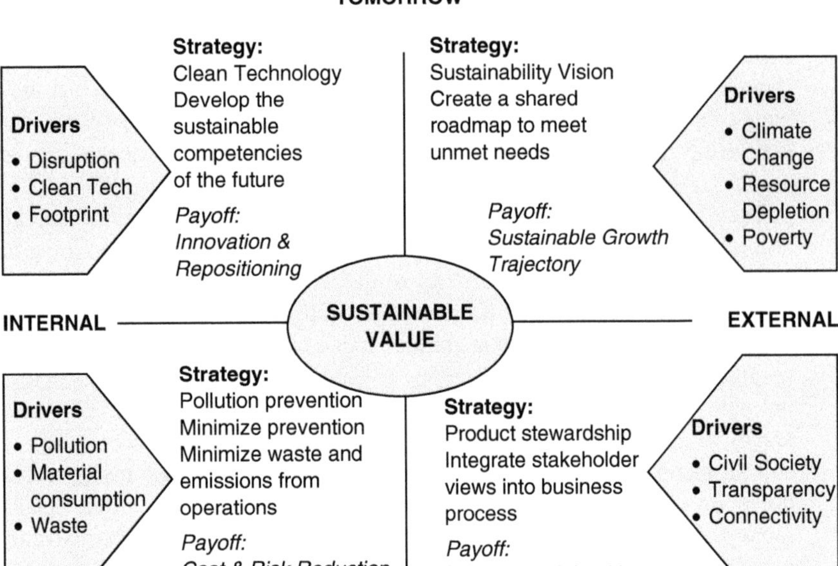

Figure 5.1 Sustainable value framework.
Source: Senge et al. (2008). Used with permission.

public eye cannot be measured yet. However, this initiative serves to exemplify what Senge, Kruschwitz, Laur, and Schley (2008) identify in their Sustainable Value Framework as those companies whose strategic vision is set on implementing a sustainable growth trajectory through innovation and repositioning (see Figure 5.1).

Regenerating the curriculum: tearing down the silos in higher education through deep listening and generative conversation

Jean MacGregor is the Senior Scholar and Director of the "Curriculum for the Bioregion" Initiative at the Washington Center for Improving the Quality of Undergraduate Education at The Evergreen State College, in Olympia, WA. She is also a Senior Advisor to the Advisory Council of the Association for the Advancement of Sustainability in Higher Education (AASHE). She recounted the story of how a collaborative task force of faculty, staff, and students effectively laid the groundwork for scaling up sustainability initiatives at The Evergreen State College, which currently involves 52 colleges and universities in the Bioregion of the Puget Sound.

For several years and up to the present, a small group of faculty has been intensely interested in sustainability at The Evergreen State College. This is a college with a very strong environmental and social conscience, which it has had since it was founded. While this small task force was very aware that Evergreen was recognized for its environmental commitment, we said to ourselves: "We still need to work on this, we can't sit on our laurels, we have good work in sustainability already under way on the campus but it's quite fragmented, it's not well organized, and we have a very, very large group of colleagues to educate in the faculty, staff and student body." So we conducted a series of Summer Institutes for faculty, staff and students over a period of years, and in 2006, the president decided that it was time to create a new strategic plan and a new campus master plan. So we took on the task to make sure that sustainability was very prominent in those two exercises to the degree that we asked the president and the provost to create a Sustainability Task Force to actually write the sustainability portion of the college's master plan. This led to the creation of a task force of about 15 people.

But the process, the story that stands out for me, is that as we decided to strike a set of goals and benchmarks on the wall according to the strategic plan's template, we decided to do a listening process on the campus, to assess the degree to which our colleagues understood sustainability and to explore what kinds of ideas they had looking to the future. And we engaged several hundred people in that listening process. We interviewed faculty across the campus; we involved the faculty involved in our two satellite campus programs and our three graduate programs. We consulted staff members, and we visited many, many student programs and asked for people's thoughts. Then we went on retreat with all our data to sort them, to prioritize them, and actually to use those data as the material to draw upon to make suggestions for the sustainability plan. It worked very well. I believe that it helped get the work quite energetically down the road, and it actually resulted in tremendous buy-in on the part of many campus leaders including our president. This was simply a good old tried and true "sensing interview" strategy that most community organizers would recognize. Now, two years later we have four foci of work, a sustainability office that's in the president's office, and a lot of good work on the way.

Among the most persistent challenges to the infusion of sustainability in higher education today are its top-down funding structure and the promotion and tenure system (Barlett & Chase, 2004; Shriberg, 2002). As with the previous example in business, the potential for driving sustainability through deep listening and generative conversation across the boundaries of potentially competing institutions is well illustrated here. In this case, however, the challenge has been in shifting institutional cultures toward a greater willingness to develop cross-disciplinary curricula in an environment that traditionally has been designed to protect programmatic boundaries in defense of the now seriously outdated principles of academic integrity and legitimacy. Faculty see little need and receive minimal institutional incentive to engage other faculty beyond the limits of their department, and for the most part tend to resent being pulled away from their work to participate in periodic college-wide cycles of program reaccreditation. The most they share, as Roland Barth (2000) points out, are heating systems and parking lots. Michael Crow, President of Arizona State University, describes this state of affairs as the stone age in which higher education is still entrenched, while indicating the need for sustainability to become the new organizing principle of universities, both "organizationally and conceptually" (Crow, 2007). In view of the current environment, the regenerative work of Jean MacGregor and her colleagues throughout the Puget Sound is remarkable, showing that it is possible to transform higher education in pursuit of a better world.

Empowering others in building sustainable community

In 2008, Dr Cecilia Campoverde was named Social Worker of the Year for Palm Beach County, Florida. Cecilia is the founder of The Guatemalan Project, the mission of which is to provide education and training to a displaced community in the province of Zacapa, a remote rural province in Guatemala. Following the Grameen Bank microfinance model, the project also provides small loans with no collateral that allow people to start up microenterprises for self-sustainability. In 2009, Dr Campoverde retired from the faculty of the College of Social Work at Florida Atlantic University (FAU), and relocated to Guatemala to continue her work with the project.

Dr Campoverde told me the dramatic story of the small Ladino community that led to the creation of the Guatemalan Project. In 1998, the torrential rains brought by Hurricane Mitch caused intense flooding along the banks of the River Motagua, devastating the community's fishing village. The storm forced the villagers to relocate inland, where they settled in the city of Gualán. Once the waters subsided, it became apparent that the destruction of the river banks and the village where they had lived presented an insurmountable challenge to their desire to return to their homes. Following the award of an area of land by the Mayor of Gualán, the villagers set up camp at a rural location and founded the village of El Triunfo. Dr Campoverde's narrative captures some of the essence of this tale of tragedy and regeneration.

> The people of the community have grown tremendously since the founding of El Triunfo. In the beginning, after the hurricane they were promised many things that never materialized, and so they learned to mistrust outsiders. They developed a lack of willingness to make the effort necessary to work with those wishing to help, and simply came to expect things to be given to them. They were therefore not very convinced at first when they realized that the mission of the Guatemalan Project was not to solve their problems for them but to help them solve their own problems in a way that suited

them. We did this through the small loans programs, and to provide the support needed to make it possible for the system to be successful we developed the practice of open community meetings.

Because of the initial distrust it wasn't easy to get things started. We ended up starting with the women, as they were willing to trust us enough to take a microloan in order to try to raise some chickens. As you may know, in Central America, the research tells us that one dollar in the hands of a woman is equivalent to eleven dollars in the hands of a man. And the women became quite successful at this, repaying the loans and taking out larger loans in order to expand and diversify their businesses. However, when the men saw that the women were beginning to be successful, they began to complain, saying "Hey, I want to be a part of that, of whatever you are doing." And this has evolved tremendously over the past few years. Today, the entire family comes to any meeting that we have at the gathering place in the village, and the men, if the women are not careful, will take up all the loans. But now all the residents know that they have the support and guidance that they need. We hold the village meetings informally, and I ask them, "How are you doing?" And they respond that they have made plans on how to save money, even if it's only 1 or 2 quetzals a day. So it's a constant way of reminding themselves, "Are we on time; are we on target; is there anything that we need to do?"

We hold these meetings at least twice a week, very informally, right in front of the house where I live. About 15 or 20 people come to each meeting. And we just sit there, and have a cup of chocolate. They just come if they want to, there is no obligation. They know that I am always there. The design of the house where I live is conducive to having people sitting outside. There is a large open space that allows people to gather. And of course the kids can play; they make a bonfire while we are over here. It's not that we are in Room 203 in a closed building. It's right there outside the house. People go back and forth in the street, they stop, they talk, they keep going, that kind of thing. I don't know if this is a new way of doing things, but that's what works there. This raises the question as to whether we are willing to go along with them or want to impose a formula for the way we conduct our meetings. In fact, we just go along, and it's doing very well.

By having these meetings they see each other more and they learn, not necessarily about other people's problems or what they are going through, but they build up a connection with each other. They don't speak out too openly yet, but it brings them together a little bit more. Everybody knows everybody. We get to know each other better and to support each other better, and I believe it has been very good for them.

Dr Campoverde's approach to sustainable community building highlights the critical importance of empowerment at the grassroots level. When engaged as described here, people in even severely challenging circumstances are able to redefine their sense of purpose, of self-worth, and of community that external

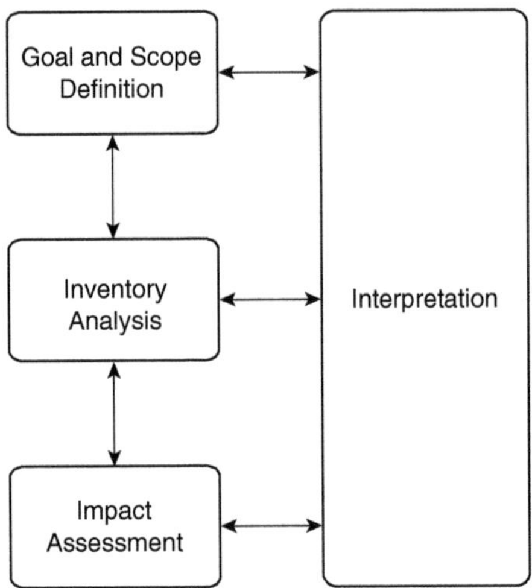

Figure 5.2 Life Cycle Assessment (LCA) as defined by ISO 14040.

intervention cannot provide. While relief work by external agencies is essential in extreme conditions of environmental degradation, conflict, or widespread disease, which Sachs (2005) defines as those that pull communities below the bottom rung of poverty, rendering them incapable of pulling themselves out of the situation, the risks of continued intervention beyond this level far outweigh the benefits. Once the basic necessities of life have been addressed, the health and well-being of individuals and communities reside in the provision of access to education, training, and the financial resources needed to enable them to build themselves out of poverty. Dr Campoverde's understanding of this notion of regeneration from within is embodied in the emergence of authentic community leadership, beginning with the women, and in the establishment of a microfinance program to support local business development. In turn, this led to the creation of the local school, the construction of a small health clinic, staffed by doctors visiting from the capital on a rotation. More recently and in good measure as a response to the success of the Guatemalan Project, plans were drawn up for a second settlement nearby, intended to attract more families away from the city of Gualán, where most of the displaced residents from the destroyed fishing village on the banks of the Motagua river had been forced to relocate following Hurricane Mitch.

Systems thinking and life cycle management

The notion of multiple stakeholder engagement is closely related to the central importance in regenerative practice of understanding the connectedness, and often invisible interdependence of all living and nonliving things (Capra, 2002). This requires the suspension of a rational, linear way of thinking about how things operate, which underpins many if not all of the processes that determine how we run our businesses, make things, dispose of waste, educate our children, and manage our communities. From the time Peter Senge brought the concept into the mainstream in 1990 through *The Fifth Discipline*, systems thinking has evolved from revolutionary techniques in inventory control such as just-in-time supply chain management into the vastly more complex field of life cycle management (LCM). Most organizations are capable of understanding and acting on their environmental impact by conducting or contracting life cycle assessments (LCAs) of the products they manufacture or consume (see Figure 5.2). They are able to make important decisions regarding how to remove toxic or environmentally destructive materials from their supply chain, decrease waste and greenhouse gas emissions, and they can devise strategic plans that will bring their organization into line with a more environmentally friendly core purpose.

Only a few leading organizations in business and industry, education, or community have undertaken, or are even familiar with, the potentially more regenerative process known as LCM or a Sustainability Life Cycle Assessment, as defined by ISO 26000. An LCM incorporates LCA, environmental life cycle costing (LCC), and social-life cycle assessment (S-LCA). Therefore, the organization not only considers environmental impacts but also the economic and social effects, from extraction to disposal, of every product and service over which it has a measure of responsibility and control. As defined by the Guidelines on Social Responsibility in ISO 26000, the Sustainability LCA includes the following:

> Responsibility of an organization for the impacts of its decisions and activities on society and the environment, through transparent and ethical behavior that contributes to sustainable development, including health and the welfare of society that;
>
> - takes into account the expectations of stakeholders;
> - is in compliance with applicable law and consistent with international norms of behavior; and
> - is integrated throughout the organization and practiced in its relationships.
>
> (International Organization for Standards; see http://www.iso.org/iso/catalogue_detail?csnumber=42546)

The United Nations Environment Program (UNEP) provides extensive assessment tools for S-LCA, listing the five main stakeholder groups as involved in the process:

1 worker
2 consumer
3 local community
4 society and
5 value chain actors.

It also lists nine main impact categories for "local community":

1 access to material resources;
2 access to immaterial resources;
3 delocalization and migration;
4 cultural heritage;
5 safe & healthy living conditions;
6 respect of indigenous rights;
7 community engagement;
8 local employment; and
9 secure living conditions.

(Source: UNEP; see http://lcinitiative.unep.fr/default.asp?site=lcinit&;page_id=A8992620-AAAD-4B81-9BAC-A72AEA281CB9)

This includes the notion of externalities, defined as people and natural environments that are eventually affected by the organization even when they do not participate directly in it. This concept has taken on greater significance with the exponential expansion of the global reach of organizations through technology and sheer size. Examples of externalities include the increasingly visible cases of diseases caused by contamination of fresh water systems, or chemical spills and nuclear accidents. Less obvious are the insidious effects of inappropriately devised public programs and services, as in the case of fragmented approaches to health care and education. Wherever systems thinking is genuinely adopted, externalities and unanticipated consequences can be mitigated and even eliminated, leading to truly regenerative practice. In conclusion, while a LCA may be an excellent step in the right direction, as evidenced by Walmart's recent implementation of their 15-point Sustainability Index served to over 60,000 of their suppliers, the LCM should be the ultimate measure of an organization's regenerative leadership.

Within the organizations reported here, it is clear that sustainability is still in the process of institutionalization and that there is still a long way to go before they can become regenerative as defined here, to come of age in their commitment to sustainability. Whereas some organizations or communities have attained a fair balance in their consideration of environmental, social, and economic issues when making decisions, the majority tend to favor one of the three dimensions over the others, and only a few genuinely consider future generations as actual stakeholders at the decision-making table. These limitations led me to return to the literature to seek out theoretical models that may offer strategic value for leaders seeking to redesign their organizations around a regenerative construct. These have provided some insights as to how organizations may approach change to go beyond sustainability toward regenerative practice. As mentioned before, this goes beyond a commitment to sustaining what we have to restoring and replenishing natural resources, and to creating a lasting impact in the local and global community. These insights are followed by cases where I have seen regenerative leadership in the fullest sense of the pursuit of the triple top line.

Seeing the world differently

If we agree with Einstein's assertion that we cannot solve current and future problems with the thinking that created them, then we can only evolve toward a regenerative and eventually a sustainable future by suspending all past ways of thinking and doing, and creating entirely new forms of human organization. Cortese (2009) calls this the difference between "creating and problem solving." From his perspective, problem solving is addressing something that is not working in order to make the issue go away, with the potential that unforeseen consequences will have a negative future impact. For example, the development of ethanol to replace fossil fuels is an example of problem solving. Recent research has shown ethanol to be as environmentally destructive and economically costly as the problem it was intended to solve. At the same time, the exponential growth of corn crops for ethanol production has had a significant impact on the price of this ubiquitous food staple. A similar comment may be made regarding the more recent introduction of GM's Chevy Volt, a hybrid that has maintained a connection to the past through its marketing slogan, "more than electric." This contrasts with the Nissan Leaf, the first wholly electric car produced for the mass market.

This last is an example of creating, which involves finding a new approach to satisfying our needs not grounded in any known system. This creative process brings with it a number of challenges. It requires that we suspend all previous patterns of thinking, going beyond Argyris and Schön's (1978) definition of single- and double-loop learning to engage in a collective process of meaningful or mindful dialog (Isaacs, 2000), known as deutero-learning (Bateson, 1972) or triple-loop learning (Romme & van Witteloostuijn, 1999). For Argyris and Schön, single-loop learning is correcting "an error in an existing strategy without altering the underlying governing variables of that strategy" (p. 263). Double-loop learning occurs when "the underlying assumptions and values that govern the action in the strategy" (p. 263) need to be changed in order for it to be corrected. In a regenerative model, the literature suggests that we need to embrace a more deeply transformative and creative approach, that of triple-loop learning within dynamic systems (Romme & van Witteloostuijn, 1999). Triple-loop learning goes beyond questioning underlying assumptions and theories of action by engaging in "learning about learning that permits insight into the nature of the paradigm itself, not merely an assessment of which paradigm is superior" (Isaacs, 2000, p. 239). This type of work requires a "collective attention and learning." The purpose of conversation in this model is to "create a setting where conscious collective mindfulness can be maintained" (p. 240). This supports the more current trends that have substituted the process of building technical infrastructure to support knowledge capture, dissemination, and collaboration, to building a human infrastructure based on dialog to create a shared field of meaning (Isaacs, 2000).

This is described by Scharmer (2007) as the field of attention, which underlies the attitudinal condition of "letting come" that leads to the crystallization of new ideas when working with potential emerging futures and developing prototypes a process that he calls Theory U. This visualization of desirable futures is defined as backcasting (Cuginotti et al., 2008), which proposes an inverted chronological approach to strategic planning, beginning from this ideal future state and working backwards to the present in order to set a strategy in place that is free of unanticipated consequences.

Ideally suited to creating this safely dangerous environment that promotes the creative flow and sharing of ideas, is the construct of the circular organization or system (Romme & van Witteloostuijn, 1999), symbolized in the regenerative leadership framework by the connected semicircles surrounding the leadership process. The circular model of organization implies a consensual decision-making structure that is embedded in the work process to offset the single flow of information and authority emanating from a hierarchical structure. Circular organizations "support and promote processes of open and free inquiry, which reflects the key condition of rigorous public testing in circle meetings throughout the company" (Romme & van Witteloostuijn, 1999, p. 451). In a regenerative organization engaged in connecting people to purpose and meaningful work, this model appears to offer great potential for evolving toward higher degrees of sustainability. However, in order to sustain its momentum and currency within an organization, Romme and van Witteloostuijn affirm, it is indispensable that this approach should not be left to the willingness of those responsible for it, particularly in times of turbulence, but that it should be institutionalized in organization policy. At its most effective, circular organization connects to triple-loop learning by "linking together all local units of learning in one overall learning infrastructure as well as developing the competences and skills to use this infrastructure" (Flood & Romm, 1996).

In my research and consulting work, I have found significant evidence of double-loop learning with regard to the development of reflective approaches to self-knowledge and awareness. There is also growing evidence that organizations engaged in sustainability efforts are actively pursuing second-order change. However, little evidence is yet available to substantiate the value of the practice of transconceptual experience as central to regenerative leadership and organizational change for regenerative practice as defined in the literature (Bartunek & Koch, 1994; Scharmer, 2007; Senge et al., 2004; Starr & Torbert, 2005; Wilber, 2001). The difficulty in overcoming resistance by organizations when this approach is suggested is perhaps the most difficult challenge facing regenerative leaders.

This is the territory that is currently being explored and mapped by the author and colleagues who understand the central importance of consciousness development in this endeavor. Figure 5.3 maps this developmental journey of leaders and organizations to regenerative practice. It collects the findings that emerged from the interviews with the study leaders, and displays them in a two-factor diagram where the individual's development is shown incrementally on the Y axis, and

THE JOURNEY OF INDIVIDUALS AND ORGANIZATIONS TO REGENERATIVE PRACTICE				
	INTEGRATED WORLDVIEW	Individual	Local/Organizational	Global 
INDIVIDUAL MINDSET/BEHAVIORS	LEVEL 5 ENGAGED World-centric (All of Us) Post-conventional moral development (Kohlberg)	• Awakening • Heightened sense of purpose • Vision beyond sustainability • Systems thinking, everything is interconnected – Global ethics • Intra & intergenerational (future) • Urgency • Fearlessness – courage • *"Inner work"* • *"... more important than me"* • *"... butterfly mindset"* • *"I get in people's faces, but in a nice way"*	• Humility and courage from purpose-driven transforming leadership • Multi-stakeholder engagement • Literally everyone is critical to the decision making process • *"Leadership from within"* *"Check your ego and logo at the door"* • *"Bring everybody involved to the table before you begin"* • *"Strategic planning for 50 years"*	• Backcasting • Triple loop learning • Transconceptual dynamics • Third order change • Circular organization • Triple top line: *"How can we grow prosperity, celebrate our community, and enhance the health of all species?"*
	LEVEL 3-4 COMPLIANT/ COMMITTED Ethno-centric (Us) Conventional (Kohlberg)	• Compliance in isolation • Ethno-centric ethics • Local perspective • Mid-term vision	• Weighting between compliance and commitment in some areas (e.g. economics, and/or education, environment and social justice)	• Global efforts that show commitment to local/organizational agenda Integration stronger than compliance and fragmentation
	LEVEL 1-2 RESISTANT/ SKEPTICAL Self-centered (Me) Pre-conventional (Kohlberg)	• Self-serving ethics • Short-term vision • Distrustful of evidence • *"Fear and greed"*	• Partial compliance with fragmented external policy and regulation • Single bottom line • *"Silo effect"*	• Forced compliance with integrated external policy and regulation • *"Sticks and carrots"*
	FRAGMENTED WORLDVIEW	Level 1 (Weak Sustainability)	Level 2 (Moderate Sustainability)	Level 3 (Strong Sustainability)
		COLLECTIVE MINDSET/BEHAVIORS		

Figure 5.3 The journey of individuals and organizations to regenerative practice.

organizational development is shown similarly on the X axis. As may be seen from this evolutionary model, on the bottom left the diagram shows the lowest level of personal and organizational development, while the top right shows the highest level. Vertically, the incremental progression of development follows the continuum from a fragmented to an integrated worldview, as shown previously in Figure 2.3 (p. 17). Horizontally, the progression goes from weak to strong sustainability (Levels 1–3) of organizations and institutions.

Organizations approaching regenerative practice

There are clear indicators that we need to do things very differently if we are not only to survive but see our world flourishing 100 years from today. A developmental or evolutionary perspective of human consciousness, as the findings here begin to reveal, would suggest that individuals and communities can learn to live productively within the limits established by the earth's systems. Were this to come about, then the external manifestations of organized human activity would have to be very different to the models currently in existence. This would have to be true for all systems, government, education, health care, business, commerce, agriculture, and even religion. But what can organizations of this kind look like, should they become fully sustainable or regenerative? Will businesses, schools, communities, religions, governing bodies, and other domains of human thought and activity become reconciled in a universal endeavor or will they insist on operating in ways that continue to deplete the earth's resources, generate more waste than the biosphere can absorb, and generally decrease future generations' capacity to satisfy their needs? Is it possible that we may find the consensus and the willingness to let go of the old approaches in order to redesign the way we live, work, and learn in an entirely new, regenerative manner?

The analysis of the findings of my own studies and the emerging framework for regenerative leadership offer some indicators of how we, as a human race, may work toward this better future. These point to the need for a higher and deeper level of awareness, pursued through conscious and deliberate practice that may serve to free our minds from attachment to the old ways of being, thinking, and behaving. In this new reality, sustainability and regenerative practice have ceased to possess meaning, as they have become the status quo. The Venn diagram depicting the three dimensions of sustainability, environment, equity, and economics, has become a unified whole where the three linked circles have become perfectly superimposed.

What kind of people can bring about this prosperous, environmentally sound, and socially equitable society? Andrew Cohen and Ken Wilber (2002) have suggested a developmental process that corroborates the findings of my own study and work, which may serve to illuminate the way to a sustainable future. They describe this process as one of evolutionary enlightenment, grounded in the authentic self, which they define as the individual who has engaged in inner work to become free of the ego and can therefore embrace a deeper and broader understanding of the meaning and purpose of life. Individuals at this stage of development are able to establish relationships at a different level, that of the "higher we," through the development and expression of a synergy of principles, which Cohen (2008) calls purity of motive and integrity of action, autonomy and community, and evolutionary tension and natural hierarchy. At this level of inner development, a group of individuals is able to generate creative conversations capable of addressing the most complex problems by integrating the collective mind, intuition, and the will to act. It may be hypothesized that in this environment issues of race, culture, gender, ideology, power, and personality should be transcended in the pursuit of the higher purpose, and that this should be true in any form of social organization, whether education, business, government, health care, agriculture, industry, and so on. This level of leadership for sustainability would reflect the capabilities McEwen and Schmidt (2007) describe as those of the leader as alchemist, that integrate "multiple

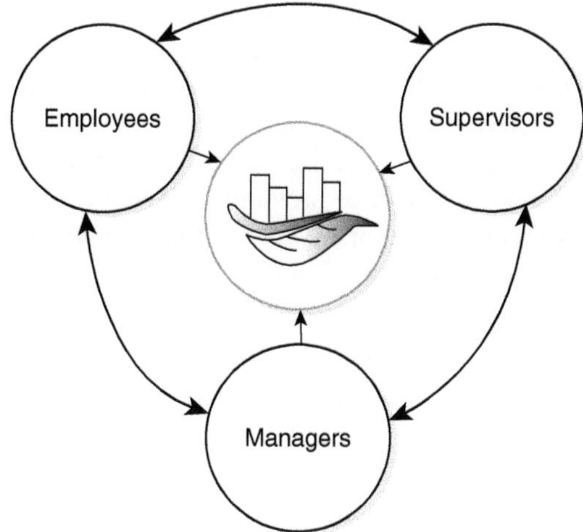

Figure 5.4 Dirt Pros' round table and inverted pyramid. Used with permission.

realms of knowing" (p. 35). However, in their own research in business, they found evidence to support this level of development in 1 percent of the sustainability leaders they reviewed. It is becoming clearer, therefore, that the problem and the challenge of sustainability, as proposed from the outset of this book, are not in the consequences of our actions, but in the source within us of the actions themselves. The three cases reported below, while still evolving, offer concrete examples that regenerative practice is not only possible but also profitable and empowering in business, in education, and in community.

The business case for regenerative leadership: Dirt Pros

In 2008, I was invited to become a senior sustainability advisor to Dirt Pros, an environmental services company based in Florida, by its President and Chief Operating Office, Marcell Haywood. At the time, I was completing the doctoral dissertation into regenerative leadership. Since that time, I have been in a privileged position to support but principally to witness Marcell's extraordinary work as a regenerative leader. In these few years, and despite the global recession, he and his staff have not only embraced the triple top line, as will be seen here, but the company has also achieved local and national ranking. At the time of writing, INC. 500/5000 ranked Dirt Pros as the 17th fastest growing company in Florida, and 232nd in the nation; this is the second consecutive year that Dirt Pros was included on the INC. 500/5000 listing. In a low-margin business within a competitive environment, Dirt Pros has done a fantastic job of building equity and managing their growth rate.

A factor of interest is the company's cultural makeup. Whereas Marcell is a young African-American whose native language is English, most of the senior management and custodial personnel are of Hispanic origin. Despite the difference in ethnicity and the language barrier, the firm boasts one of the lowest employee turnover rates in the industry. More uniquely, Marcell leverages the power of each and every member of his staff to deliver safe and healthy environments. Together, Everyone Achieves More (T.E.A.M.) is the philosophy that ultimately drives the company's success; and is one that will undoubtedly keep Dirt Pros well positioned to continue providing impactful solutions to both customers and employees alike for years to come. With 280 employees to date, Dirt Pros is described on their website as

> A single source, full service, integrated facilities maintenance firm whose service portfolio spans several specialty divisions throughout the state of Florida. Dirt Pros both designs and provides Maintenance & Repair Operation (MRO) Programs, Housekeeping, Custodial, Grounds Maintenance, & Corporate Services Programs for clients of all sizes in the Healthcare, Commercial Real Estate, Education, Hospitality, Retail, & Public Venue industries.

The company has not limited its sustainability plan to environmental efforts. In addition to using 100 percent green cleaning products, low energy and water consuming equipment, adopting a paperless administrative system and supplying its senior managers with hybrid cars, Dirt Pros has developed what can be considered a mature philosophy and practice in corporate social responsibility. The overall impact on the South Florida community at large remains a motivating force behind the company vision: " . . . to be a socially responsible change agent in the facilities-management industry." While many companies have diminished corporate social responsibility efforts in today's unfavorable economic climate, Dirt Pros has remained vigilant in this area, making contributions to Haiti relief efforts, participating in youth outreach programs in the tri-county area, and donating regular services to area organizations.

Going beyond traditional philanthropy, the personnel are encouraged to leverage the firm's core business to benefit the local community. Staff can use the company' products at wholesale prices, and its equipment to service local non-profit organizations with which they are connected. They are also supported through scholarships and soft loans so that they may complete their education at the secondary and college level. Ultimately, Marcell has built a company with a higher commitment recognizing that its responsibility is not just to its own stakeholders but also to the broader community (Figure 5.4).

Breaking down the silos in higher education: Florida Atlantic University

In the course of the doctoral research into sustainability leaders in business, education, and community, I became increasingly involved in the sustainability efforts at FAU. In August, 2007, former university President Frank T. Brogan signed the American College and University Presidents' Climate Commitment (ACUPCC).

Along with the pledge, President Brogan charged that a Sustainability Committee be created. This led to the creation of the FAU Sustainability Committee, an *ad hoc* group of faculty, staff, and students. Through a broad consultation process, the committee developed a mission and strategy, which led to the creation of a number of subcommittees charged with developing specific sustainability-related agendas in a number of areas, as indicated below:

- academics and research;
- community engagement;
- facilities/landscape and waste management/energy and water;
- food services;
- housing;
- purchasing;
- transportation.

This initiative led to the preparation of the university's first greenhouse gas emissions audit in 2008, and subsequently to the FAU Climate Action Plan. Having been retained to write the plan by the Architect's Office in July 2009, I was placed in a strong position to put regenerative leadership strategies to work. The immensely complex task of mobilizing a public university, with its highly fragmented governance, academic, and operational structure, was a daunting but exciting challenge for all of those who were involved in developing the best possible plan, which may be accessed from the ACUPCC website (see http://acupcc.aashe.org/search/?institution_name=florida + atlantic + university&carnegie_class=%3F%3F&;state_or_province=%3F%3F). Shortly after her appointment as President of the University in the summer of 2010, President Mary Jane Saunders created the position of Sustainability Liaison. Parallel to this work, and of even greater significance, was the establishment of the Climate Change Research Initiative at the University, a multidisciplinary effort that crosses most if not all departments and colleges.

Following from this work, in the summer of 2009, I developed and submitted to the College of Business a syllabus on Sustainability Leadership for Entrepreneurs (MAN 6931/4930), which was offered as an elective course open to graduate, undergraduate, and non-degree seeking students, thereby making it accessible to the wider community. The following semester, I was asked to develop a similar course for the College of Engineering's Innovation Leadership Honors Program, the College's interdisciplinary undergraduate program. In the ensuing semesters, in the search for a more self-directed, multidisciplinary curriculum, this has evolved toward an approach that the program Director has come to call "Montessori for engineers." Both sustainability leadership classes incorporated academic service-learning team projects, involving students in addressing sustainability issues in the FAU and wider community. These opportunities for experiential learning have included working with a number of nonprofit organizations in southeast Florida, and on diverse sustainability issues affecting the university. These have included waste management, LCAs, sustainable

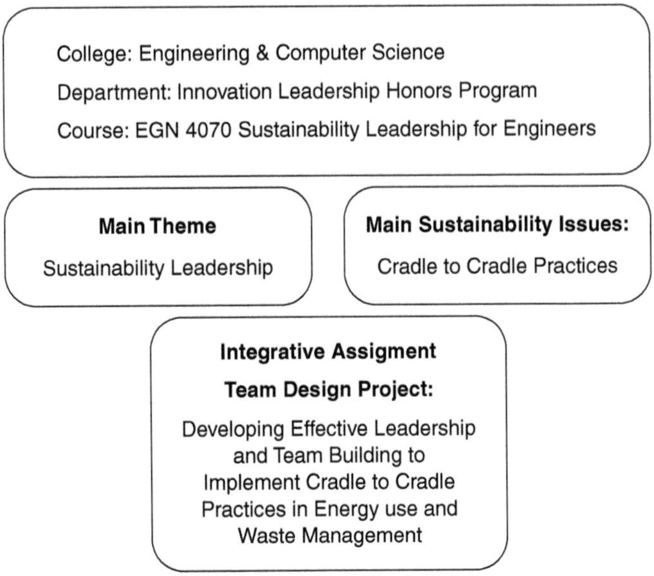

College: Engineering & Computer Science

Department: Innovation Leadership Honors Program

Course: EGN 4070 Sustainability Leadership for Engineers

Main Theme

Sustainability Leadership

Main Sustainability Issues:

Cradle to Cradle Practices

Integrative Assigment

Team Design Project:

Developing Effective Leadership and Team Building to Implement Cradle to Cradle Practices in Energy use and Waste Management

Figure 5.5 Framework for the infusion of sustainability in the engineering curriculum.

community development planning, building retrofits, efficiency audits, sustainable networking websites, the design of organic community gardens, and related curricula, among numerous others. Most recently, these projects have begun to involve collaborations with other faculty across course boundaries, leading to interdisciplinary initiatives that have provided expanded opportunities for addressing complex problems.

The Dean also retained my services to facilitate the process of infusing sustainability and regenerative practices into the engineering curriculum. The College has undergone significant consolidation efforts over the past year. A number of faculty were laid off, some of these tenured, and some of the departments were merged to streamline the delivery of core courses. This presented a challenge, as this had led to strong skepticism and resistance regarding further changes emerging from the Dean's office. However, it also presented an opportunity to enable faculty to work across their former silos in this new academic environment. The work itself involved convening a voluntary faculty task force over the spring semester to engage in collegial, interdisciplinary, purposefully generative conversations intended to show how the principles of sustainability were relevant to syllabi, programs, and the curriculum as a whole, so that connections might be made across subjects, disciplines, and departments that could lead to an integrated undergraduate and graduate curriculum. An exciting and motivating backdrop to this process at the time was the ongoing construction of the new Engineering building, inaugurated in the fall of 2010, the first university construction in southeast Florida seeking LEED Platinum level certification.

To engage the process, I was able to capitalize on my research, as reported earlier, with successful sustainability leaders in higher education such as Jean MacGregor at Evergreen State College, Mitch Thomashow at Unity College, Tony Cortese at Second Nature, Judy Walton at the AASHE, and my own colleagues at FAU Len Berry, Daniel Meeroff, Jaap Vos, Jim Murley, and MaryBeth Burton. With a small group of willing faculty, from the departments of Computer Science, and Civil, Mechanical, Electrical, and Ocean Engineering, we were able to engage in a highly productive generative conversation over the course of the following 3 months. I summarize here the guiding principles we applied to promote the success of the process, which led to significant revisions in the faculty members' syllabi. Readers interested in accessing the full report, may download this from http://regenerativeorganizations.com.

Initially, there was concern about the Dean's underlying intentions with regard to the initiative, and there was an understandable unwillingness to engage in an effort that might jeopardize the faculty's relationships with colleagues. At my invitation, this concern was dispelled at the outset by having the Dean attend the first meeting of the task force. On this occasion, the Dean made a very strong case for the value of sustainability and its central relevance to the engineering curriculum. He also endorsed the fundamentally important role of the group in the process due to their individual and collective expertise, which effectively removed him from the position of exclusive decision maker. These statements made it possible to bring into play two critical regenerative leadership principles. The first was that of the purpose-driven, collaborative nature of regenerative leadership itself. By placing the project at the core of the task force's mission, it became possible to "check egos and logos at the door," relieve anxieties, and thereby tap into the group's more creative energies.

A second issue related to some of the faculty's concern with regard to the implications of bringing the principles of sustainability into their programs. Their major worry related to the potential risk of losing foundational content from their textbooks. This initial resistance was overcome by reviewing the principal definitions and frameworks of sustainability such as those contained in the Brundtland Report (1987), Karl Henrik Robèrt's (1991) Natural Step, the Earth Charter, and so on. From this introduction, it became possible for the task force to establish a clearer vision of the futures they considered most desirable for engineering students at both the undergraduate and graduate level. More specifically focused readings were brought in to build the group's knowledge base, including the comprehensive EPA-sponsored *Benchmarking Sustainable Engineering Education: Final Report*, by Allen et al. (2008). From the resulting conversations, it became clear that it was possible to integrate and infuse social, economic, and environmental concerns as integral components of every course without having to substitute essential content knowledge. Once this was understood, the conversations became far more productive. In fact, when this resistance had been overcome, faculty became interested not only in amending their own syllabi but also began to notice the connections between their programs and those of colleagues, some of whom belonged to different departments. To facilitate the infusion process, I introduced the framework that Jean MacGregor had employed at The Evergreen State College, as reported in Chapter 4 (see sample in Figure 5.5). This is also included in the online report at http://regenerativeorganizations.com.

This then gave rise to conversations that had to do with linkages and common interests both in teaching and research, and later in community engagement. The artificial nature of the boundaries between disciplines became more evident as the conversations progressed. For example, faculty teaching concepts like structure and materials in civil engineering became aware of the implications that their course content had for faculty working in the areas of transportation in mechanical engineering, who in turn began to make connections to instructors teaching and conducting research in the areas of hydrocarbons and renewable energy. At the time of writing, in addition to modifying existing syllabi, several faculty have created entirely new courses focusing on issues having to do with sustainable materials and structures, renewable energy, and LCAs and of the toxicity in the chemical composition of products.

Some of these have led to team projects involving businesses and nonprofit organizations with the purpose of developing real-world sustainable solutions in the community. At the time of writing, several faculty members have submitted their syllabi to the University's Academic Service Learning Faculty Learning Community so that these may receive the designation of academic service-learning courses. The projects resulting from these courses will participate in the recently instituted Earth Day Sustainable Solutions Competition, to be held each April.

Neighborhood regeneration: the 79th Street Corridor Initiative in Miami-Dade

Early in 2010, as a member of the Sustainability Committee of the southeast Florida District Council of the Urban Land Institute (ULI), an important nonprofit organization dedicated to improving stewardship in land use and real estate development throughout the United States, I joined a number of professionals and policymakers in the creation of a sustainable community development framework. This was to be offered to cities and communities in southeast Florida, first as a pilot project and, if successful, replicated throughout the region and further afield. Over a period of several weeks, the Sustainability Committee consulted with experts, conducted research, and held generative conversations that led to the development of a strategic planning tool intended to engage communities in a process that would empower residents to envision, design, and implement their own regenerative approach to creating an identity, a vision, and a process for a prosperous, thriving community. Two cities and a community group applied to participate in the project, and completed a questionnaire intended to determine which of the groups would be most likely to offer the best chances of conducting a successful pilot. After analyzing the responses and conducting face-to-face interviews with representatives of the three applicants, in the fall of 2010, for this first project the committee selected the 79th Street Corridor Neighborhood Initiative, a nonprofit community organization committed to revitalizing a large blighted urban area in unincorporated Miami. With the support of three

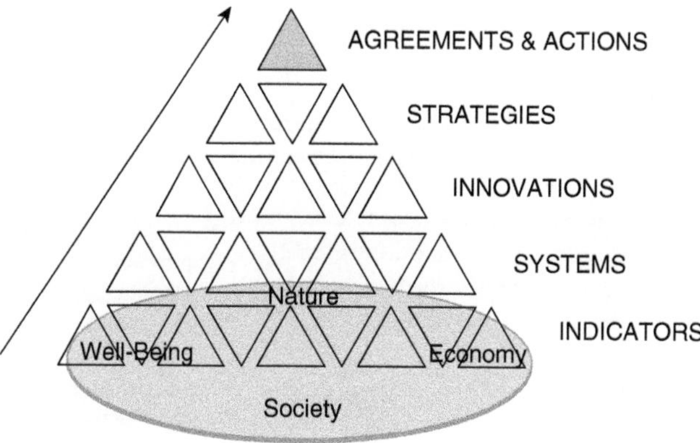

Figure 5.6 Pyramid process.
Source: AtKisson, 2008, *The ISIS Handbook.*

other members of the committee, I facilitated the initial sustainability strategic planning process, culminating in a full-scale half-day workshop in September.

Applying the regenerative leadership framework principle of multiple stakeholder engagement, we met with the Initiative's executive committee in order to help them identify the most representative group of community leaders to ensure comprehensive participation in the workshop. From these sessions, 24 community leaders, from business, education, nonprofits, city officials, and concerned citizens, most of whom were representatives of the overwhelmingly Black and Hispanic community, were convened to the workshop, held at Miami-Dade College, in September 2010. For this workshop, I developed a combined approach, using the regenerative leadership framework and the sustainability planning process known as the Pyramid, developed by Alan AtKisson of the AtKisson Group (see http://atkisson.com).

The pyramid served as the sustainability planning tool that allowed the group to identify the sustainability indicators and systems that were impacting the community and to agree on the innovations and strategies that would serve to empower the community to move forward on a desired path to well-being. However, the leaders did not know each other, had not all worked together before, and they represented different interests within the community. It was important that a number of basic ground rules be established before beginning. Therefore, I presented the principles of the regenerative leadership framework to the group. The first principle presented emphasized the notion of multiple stakeholder engagement, as was evident from the racial and cultural diversity in the room. This brought into play the value of "checking egos and logos at the door," which highlighted the critical importance of placing the whole community rather than sectorial agendas at the center of the process. To do this effectively, it was clear that decisions had to be reached through collaborative and cross-organizational dialog, which demanded that people exercise deep listening skills

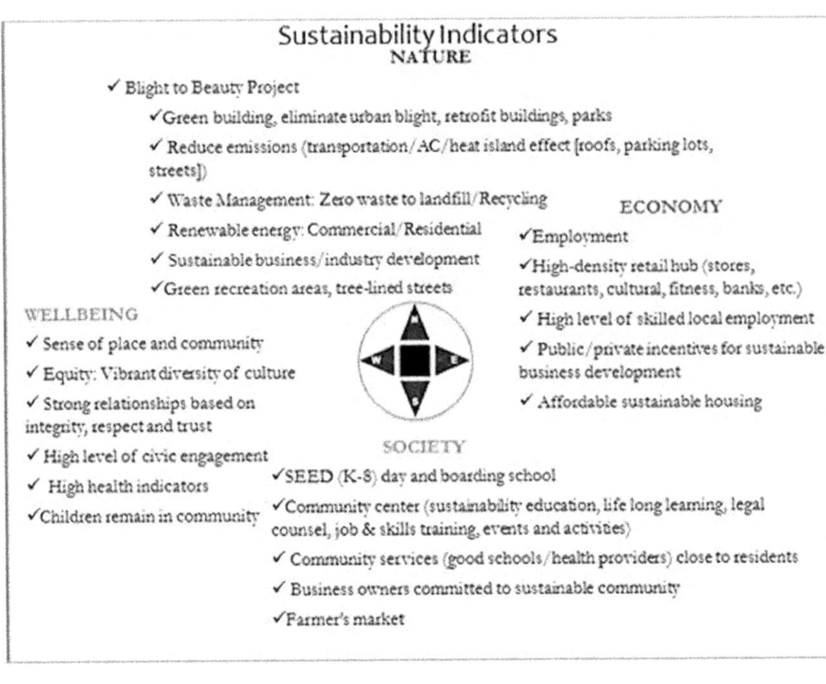

Figure 5.7 79th Street Corridor Neighborhood Initiative workshop sustainability indicators.

in order to identify common values and interests and to downplay and defuse factors of separation. From this collective mindset it would become possible to envision and implement the most desirable future for the entire community.

Once these principles had been presented, discussed, and agreed, we divided the leaders into the four teams that would build the pyramid's indicators, systems, innovations, and strategies (ISIS) in each of the four dimensions of environment, economy, society, and well-being, as established by AtKisson's Pyramid Process (see Figure 5.6).

The work of the teams resulted in four thematic concept maps that focused respectively on Blight to Beauty (Nature or Environment), Employment (Society), Economic Opportunities (Economy), and K-12 Education (Well-being) (see Figure 5.7). From these four themes, the plenary was able to come to a capstone agreement that considered Blight to Beauty, or the revitalization of the neighborhood, as its first priority. Decreasing unemployment by incentivizing new businesses and through the creation of new jobs became a clear need to support the first priority, and this in turn flagged up the critical importance of providing education and training opportunities.

From the capstone agreement, it then became possible for the group to charge the convening committee to establish a clear strategic plan. Over the following weeks, the committee met with business owners, external investors, educational

Figure 5.8 79th Street Corridor Neighborhood Initiative sustainable community wheel.

authorities, city officials, and additional residents to create a viable action plan to benefit the community. At the time of writing, the 79th Street Corridor Neighborhood Initiative has established partnerships with the new proprietors of the neighborhood mall, which has begun investing heavily in restoring and expanding this formerly rundown facility. This project will serve to provide a host of new jobs as well as contribute to the regeneration of the surrounding residential and commercial area. A second session of some 15 of the community leaders refined the initial sustainability pyramid, resulting in the organization of the community project as displayed in Figure 5.8.

The Initiative has also begun to work with a large real estate developer. This company has designed a major project next to the Tri-Rail train station in the heart of the community, which will include affordable housing and retail stores. One of the community leaders, executive director of the entrepreneurship program at Miami-Dade College, is currently leading a project to create a new K-12 school intended to serve as both a boarding and day school for the community.

The Initiative's Executive Committee has held meetings with the area's city commissioner, with a view to having representatives appointed to the Commission who may then support policies and legislation conducive to sustainable development within the community.

Chapter summary

While their scope may not be on the scale of grander global initiatives that make the news, the increasingly practical examples in the field described in this chapter are intended to underscore the value and describe the outcomes of incorporating the key principles of the Regenerative Leadership Framework into sustainability work in a wide range of organizations. Continued observation appears to confirm that the sustainability achievements of these companies, communities, and institutions of higher education could not have been accomplished without a heightened sense of collective purpose grounded in the inner work of committed individuals. Time and again, the latter have acknowledged the importance of working on the individual and collective mindset as a prerequisite to effective regenerative practice. Indeed, a considerable number of them have reported that they themselves favor practices and activities that stimulate and sustain their personal growth and consciousness, whether through yoga, meditation, martial arts, music, contact with nature, and prolonged retreats. For centuries, contemplative practices such as these have helped individuals sustain their resilience and lead healthier, more productive, and fulfilling lives. However, while increasing numbers of people have come to recognize the value of these practices in their lives, they have yet to become widespread practice in the workplace. The next chapter describes an approach to one of these practices in particular, explicitly connected to the Regenerative Leadership Framework. We have found this technique, composed in this case of a set of four meditative practices for groups, to be very effective in cultivating a higher level of collective awareness and greater willingness to engage in deep listening, to relinquish past ways of thinking, in order to activate what we have described in the framework as the transconceptual dynamics of triple-loop learning and third-order change.

6 Cultivating regenerative leaders in the organization

> Taking even one step in mindfulness can benefit all beings on Earth.
>
> (Thich Nhat Hanh)

In our work with organizations in the corporate and nonprofit sectors, sustainability and emerging regenerative leaders speak increasingly of the need to engage their organizations in new and more creative ways than ever before. This is necessary to cope successfully with a range of challenges. Foremost in many people's minds is risk management due to cash flow constraints and diminishing resources. This entails looking at innovative approaches to reducing operating costs in order to sustain a healthy bottom line. But they must balance this search for lean financial efficiency with the need to accelerate the process of redesigning products and services in a complex, fast-paced global environment fraught with unanticipated risks. The far-reaching environmental, sociopolitical, and economic fallout of the 2011 nuclear tragedy in Japan, coming a year after the BP oil spill in the Gulf of Mexico, continues to bring this fact to our awareness day after day. Similarly, the spread of democratic unrest in the Middle East, and its effect on things "back home," wherever home may be, reinforces the sense of the global pervasiveness of distant events. The growing consensus that major environmental issues such as climate change, pollution, topsoil depletion, and diminishing reserves of food and clean water are here to stay and that we are responsible for originating and therefore solving them is forcing organizations to reassess previously unexamined behaviors such as the life cycles of their products from extraction to disposal. And for good or evil, the treatment evidenced by organizations toward their own personnel and external stakeholders is increasingly open to the global scrutiny provided by social media, interest groups, and governmental oversight. And this is all occurring within a global context of financial unpredictability, downsizing, and competition for diminishing physical resources.

This complex range of internal and external tensions has led to unprecedented levels of stress in the workplace, which research has shown to be one of the most effective inhibitors of creativity in individuals and teams (Baas, De Dreu, & Nijstad, 2008). At least two considerations may be extracted from this conclusion: To begin with, can it be possible to measure the level of capacity at which individuals and teams are actually operating? Secondly, if and when this level of capacity has been determined, how can it be increased effectively and systematically?

With this specific intent, the Regenerative Capacity Index (RCI) was developed as an organizational self-assessment tool (see Appendix 1 for a copy of the questionnaire and instructions on how to administer it). Structured to address the components of the Regenerative Leadership Framework, the RCI measures the regenerative capacity of the individuals in any given organization or community (Quadrants 1–4), and their capacity to operate at what is defined here as the system leadership level. The latter measures the extent to which the organization is operating effectively across internal and external boundaries from the local to the global level. The assessment is enlightening and useful in that it determines the current state of engagement and emerging consciousness of the organization as a whole, offering a clear picture of the strengths and weaknesses of its regenerative capacity. The process in itself tends to bring a deeper awareness of the developmental needs of the organization, as the individual perceptions of internal and external stakeholders are collected to reveal its overall worldview. As illustrated in Figure 2.3, this may range from fragmented to integrated, which is a strong predictor of the organization's readiness to successfully embrace the triple top line (TTL). From this understanding, it becomes possible to design and implement strategies to bring the collective capacity closer to a regenerative mindset and the higher level practices this engenders.

Across different fields of endeavor, regenerative leaders consistently mention that they engage in personal practices that serve to stimulate higher levels of consciousness, engagement, and performance. From the enhanced awareness they engender, they indicate that these contemplative practices have fostered new behaviors. They mention increased physical health through the modification of ingrained eating and drinking habits, clearer focus when making decisions, greater connectedness and mindfulness in relationships, and overall a deeper sense of personal purpose and meaning. The time set aside for these activities, therefore, has tended to become highly valued and therefore protected. The greatest challenge, they find, is in how to bring these practices into the workplace so that they may have a similar impact on their organization's capacity to perform at the highest possible level.

The program that follows has been designed specifically to address this challenge. This was developed principally by my wife, Patricia, as a result of her training in group dynamics, psychotherapy, Reiki, yoga, and meditation. Synthesized from several Eastern traditions, the program is designed as a set of simple relaxation and breathing exercises that can be practiced individually and/or collectively. As mentioned, used systematically in the manner described, they prepare groups to engage their collective creative faculties through transconceptual dynamics conducive to generative conversation, triple-loop learning, and third-order change.

In organizations, the beneficial effects of health and wellness programs focusing on stress reduction for improved productivity and job satisfaction are well documented in the literature. In our experience, however, while corporate health and wellness programs often promote these practices on a voluntary basis for

	Enacting emerging futures		
Primacy of the whole	**Generative Dialogue** Presencing and flow Collapse of boundaries Listening from future self	**Reflective Dialogue** Inquiry I can change my point of view Empathic listening	Primacy of the parts
	Talking Nice Downloading Politeness and caution Listening is projecting	**Talking Tough** Debate and clash I am my point of view Listening from outside	
	Re-enacting patterns of the past		

Figure 6.1 Four structures of conversation.
Source: Scharmer (2007). Used with permission.

individuals, they are rarely adopted as an integral component of the workplace routine. There appears to be a disconnect between the recognized, measurable long-term benefits of these practices at the level of the individual and their potential value for promoting increased collective consciousness and performance. In some cases, the unwillingness to incorporate them may arise from a notion that they are incompatible with organizational culture, the "way we do things around here," and they may be dismissed as mystical or even religious practices. In other cases, the difficulty arises simply from a lack of training in how some of the more effective of these techniques can be applied in the workplace.

Those leaders who have reaped the benefits from these personal practices are more willing to seek to introduce them in their organizations to increase collective awareness and performance, particularly as they can relate them to the core regenerative issues of increased revenue, and environmental and social governance (ESG). It has become more frequent therefore, that we receive questions on how some of these techniques may be incorporated as an integral aspect of the work of a team or an organization to increase performance. Otto Scharmer (2007) offers a framework to show the different levels at which individuals interact in organizations, which he has called the four structures of conversation for generative dialog (see Figure 6.1). In an environment conducive to generative dialog, Scharmer proposes, participants are able to enter into a state of "presencing" and flow, which in turn leads to the collapse of separation and boundaries, allowing for the development of an increased capacity to "listen" from our future rather than our old selves.

What follows, therefore, is a brief rationale for the value of contemplative practices as a means to developing the aspects described in Quadrants 1 and 3 of the regenerative leadership framework as the collective mindset, purpose, and worldview, and the corresponding collective behaviors, competencies, and skills described in Quadrant 4. Four techniques are introduced, crafted from personal and professional practice, and these have been refined through working with individuals and teams within organizations seeking to build their capacity for innovation and creativity as a core dimension of their decision-making process. Central to this practice is the intention to deepen what is described in the Regenerative Leadership Framework as the field of engagement and emerging consciousness (depicted in Figure 2.2). As will be remembered from its description in Chapter 2, this is located intentionally between the subjective and objective quadrants of the framework, representing the metaphorical "topsoil" of consciousness, an idea adapted from Otto Scharmer's account in *Theory U* (2007) of the field walk his father would take the family while on their farm in Germany during his childhood. During these walks, his father would pick up and sift through a handful of rich earth holding earthworms, talking all the while about its critical importance to human survival. In the regenerative leadership framework, this notion of the importance of topsoil is translated as a metaphor of human consciousness, the "fertility" and ability to flourish of which is directly proportional to the systematic work invested in its development.

Thich Nhat Hanh, arguably the second most well-known Buddhist monk after the Dalai Lama, divides this field in two levels. The top of these he calls the living room where we display the flowers of our consciousness. Below this lies the storeroom where we keep the seeds of our awareness. Among these we can find the seeds of mindfulness, joy, peace, love, hope, and prosperity, and also the seeds of anger, jealousy, fear, guilt, hatred, and greed. As Thich Nhat Hanh explains, if we water the good and not the bad seeds with our attention and intention, into the living room of our lives we will bring forth beautiful flowers to be shared with others. However, if we water the bad seeds, we will cultivate the weeds of negative thinking that will compete and push out the good plants.

To continue the metaphor, as we cultivate the good seeds in the field of engagement and emerging consciousness, we are able to expand our awareness and in consequence gain access to higher levels of creativity, thereby enabling us to become socially, environmentally, and economically regenerative. As described more fully in Chapter 2, below the field of engagement, Quadrants 1 and 3 represent the interior, subjective world of the individual and collective mindset, purpose and worldview. Above the field, Quadrants 2 and 4 depict the exterior objective world of individual and collective behaviors, systems, competencies, and skills. As individual and collective consciousness increases, the reasoning goes, generative conversation must lead to better decisions by virtue of the expanded state of awareness and increasing resonance of those participating in the process. At this level of awareness, hierarchies are flattened, and social entropy between individuals and teams is continually reduced, leading to the highest quality outcomes from an economic, environmental, and social perspective.

Introduction to meditation

The scope of this chapter does not allow for an extensive study of meditation, its origins, and diverse traditions, and this information is readily accessible elsewhere to the interested reader. We have opted, therefore, to provide only an introductory overview for the lay reader, and have focused principally on its practical application to the consciousness development of individuals and groups.

Physiological effects

Numerous scientific studies of the brain's activity during meditation have led to an understanding of how its practice affects its functioning (see Ospina et al., 2007). Using an electroencephalogram to analyze brain activity during meditation, the brain's electrical impulses can be seen to go from beta waves (normal waking activity at 15–30 Hz) to a coherent configuration of alpha waves (relaxed calmness and creative state at 9–14 Hz). During deeper stages of meditation, the brain can descend to theta waves (profound relaxation leading to enhanced problem solving, at 4–8 Hz). Studies such as this have concluded that meditation can lead to lower cholesterol levels, improved blood pressure, and reduced anxiety. Complementary to meditative practices that regulate the frequency of the brain are those techniques that help harmonize the frequency of the heart, the most powerful organ in our bodies, responsible for sustaining our physical and emotional energy. Aligning the heart and brain frequencies releases creative energy through the suspension of emotions such as fear, anxiety, and attachment to the ego, arguably the greatest obstacle to collective creativity and performance.

Meditation as a tool

Different meditation techniques can be classified with regard to their focus. Some focus on the field of perception and experience, also known as mindfulness meditation. Others focus on a specific object of attention, which may be defined as meditation concentration. While emphasizing mindfulness meditation, the practices described here can also be used to focus on specific issues and projects, particularly when guided by specialized facilitators.

Meditation and diverse traditions

In the Zen tradition, meditation is the natural state of human consciousness which is capable of comprehending the meaning of its own existence. Within Buddhism, each school has developed specific approaches to meditation, some of which can be summarized as follows:

- observation of the breath;
- visualization of thought;
- focus on an object or image (such as a Mandala).

In Indian yoga, meditation is considered to be:

- a state of concentration on the reality of the present moment;

- a mental state experienced as dissolution of the mind when it is liberated from its own thoughts;
- focusing on a single object of perception, such as the breath.

The meditation practices

The four exercises described here can be conducted as a single session lasting approximately 60 minutes, or they can be broken down into single practices of shorter duration according to the specific purposes to which they may be applied. While they may be practiced by individuals, they are designed also to be conducted in groups, which can be of any size depending on the space available. It is recommended that the full session be conducted when engaging in new projects or addressing critical events that require the fullest capacity of the organization's consciousness.

Practice 1 – open mind meditation

Purpose: awakening to the field of engagement and emerging consciousness

This technique is directed at quieting the mind, freeing it from the distraction of internal thoughts and emotions and from external stimuli. It helps to establish the present place and moment as the focus of attention. From this state of awareness, we are able to disengage from habitual thinking and resistance to new ideas. In essence, we become able to integrate the different parts of our brain, left and right hemispheres, frontal and occipital lobes, so that our minds can operate coherently and effectively, engaging fresh perspectives and ideas creatively and without judgment. In this state, it is possible to engage in humble inquiry, and the eternal question, "What do I want?" can be asked within a broader context, where self-seeking impulses can be balanced against natural and universal laws.

Technique

This initial short meditation (10 minutes) applies the breathing technique of Pranayama yoga. The practice begins by having the participants sit with eyes closed, hands in their laps, in an upright posture with back straight but relaxed. The meditation facilitator brings the participants' attention to their breath for a few moments, and then proceeds to guide them through a process of physical relaxation of the body, beginning with the feet through to the top of the head. This is followed by a short silent meditation before returning to the normal state of alertness.

Practice 2 – open heart meditation

Purpose: sensing from the field of engagement and emerging consciousness

The open heart meditation produces a shift in the energy field of the group and of the physical environment where it is practiced. This can be considered as a change in the intensity level of the energy field. Breathing becomes calmer, and emotional intensity is decreased. Thoughts and emotions become clearer and more balanced, leading to an enhanced sense of creative freedom and expression. The level of trust within the group is expanded, leading to a more conscious and dispassionate capacity for collective reflection on the root causes of the problems confronting it, and in consequence on how they may be solved.

Technique

Deep breathing technique to enhance relaxation (15 minutes). The practice includes the use of polarity breathing, which consists of using the thumb and middle finger to close and open the right and left nostril, respectively. In this manner, the breath is first taken in on the left side and released through the right nostril, and the process is inverted to complete the cycle. The practice is repeated ten times (2 minutes). This practice serves to further balance the right and left hemispheres of the brain and increases the body's energy. The participants' attention and intention are then brought to focus on the heart through the slow, rhythmic repetition of four heart *sutras* (from the Sanskrit meaning a thread or line that holds things together). The four sutras are "peace, harmony, laughter, love." Through this practice, it becomes possible to activate the right emotions of compassion, empathy, harmony, and love. This also has the effect of opening the throat chakra, associated with the free expression of truth and effective communication.

Practice 3 – open will meditation

Purpose: activating the field of engagement and emerging consciousness

This technique is designed to break down our instinctive fear of and resistance to change, allowing participants to relinquish any excessive tendency to control oneself and others, and thereby enabling the will to act to emerge naturally and spontaneously even when major challenges lie ahead. In this meditation, there is a deeper sense of merging with the group, the "ego" is willingly suspended and can even be felt to disintegrate. In the most successful practices, the progression through these first three meditations fosters a profound understanding of the group's creative power, breaking the illusion of individuality and raising the group's potential for visualizing what Scharmer (2007) has called "desirable emerging futures."

Table 6.1 The seven major chakras

Sanskrit name	*Location*	*Color*	*Sound*	*Meaning*
Sahasrara	Crown	White	OM	Pure consciousness – the source of stillness that connects to the whole
Ajna	Brow	Violet	Sham	Clarity of vision – wisdom and intuition
Vishuddha	Throat	Blue	Ham	Expression of truth – communication
Anahata	Heart	Green	Yam	Harmony – compassion – empathy – mindfulness
Manipura	Solar plexus	Yellow	Ram	Processing – will to act – creative energy
Swadhisthana	Sacral (coccyx)	Orange	Vam	Change – flexibility – plasticity – intimacy
Muladhara	Base/root (perineum)	Red	Lam	Groundedness – stability – security

Technique

Guided and stillness meditation (15 minutes) that touches upon the seven major chakras, accompanied by visualization of each chakra's color and sound frequency (see Table 6.1).

Practice 4 – emerging meditation

Purpose: materializing the field of engagement and emerging consciousness

This longer silent collective meditation is designed to promote and sustain the group's capacity to visualize and materialize regenerative practices as innovative prototypes that may not emerge through conventional modes of decision making.

Technique

Deep silent meditation (20 minutes), beginning by focusing briefly on the seven major chakras covered in the open mind, heart, and will meditations, followed by placing the attention on the breath, and then allowing one's inner stillness to emerge. This stillness is the deepest source of awareness available to us, and allows us to develop a powerful sense of wholeness and connection to others induced by the state of complete relaxation in the present moment. When effectively practiced, this technique promotes the world centric or integrated worldview (Level 5) that leads to the global ethics described in the regenerative leadership framework. At this level of consciousness, the group enters into a state of resonance and increased clarity, where the faculties of reason, intuition, heart, and the will to act become an indivisible whole. As the group is brought back from this state of being fully present, its capacity to engage in generative conversation and the co-creation of TTL solutions is enhanced through the integration of all faculties.

Discussion

The practices described here may appear at first glance as foreign and impractical in business environments that place greater importance on shareholder management rather than stakeholder engagement, on quarterly reports and returns on investment rather than on long-term collective visions and efforts seeking to create a more prosperous global society within a healthy biosphere. In response to this, it can be argued that the traditional business mindset and model has played a major role in creating, even if unconsciously, a society with increasing disparity of wealth, rapidly depleting renewable and non-renewable natural resources, and a degraded, impoverished environment that will be incapable of offering future generations the quality of life that we have taken for granted for so long. This way of doing things is no longer acceptable. The search for alternative design and decision-making processes through techniques such as these can provide fresh insights into how we can engage in growing prosperity, celebrating community, and enhancing the health of all species for all time.

Conclusion

Deepak Chopra tells us that our knowledge is the prison of our past, and that to break out of this prison we must awaken and look at the world as if for the first time (Chopra & Plack, 2008). We live in a society where the past plays a dominant role in how we envision and design our futures. The suspension of prior assumptions, knowledge, and skills in order to create better futures is a daunting challenge for most of us. However, a review of existing systems, government, economy, education, health care, security, agriculture, business, and industry reveals deep structural flaws in our understanding of who we are, why we are here, and what we do. These flaws have led to a human condition incapable of ensuring personal fulfillment or equitable prosperity for all within a healthy biosphere, but rather the contrary. The solutions to our problems cannot come from a fragmented worldview grounded in a mindset of self-serving, ethnocentric competition rooted in outdated beliefs and assumptions about reality and about ourselves. While many of us recognize these increasingly evident truths, we have yet to find the courage, the skills and the tools to extract us from the oppression of our own minds and to engage in doing things in entirely new ways uncontaminated by prior assumptions. Yet a possible world for us all can only be based on a new, integrated mindset on a global scale capable of suspending the old ways that no longer work for us and the planet, despite the fear and anxiety that this may cause. Anything less will not get the job done.

The regenerative leadership framework and the RCI offer some pointers as to what a roadmap to a more desirable future might look like. The values, attributes, skills, and behaviors described here have emerged from systematic research into the work of successful leaders in high-performing organizations that are making significant strides in mapping effective leadership and organizational journeys to regenerative practice. It is my hope that their collective experience may serve to inspire us all to discover our own internal regenerative leader, and to allow us to find personal and professional fulfillment by working to address the most critical challenges we face as a species. Our fate, and that of our children and their children, is in our minds, our hearts, and our hands. As Majora Carter, the South Bronx environmental justice activist, said not so long ago, "we have nothing to lose, and so much to gain."

Appendix 1: The Regenerative Capacity Index

Introduction

The Regenerative Capacity Index (RCI) emerged from the Regenerative Leadership Framework (see Figures A1.1–A1.4), which was developed through systematic research and process consulting work with successful sustainability leaders in business, education, and community beginning in 2007. By responding to the following questionnaire, you and your team(s) will be in a better position to understand the organization's capacity as a regenerative force in the local and global community while sustaining a healthy bottom line. It will also help you drill down into those areas of the organization that need to be improved if it is to become more effective in identifying those aspects of individual and collective awareness and behaviors that will bring you closer to the triple top line.[1]

The assessment instrument is divided into five sections, following the four quadrants of the Regenerative Leadership Framework, complemented by a fifth section that collects data on the organization's capacity for system leadership. Designed as an active spreadsheet, the responses are automatically loaded into tables and charts for immediate viewing and discussion. See Figures A1.1–A1.4 on the following pages.

Note

1 Growing prosperity, celebrating community, and enhancing the health of all species for all time.

REGENERATIVE CAPACITY INDEX

TEAM/ORGANIZATION
FACILITATOR
DATE

The Regenerative Capacity Index (RCI) is divided into four main domains or quadrants, followed by a section on system leadership. Each section lists items rated from 0-3. Please rate your responses to the best of your ability. There are no wrong answers. The tables and charts to the right will be populated as you respond, providing an overview of the team/organization's areas of greatest strength and in need of improvement based on your assessment. When consolidated with the responses of the rest of your team(s), you will have a clear idea of your organization's capacity to engage in regenerative practice.

QUADRANTS 1 and 2: Individual Subjective and Objective Domains

The following questions refer to your perception about your regenerative capacity at the level of inner awareness (Q1) and your behaviors (Q2). As you provide each response think of a specific project and the organization responsible for it.

QUADRANT 1: Personal mindset, purpose, and worldview

1. Possession of a sense of personal engagement with the issue or project
Enter 0-3 — *Low (0) to very High (3)*

2. Capacity to engage different ways of approaching the issue or project
Enter 0-3 — *Tend to repeat past ways of thinking (0) to engaging entirely new ways of thinking (3)*

3. Capacity to understand the inter-connections of nature, society, economy, and well-being in the issue or project
Enter 0-3 — *Linear cause and effect thinking (0) to integral perspective (3)*

4. Capacity to balance benefit for oneself, for all, and for the future
Enter 0-3 — *What's in it for me (0) to what's in it for all of us (3)*

0 — ***SUBTOTAL***

Figure A1.1 RCI (intro and Quadrant 1).

QUADRANT 2: Personal leadership behaviors, competencies and skills

1. Capacity to support the common issue or project by suspending personal agendas
Enter 0-3 — *It's about one person's idea (0) to it's important to us all (3)*

2. Willingness to observe best practices related to the issue
Enter 0-3 — *Did it alone (0) to extensive observation of best in field (3)*

3. Capacity to value the ideas of others
Enter 0-3 — *Disengaged (0) to highly engaged (3)*

4. Capacity to engage a diverse range of stakeholders
Enter 0-3 — *Some engagement (0) to engagement of a broad range of internal and external stakeholders (3)*

0 — ***SUBTOTAL***

QUADRANTS 3 and 4: Organizational Subjective and Objective Domains

The following questions refer to your perception about the regenerative capacity of the organization at the level of collective inner awareness (Q3) and behaviors (Q4).

QUADRANT 3: Collective purpose, mindset and worldview

1. Capacity to operate from a heightened sense of shared purpose in the team/organization
Enter 0-3 — *Low (0) to very high (3)*

2. Capacity to operate in an environment of high trust for generating new ideas
Enter 0-3 — *Low quality (0) to highly generative conversations (3)*

3. Willingness to engage other faculties in addition to logic (e.g. intuition, imagination)
Enter 0-3 — *Logical only (0) to multiple faculties (3)*

4. Willingness to suspend all prior assumptions when designing solutions
Enter 0-3 — *Can't let go of old paradigm (0) to high willingness to cultivate new paradigm (3)*

0 — ***SUBTOTAL***

Figure A1.2 RCI (Quadrants 2 and 3).

QUADRANT 4: Collective behaviors, competencies and skills

1. Collective capacity to envision shared desirable futures
Enter 0-3 — *Low (0) to very high (3)*

2. Collective capacity to implement complex new solutions
Enter 0-3 — *Ineffective (0) to highly effective (3)*

3. Collective capacity to generate small-scale regenerative solutions
Enter 0-3 — *Low (0) to high (3)*

4. Collective capacity to scale up environmentally, socially, and economically regenerative solutions
Enter 0-3 — *Low (0) to very high (3)*

0 — ***SUBTOTAL***

SYSTEM LEADERSHIP

The following questions refer to your organization's capacity to operate effectively across departments, and the local, national and global community.

1. Internal - Capacity for cross-departmental integration
Enter 0-3 — *Fragmented (0) to fully integrated (3)*

2. Consortium building - Capacity for cross-organizational engagement in same industry, community.
Enter 0-3 — *Low (0) to very high (3)*

3. Coalition building - Capacity for effective multilateral engagement across industries, communities, educational systems
Enter 0-3 — *Low (0) to very high (3)*

4. Global networking - Capacity for effective engagement across political, socio-economic, cultural, ethnic, religious boundaries
Enter 0-3 — *Low (0) to very high (3)*

0 — ***SUBTOTAL***

Figure A1.3 RCI (Quadrant 4 and system leadership).

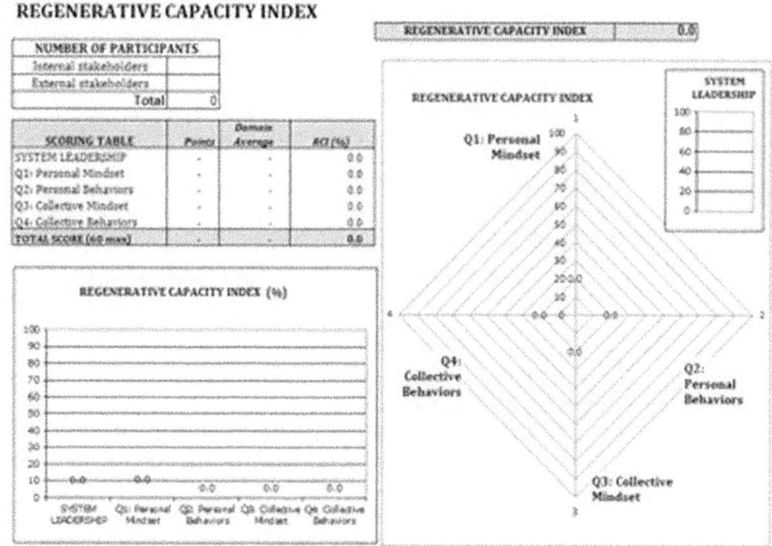

REGENERATIVE CAPACITY INDEX

NUMBER OF PARTICIPANTS	
Internal stakeholders	
External stakeholders	
Total	0

SCORING TABLE	Points	Domain Average	RCI (%)
SYSTEM LEADERSHIP	-	-	0.0
Q1: Personal Mindset	-	-	0.0
Q2: Personal Behaviors	-	-	0.0
Q3: Collective Mindset	-	-	0.0
Q4: Collective Behaviors	-	-	0.0
TOTAL SCORE (60 max)	-	-	0.0

REGENERATIVE CAPACITY INDEX	0.0

Figure A1.4 RCI (results – tables and charts).

Appendix 2: List of regenerative leaders

Summary list

Business	
Michael Singer	Michael Singer Studio
Joe Laur	Greenopolis, Waste Management/Cofounder, Sustainability Consortium of the Society for Organizational Learning (SOL)
Martin Melaver	CEO, Melaver, Inc., Real Estate
Roger Vardan	General Motors, Founder of Strata-gems LLC, Cornell
Darcy Winslow	GM of Women's Global Business and Senior Advisor, NIKE Foundation
Gregor Barnum	Director of Corporate Consciousness, Seventh Generation
Seetha Coleman-Kammula	Shell/Founder of Simply Sustain LLC
Marcell Haywood	President and COO, Dirt Pros EVS
Community	
Eve Williams	Program Architect, City of Tallahassee
Cecilia Campoverde	Founder, The Guatemalan Project
Rebecca Bardach	United Nations High Commission for Refugees and the Center for International Migration and Integration of the American Jewish Joint Distribution Committee
Debbie Koristz	Assistant Director of Israel & Overseas Projects, Jewish Federation of Palm Beach County
Jim Murley	Secretary of Community Affairs, Florida, Executive Director, Center for Urban and Environmental Solutions (CUES) at Florida Atlantic University (FAU), Chair of the Florida Energy and Climate Change Commission
Nathan Burrell	Founder, The Honey Project, President of the Minority E-Commerce Association, Inc. (MECA)
Steve Seibert	Executive Director, Century Commission for a Sustainable Florida
John Elkington	Founder, Volans Ventures, Visiting Professor, Doughty Centre for Corporate Responsibility, School of Management, Cranfield University, UK

(*Continued*)

(*Continued*)

Education	
Anthony Cortese	President, Second Nature
MaryBeth Burton	Associate Director, Center for Urban and Environmental Solutions, Florida Atlantic University
Leonard Berry	Director, Florida Center of Environmental Studies
Jaap Vos	Associate Professor and Chair of the Department of Urban & Regional Planning, Florida Atlantic University
Judy Walton	Executive Director, Association for the Advancement of Sustainability in Higher Education (AASHE)
Jean MacGregor	Director, Curriculum for the Bioregion Initiative, Washington Center for Improving the Quality of Undergraduate Education, The Evergreen State College
Daniel Meeroff	Professor of Environmental Sciences/Dept. of Civil Engineering, Florida Atlantic University (FAU)
Mitchell Thomashow	President, Unity College, Maine

Biographical sketches

Business

Michael Singer

Visiting Scholar, College of Integrated Science and Technology, James Madison University. www.michaelsinger.com

Michael Singer has received numerous awards, including fellowships from the National Endowment for the Arts and the John Simon Guggenheim Foundation. His works are part of public collections in the United States and abroad, including the Australian National Gallery, Canberra; Louisiana Museum of Modern Art, Humlebaek, Denmark; Guggenheim Museum, New York; The Museum of Modern Art, New York, and the Metropolitan Museum of Art, New York. He had several one-person shows, most notably at the Guggenheim Museum, New York City. In 2011, he will be holding an exhibition of his work at the Utzon Center, Denmark, from June to November.

Throughout the 1970s and 1980s Michael Singer's work opened new possibilities for outdoor and indoor sculpture and contributed to the definition of site-specific art and the development of public places. His most recent work has been instrumental in transforming public art, architecture, landscape, and planning projects into successful models for urban and ecological renewal. In 1993, *The New York Times* chose Singer's design of a massive waste recycling and transfer station in Phoenix as one of the top eight design events of the year.

In recent years, Singer has been involved in a variety of landscape and outdoor environment, planning, and infrastructure projects in the United States and Europe. He has completed a woodland garden and sculpture for a 2-acre site on the Wellesley College campus, Wellesley, Massachusetts. In Stuttgart, West Germany, Singer completed a 1-acre sculptural garden commemorating "Those

Who Survived'' as part of a new public park. In 1994, a sculptural floodwall and walkway that serves as a model riverine reclamation project designed by Singer for the Grand River East Bank in Grand Rapids, Michigan, was completed. For the Denver International Airport, Singer completed a large interior sculpture garden design and installation for Concourse C. At the Isabella Stewart Gardner Museum in Boston, Singer developed a master plan for the use and redesign of the outdoor gardens as part of a 2-year residency. Singer's design of air and water purification gardens for the Institute for Forestry and Nature (Alterra, IBN), Holland, has been featured in many journals as one of the leading examples of esthetically outstanding green sustainable design. The Canal Corridor Association and Chicago Parks Department selected Singer to design a new urban park on the Chicago River that interprets the history and impacts of canals on the city, as well as reclaims wildlife habitat and restores a wetland ecosystem. With support from the Rockefeller Foundation, he leads a multidisciplinary team with the environmental group River Watch Network on the master plan for Troja Island Basin in Prague, Czech Republic.

The recently opened AES Londonderry, New Hampshire Cogeneration Facility buildings, site, and surrounding land holdings (US$400 million) was designed by a team led by Michael Singer. The Singer Team design identified many strategies by which the facility will set a new standard for the power industry, making this power facility an asset to its surroundings; demonstrating how essential services like power generation can become integral parts of a community's social fabric. As a result of Singer's work for AES, several companies in the electric power industry have engaged him to work on new facility design. The Singer Team developed the design for Trans Gas Energy's Greenpoint, Brooklyn site. The Singer Team design is included in the New York State Article 10 Regulatory Application. The design reveals many exciting possibilities for integrating the facility water and waste heat systems into design and programs that are amenities to the community. The design defines an ''Urban Eco-Sustainable Network,'' including habitat creation, education, recreation, water preservation, and urban agriculture as part of the electric generation facility building and site.

The EcoTarium in Worcester, Massachusetts, recently completed two phases (US$16 million) of a Singer-led master plan and design for the institution's 60-acre site. The design includes extensive renovation, new buildings, museum store, telecommunications center, exhibitions, major site and landscape improvements, and animal habitats. The project and Singer's work were a feature in the ''New York Times Sunday Arts and Leisure Section.'' Singer completed an artist in residence grant at the Armory Art Center in West Palm Beach as the leader of ''Imagining Howard Park,'' a creative urban planning exercise. For this residency, Singer led a ''think tank'' of community participants, regional artists, design and planning professionals, students, and members of the general public. The Plan identifies design and program opportunities that inform the City about revitalizing and interconnecting the park to the residential, commercial, cultural, environmental, and civic interests encompassing it, and to bring attention to the special qualities of the indigenous South Florida landscape. Singer is currently the Dorothy F. Schmidt Eminent Scholar Chair at Florida Atlantic University. His work with FAU PhD students resulted in proposals for a new retention pond policy at the university, and an innovative visitor center for the South Florida Water Management District.

The Jewish Community Center on the Upper West Side: New York City commissioned Michael Singer to propose a public work of art for the new Samuel Priest Rose Building on 76th Street and Amsterdam Avenue in Manhattan. Singer designed and fabricated "Welcoming Garden," a vertical 40-foot narrow sculptural garden positioned, like a crevice, into the stone wall. "Welcoming Garden" is set into a "field" of Jerusalem Stone. The vertical garden is a series of textured cliff-like shelve forms made of copper and bronze castings. The garden's channel extends behind the plane of Jerusalem stone, revealing deeper layers. Vine plants are distributed within the 16-inch-wide inner chamber. Water flows very slowly within the crevice, dripping from level to level before collecting in a small reservoir. The project was completed in April 2002 and sponsored by the Jewish Community of the Upper West Side.

In 2003, Michael Singer completed the Palm Beach County Courthouse Security Barrier: West Palm Beach, Florida. Michael Singer was selected through a competition to design and fabricate a US$350,000 security barrier for two plazas of the County Courthouse. This project uses public art as way to esthetically enhance a functional security need.

In January 2003, The New York City Economic Development Corporation hired Michael Singer to form a core team with Margie Ruddick Landscape, and Michael Sorkin Urban Planning to provide planning, streetscape, and landscape design for the public spaces in Queens Plaza near the Queensboro Bridge in Long Island City, New York. The focus of the design is a sustainable urban environment using storm water runoff from the Queensboro Bridge to implement systems including plantings and streetscapes that filter and cleanse a portion of this water. Public art was designed to enhance the functional elements needed at the site, providing amenities for solar collection, wind abatement, and sound attenuation, as well as the armature for information and interpretation of the environmental and cultural history of the site. The project was completed in the year 2006.

In October 2004, Michael Singer completed a sculpture garden commission by Middlebury College. "Garden of the Seasons" is located adjacent to the new Middlebury College Library. The sculpture garden functions as a filtration system for storm water runoff on the upper campus as well as an outdoor seating and gathering space. Native plantings are set around a granite seating, sunken gardens, and water wall that becomes a winter ice wall.

The city of West Palm Beach hired Michael Singer with TDG Planners and CH2MHILL Engineering to design a new central waterfront park, City Commons, on 1 mile of the Intercoastal in the downtown area. The planning and conceptual design was completed in November 2005. Environmental enhancement was an important theme of the proposal along with floating islands that help purify the Intercoastal water and are connected to land by a series of piers and water surface walkways. A planted and stepped transitional edge was proposed for the sea wall. There were interpretive programs for all ages to help people understand the environmental, cultural, social, and historical layers of the site.

In 2005, Whole Foods Market engaged Michael Singer to develop alternatives to the types of shopping centers the store is proposing to anchor. In June 2005, Singer completed "Outside the Box," a visual and written report on the potential for Whole Foods Market and their host shopping centers to address esthetic, cultural, and environmental issues that would distinguish these "big box" places from what is the norm. Singer completed design concepts for a new Whole Foods Market store in Orlando and continues to work with Whole Foods Market on the stores they are opening in the Florida region.

Michael Singer was recently awarded the commission to design and install the new entry gardens and sculpture for the American Embassy in Athens, Greece. Working with architects Kallmann, McKinnel, and Wood, Singer proposed a stone and water garden be completed by fall 2006.

Joseph Laur

Content VP, Greenopolis: http://greenopolis.com/

Sustainability Consortium of the Society for Organizational Learning: www.solsustainability.org

Joe Laur is Vice President of Content for Greenopolis, a web-based social network, media, and educational center, marketplace and playground fostering learning and collaborative action on green issues. Joe was a founding partner of SEED Systems, a consultancy dedicated to learning and action for sustainable enterprise, applying systems thinking, scientific frameworks and organizational learning to foster innovation in companies engaging with environmental and social issues. In partnership with the Society for Organizational Learning (SOL) (www.solonli ne.org), Mr Laur along with colleagues Peter Senge and Sara Schley established the SOL Sustainability Consortium (www.solsustainability.org), an active group of industry leaders in learning and sustainability. He still serves as steward of this consortium, leading collaborative projects among the members as well as coachi ng individual member projects. This consortium includes members from BP, Ford, Coca Cola, Harley-Davidson, UTC, Green Mountain Coffee Roasters, Ni ke, Seventh Generation, Waste Management and more. He is coauthor with Peter Senge of *Learning for Sustainability* (2007), and the Doubleday book, *The Necessary Revolution: How Individuals and Organizations Are Working Together to Create a Sustainable World* (June 2008) written with Peter Senge, Sara Schley, and Brian Smith, and with Sara Schley, coauthor of "The Sustainability Challenge" published in *The Systems Thinker* and "Creating Sustainable Organi zations" published in the *Pegasus' Innovations in Management Series*.

Mr Laur is one of the designers and facilitators of SOL's Sustainability Forum on Business Innovation for Sustainability in 2004 and 2007. He has spoken at numerous business gatherings including the Natural Step Conference, The Power of Systems Thinking Conference, and the Systems Thinking in Action conference on issues of sustainable business. Participants in his work in organizational learning and sustainable business have included:

- BP
- BSR
- Burlington Chemical
- California EPA
- CERES
- Chrysler
- City of Fitchburg
- The Coca-Cola Company
- College of Notre Dame
- Detroit Edison
- DTE
- Ford Motor Company
- Great Lakes Commission
- Green Mountain Coffee Roasters
- Harley-Davidson Motor Company
- Hewlett Packard
- Interface, Inc.
- Missouri Botanical Gardens
- New York State Department of Environmental Conservation
- Nike
- Northeast Utilities
- Open Society Institute
- Plug Power
- PV2
- Schlumberger
- Seventh Generation
- Shell Oil
- Strata-gems
- Sustainability Institute
- Sustainable Food Lab
- Unilever
- United Technologies
- UTC
- Visteon Corporation
- World Bank
- Xerox
- and more

Mr Laur was the Executive Director of the Mankind Project (formerly New Warrior Network) from 1992 to 1996, expanding the organization into Canada and Europe, tripling training facilities, leadership capacity, and revenues during his tenure. He has spent the last decade as a consultant to organizations in all sectors, focusing on organizational learning, personal effectiveness skills, and sustainable development. He studied with Dr Karl Henrik Robèrt of The Natural Step and has facilitated learning courses and conferences with Amory Lovins, Paul Hawken William McDonough, John Elkington, Janine Benyus, and Michael Braungart, and others. Mr Laur has worked with whole systems change for over 30 years and is a certified practitioner of Structural Integration, an applied physiology practice invoking whole systems change in human body structures. He received his BFA in 1975 from the University of Wisconsin. He is the father of five children.

Martin Melaver

http://melaver.com/

Martin Melaver is Vice President and CEO of Melaver, Inc., a third-generation, family-owned business based in Savannah, Georgia. Melaver, Inc.'s vision is to become a vertically integrated, truly sustainable real estate company. Melaver Inc.'s triple-bottom line notion of sustainability harkens back to its predecessor days as a grocery business (1940–1985) deeply integrated into the needs of the local community. After selling the grocery business to Kroger in 1985, the company has focused its attention on doing real estate a different way, by attending to the overall health and well-being of land and community.

Melaver, Inc., currently accounts for about 1 percent of all the LEED certifications[1] in the United States, including participation in three distinct pilot programs for sustainable development. The company's renovation of The Whitaker Building was one of the first in the nation to be listed on The National Register of Historic Places and to be LEED certified. Melaver, Inc., developed Abercorn Common, the first all-retail LEED shopping center in the country, including the first LEED McDonald's in the United States. The company has also created one of the first sustainable real estate portfolios in the United States and has approximately 13 other LEED projects in the pipeline – office, hotel, residential, and retail – located in various communities throughout the Southeast. Other accomplishments include winning the Southface Institute's annual Argon award for visionary leadership and stewardship of the environment (prior winners have included Ted Turner and Arthur Blank) and an Excellence in Development award from The Urban Land Institute.

Martin grew up in Savannah, Georgia, and received his BA from Amherst College. He holds a Masters and PhD from Harvard University and an MBA from the Kellogg School of Management at Northwestern. He is a past Fulbright scholar to Tel Aviv University, a recipient of a Mellon fellowship to Jesus College, Cambridge University, and a Lady Davis Fellowship to Hebrew University in Jerusalem. He is the author of numerous articles on sustainable building practices as well as a featured/keynote speaker at various conferences and guest lecturer at Harvard, Dartmouth, and other academic institutions.

Martin currently serves as the Board Chair of the Georgia Conservancy, and is a board member of Urban Land Institute's Sustainability Council, The Ossabaw Island Foundation, Skidaway Institute of Oceanography, Savannah Country Day School, and United Community Bank (Savannah).

Dr Roger Vardan

Founder and Managing Director, Strata-gems LLC

Executive in Residence, Center for Sustainable Global Enterprise, Johnson School of Management, Cornell University, NY

Center for Sustainable Enterprise

Dr Roger Vardan is the Managing Director of Strata-gems, an international management consultancy, which provides strategy consulting to leading companies around the world. His consulting practice and research interests revolve around the nexus between strategy and sustainability. Previously, Dr Vardan directed global strategy for the Powertrain Group at General Motors, where he led strategy development in such diverse areas as value chain design, future of automotive propulsion and its implications for sustainable mobility, global business alliances, new product development, and marketing. He also represented the company in the International Motor Vehicle Program. Prior to his tenure at General Motors, he served as the manager of the Systems Analysis Group at Battelle Memorial Institute, one of the leading think-tanks in the world. Dr Vardan has been an active member of the Sustainability Consortium, consisting of progressive multinational companies collectively striving toward sustainability, and consults with the consortium's member companies. He also serves as a consultant to premier business organizations in India and Japan, and as a director for the Real Options Group. Over the years, Dr Vardan has been collaborating with world-renowned strategic thinkers, including Dr Peter Senge of MIT, and Dr Noriaki Kano of Japan, a pioneer in TQM and Chairman of the Deming Prize Committee. Dr Vardan is a frequent speaker at many international conferences and leading academic institutions around the world. His most recent paper appeared in the Sloan Management Review. He volunteers for various organizations that advocate preservation of nature, welfare of young children, and teaching "systems thinking" to high-school students.

Darcy Stallings Winslow
Nike Foundation: www.nikefoundation.org

At the time of our interview, Darcy Winslow was on a 1-year Senior Advisor assignment with the Nike Foundation, which seeks to empower disadvantaged female athletes aged 10–19 years through poverty alleviation and creating economic livelihood opportunities. She co-led a holistic Business Re-Alignment effort within the Nike Brand. In 2009, she launched her own sustainability-consulting firm, DSW Collective, LLC.

Darcy worked at Nike for 20 years, where she held many positions within the business, including Biomechanical Researcher, Director of Footwear and Apparel Product Testing, Product Development Manager, core team member of Nike's Footwear Business Reengineering initiative, Director of Advanced Research and Development, Global Director for Footwear Research, Design and Development, General Manager of Sustainable Business Strategies, a role focused on developing and implementing more environmental and socially sustainable business strategies across the organization. In 2001, she led the creation of the Women's Footwear Division as General Manager, and then in 2004, she led the creation of Nike's Global Women's Fitness Footwear, Apparel and Equipment business as General Manager.

Winslow is currently a Senior Sustainability Strategist with Brightworks, Inc., an Executive-in-Residence and Senior Lecturer at the MIT Sloan School of Management, Program Director for Willamette University's Sustainable Enterprise Program, and is an Adjunct Faculty member with the Center for Creative Leadership.

Winslow received her BS in exercise science and MS in exercise physiology and biomechanics, and is a 2003 graduate of the Stanford Executive Program. She currently serves on the Board of Advisors for NorthWest Earth Institute, Portland State University's Institute for Sustainable Solutions, and as a

Technical Advisor to the Oregon Innovation Council; the Board of Directors for Portland Oregon Sustainability Institute, Greenopolis, The Cloud Institute for Sustainability Education, and the Council for Responsible Sport. She is an active member of the Society for Organizational Learning and Sustainability Consortium and was recently named one of the inaugural Pivotal Leaders, a Northwest-based network of clean-tech business leaders.

Nike Corporate Responsibility Report

http://www.nikebiz.com/nikeresponsibility/#home/

Nike Foundation: improving the lives of adolescent girls. The Nike Foundation in 2005 began investing in adolescent girls as powerful agents of change in the developing world. This focus emerged from the company's desire to support the world's developing countries, recognizing the benefits that both Nike's business and consumers derive from emerging economies. Funded by Nike, Inc., the Foundation leverages the brand's drive for innovation and positive change, and its ability to inspire both. We believe that when girls receive support and realize opportunity for their futures, they can become an unexpected and powerful force in transforming their families, communities, and the world. Learn more by visiting www.nikefoundation.org.

Gregor Barnum

Director of Corporate Consciousness, at Seventh Generation:

http://www.seventhgeneration.com/

Gregor Barnum, Director of Corporate Consciousness at Seventh Generation, the leading brand of natural household products in the United States, is the grandson of Walter Rockwell of Rockwell International. In the late 1980s when Rockwell was sited for environmental injustices, Gregor thought it to be a call to educate corporate America on incorporating environment into the very fabric of the corporate strategy. As a result, he helped engage and grow a New Haven-based corporate environmental management-consulting firm that was later sold to a division of Thermo Electron Corporation.

He was the Director of Operations/Business Development for o.s.Earth, Inc., in New Haven, an educational company, building global and regional simulation events for both education and corporate markets. (The product was originally created by R. Buckminister Fuller and called The World Game.)

He presently is the Director of Corporate Consciousness at Seventh Generation, Inc, in Burlington, Vermont. He works with Jeffrey Hollender, President of Seventh Generation, in evolving the company's corporate responsibility program. He has his Masters Degree (MAR) from the Yale Divinity School with a focus on ethics.

Dr Seetha Coleman-Kammula

Founder, Simply Sustain LLC, Delaware

Simply Sustain, LLC: http://www.simplysustain.com/a/

Dr Seetha Coleman-Kammula guides companies to be profitable by doing business in ways that benefit the environment, shareholders, and society. Simply

Sustain specializes in connecting and engaging companies in the plastics value chain from producers, fabricators, consumer product companies, retailers, and recyclers to reduce the use of energy, materials, and waste by collective action.

2000–2005: Senior Vice President Strategic marketing and Innovation Basell Polyolefins Delaware; Board member, Indelpro, a Basell/Alfa Joint Venture in Mexico
1999–2000: Mergers and Acquisition leader, Shell Chemicals, Houston
1998–1999: Global Business Director, Epoxy Resins, Shell Chemicals, Houston
1997–1998: Global Strategy Director, Epoxy Resins, Shell Chemicals, Houston
1995–1997: Director Technology, Epoxy Resins, Royal Dutch Shell, Belgium
1992–1995: Section Head, R&D, Epoxy Resins, Royal Dutch Shell, Belgium
1987–1992: New Business Development Manager, Shell Chemicals UK
1977–1987: Research Associate, Royal Dutch Shell Research Labs, Amsterdam
1975–1977: Instructor, Organic Chemistry, Princeton University

- Affiliated with the Sustainable Development Consortium at MIT, Society for Organizational Learning.
- Member of Dow Chemical's Corporate Environmental Advisory Council.
- Board member at Developing Indigenous Resources – a nonprofit organization that helps with preventative health care in rural slums in India.
- Advisory Board member, Greenoplis – the first "green," interactive, collaborative, educational website to bring together communities, environmental organizations, universities, foundations, and corporations to reward individuals for making incremental positive environmental changes.

Education:

- Post Doctorate Research Associate, Princeton University,
- PhD in Organic Chemistry, Auburn University,
- BSc at Osmania University, Hyderabad, India.

Marcell Haywood
President and COO, Dirt Pros EVS
http://dirtpros.com

Community

Eve Williams
City of Tallahassee Project Management: http://www.talgov.com/you/solid/green_building.cfm

Eve Williams, Program Architect for Facilities Management, City of Tallahassee, received her Masters of Architecture, with an emphasis on

Environment and Behavior, from Georgia Institute of Technology in 1982. As a LEED Accredited Professional (AP), Williams leads the City's green building efforts, which has completed works such as the renovation of the City's waste management building, the 30-year-old Solid Waste Services Administration building. During initial planning of this renovation and addition project, the City decided that the renovated building should set a standard for environmentally responsible design and building practices. To this end, the City completed the renovation obtaining a Green Building Silver Certification through the United States Green Building Council's Leadership in Energy and Environmental Design (LEED) Rating System®. She continues to pursue the City's goal of obtaining LEED certification, Florida Green Building Coalition (FGBC) Certification, or the Green Building Initiative (GBI) Green Globes building certification for all of their new, renovated, and existing buildings.

Dr Cecilia Campoverde

The Guatemalan Project: http://guatemalanproject.com/

Dr Cecilia Campoverde was born in Ecuador; after graduating from High School, at the age of 19 she immigrated to the United States. She completed her undergraduate and graduate college education in New York State. Dr Campoverde has founded four nonprofit organizations to serve the Latin American community. She is committed to building sustainable efforts, not only at the community level but also at the personal level. Dr Campoverde teaches at FAU where she teaches Policy, Research, International Social Work, and Counseling in Groups within the Social Work Department. She is also a consultant to local agencies and conducts workshops in communication, cultural diversity, and international social work. Since 2002, Dr Campoverde has guided the Guatemalan Project, a nonprofit organization into a very successful economic and social venture. The National Association of Social Workers acknowledged Dr Campoverde as the best social worker of the year in 2007.

Dr Campoverde does not believe in charity and claims that poverty exists because social justice does not. Therefore, her work revolves around bringing social justice which, she defines it as "the celebration of human dignity." Dr Campoverde says that when people receive "fair" wages and have opportunities for economic development they strive to meet their potential. The lack of fair wages and financial opportunities indicates a lack of respect for human dignity; a social injustice. Dr Campoverde relates the tremendous need for mental health as a result of living in an unfair society where human dignity is not celebrated.

Rebecca Bardach

The Center for International Migration and Integration: http://www.cimiglobal.org/

A native of Berkeley, California, Rebecca Bardach earned her BA in English Literature at Columbia in 1995 and her MPA in Public Policy and International Development at New York University's Robert F. Wagner School of Public Policy in 2007. For her MPA she was a recipient of the Luther Gulick Fellowship for International Public Service and the Hammad Fund International Leadership and Scholarship Award Prize. Since college she has worked continually on international migration and development issues. In 1995–1996, she headed a grassroots relief organization assisting refugees from Bosnia and Yugoslavia in several areas including return to Bosnia and resettlement. This experience motivated her to work with refugees returning to their homes in postwar Bosnia, where she managed return and reintegration programs for the American Refugee Committee.

From 1999 to 2002, Rebecca worked in Israel for the UN High Commissioner for Refugees (UNHCR) to develop a national system for managing asylum requests, design refugee and asylum-seeker policies, and process refugee claims from Africa, the Middle East, and elsewhere. Since then she has worked for the Center for International Migration and Integration (CIMI) with issues of immigrant integration, diaspora-homeland partnerships, labor migration, and trafficking of women. She has also helped CIMI's parent organization, the American Jewish Joint Distribution Committee (JDC) establish its tsunami relief program in Sri Lanka in 2005, and is currently working with JDC to develop microfinance and employment programs internationally and an HIV/AIDS prevention program in Ethiopia.

Debbie Koristz

Jewish Federation of Palm Beach County: http://www.jewishpalmbeach.org/index.aspx?page=1

Debbie Koristz is the Assistant Director of Israel and Overseas Projects, Jewish Federation of Palm Beach County. She has worked in the Israel and Overseas Department at the Jewish Federation of Palm Beach County since 2005. Prior to her work at the Jewish Federation, Ms Koristz worked at Hadassah Women's Zionist Organization and the Melton Center for Jewish Education at the Hebrew University in Jerusalem. Ms Koristz has a BA in Education and Sociology and an MA in Education and Cognition from the Hebrew University in Jerusalem. Born in the United States and raised in Guatemala, Ms Koristz immigrated to Israel in 1996 where she finished her studies and moved back to the United States in 2005.

James F. Murley, Esq.

Chair, Florida Energy and Climate Commission

Assistant Dean, College of Design and Social Inquiry, Florida Atlantic University.

Former Executive Director, Florida Department of Community Affairs: http://www.dca.state.fl.us/

Former Executive Director, Center for Urban and Environmental Solutions at Florida Atlantic University: http://www.cuesfau.org/aboutus_files/staff.asp

In February 1999, James Murley became the Director of the Center for Urban and Environmental Solutions in Fort Lauderdale, Florida. The mission of the Center is "to work with policy makers and the public in their pursuit of options for managing growth while preserving natural systems, promoting a strong economy and planning livable communities.''

Jim is a 1974 graduate of the George Washington University Law School where he specialized in environmental and land use law. Before coming to Florida, he worked for the National Atmospheric and Oceanographic Administration in coastal zone management.

He first joined the Florida Department of Community Affairs in 1983 as its director of Resource Planning and Management. In that position, Jim helped draft and gain passage of Florida's landmark Growth Management Act.

In 1987, Jim left DCA to head 1000 Friends of Florida, a nonprofit, public interest group that works to promote sensible planning, economic development, and environmental preservation. Jim was then appointed Secretary of DCA by Governor Lawton Chiles, who called him a ''seasoned leader on growth management issues with nearly two decades of experience under his belt.''

Jim is currently the Cochair, Urban Infill Working Group, the Miami River Commission; Fellow of the National Academy of Public Administration; Member, Board of Directors, the Seaside Institute and the Congress of New Urbanism; Vice-Chair, Academia, The Urban Land Institute, SE Florida/ Caribbean District Council; FAU's Representative, Board of Governors, Consortium of Oceanographic Research and Education (CORE); Member, Board of Directors, Dade County Land Trust; Secretary, Board of Directors, Florida Ocean Alliance; Member, Water Resources Advisory Commission, South Florida Water Management District; Member, Florida Chapter, American Planning Association; Member, Florida Bar Association; Member, Steering Committee, VisionBroward; Moderator, South Miami Dade Watershed Technical Review Committee; Advisor, Biscayne Bay Regional Restoration Coordination Team; and Alumni, Leadership Florida, Class IX.

Nathan Burrell

The Honey Project: http://honeyproject.com/

Mr Burrell is a ''social'' entrepreneur with unique experience in both the public and private sectors of industry. He is the Founder and President of Helping Our Nations Empowering Youth Ventures, Inc. (HONEY Ventures), formally known as The Minority E-Commerce Association, Inc., a nonprofit organization founded to promote economic development through the utilization of technology and social enterprise. HONEY Ventures is responsible for instituting Community Technology Centers and Technology Business Centers. Currently, he serves as the Director of the award-winning Helping Our Nations Empowering Youth Project (HONEY Project) the flagship program under HONEY Ventures that seeks to produce the next generation of social entrepreneurs.

He was formerly President and CEO of VirtuPass Corp., an alternative payment platform company that provided secure and anonymous e-commerce transactions. In this role, Mr Burrell successfully guided the company from start-up and capital acquisition to product launch.

Prior to VirtuPass, Mr Burrell was VP of business development and marketing for the consulting firm Choices & Associates Inc., where he was responsible for managing and developing new business for the firm, as well as advising clients on go-to-market strategies and new product development.

Mr Burrell is currently a Digital Divide Council Member for the State of Florida. He is a former member on the Board of Governors for Keiser University and served on the Board for Junior Achievement South Florida. He is past chair of the Digital Divide Committee for the InternetCoast, served on the advisory board for the Metro-Miami Action Plan's Technology Business Center, and was a Broward County Zoning Board Member. Nathan holds a Bachelor's degree from Jacksonville University in Business Administration with a concentration in Marketing.

Steven M. Seibert

Secretary of Florida's Department of Community Affairs

Executive Director, Century Commission for a Sustainable Florida

Board of Directors, The Mosaic Company

Director of Strategic Visioning, Collins Center for Public Policy

Steven M. Seibert's career as a lawyer, mediator, business owner, corporate board member, elected official, and statewide agency director is founded upon innovative leadership and a successful knack for resolving difficult disputes. *The St Petersburg Times* described Seibert as "a consensus builder with an eye to the future."

He has extensive experience in strategic and long-term planning; issues relating to transportation, water and energy supply, affordable housing, community design, public administration, alternative dispute resolution, and disaster preparedness, and recovery. Seibert is an experienced public speaker and author of many articles addressing public policy challenges.

Of particular note is Seibert's current service as a member of the Board of Directors of *The Mosaic Company* (NYSE: MOS). Steve was a charter Board member (created in 2004) of what is now recognized as the world's largest crop nutrition company and has served on the Compensation, Governance and the Environmental, Health and Safety Committees.

Seibert is a 1977 graduate of The George Washington University, where he was chosen for *Phi Beta Kappa*, and is a 1980 graduate of the Law School at the University of Florida. For the succeeding decade, he practiced environmental and land use law in both the public and private sectors.

Seibert was elected to the Pinellas County Commission in 1992, and in that capacity served as its Chairperson twice, as Chair of the Tampa Bay Regional Planning Council, the Metropolitan Planning Organization (MPO), the Agency on Bay Management, as a charter member of the region's water supply authority (Tampa Bay Water), and as a member of the Tampa Bay National Estuary Board.

After reelection without opposition in 1996, Steve was tapped by Governor Jeb Bush to head Florida's Department of Community Affairs (DCA) in 1999, and he served in that capacity until 2003. DCA is the state's land planning agency, and during his years of service, also coordinated community redevelopment efforts and disaster management. As Secretary of DCA, Seibert was a member of numerous statewide bodies, including the Florida Housing Finance Corporation, the Governor's Growth Management Study Commission and the Florida Community Trust Governing Board.

Governor Bush called Seibert ''an outstanding public servant'' and noted ''his ability to bring people together to achieve meaningful reforms will be his lasting legacy.''

Steve Seibert is a certified mediator and has gained a statewide reputation for helping to resolve contentious environmental and land use disputes. He was awarded the statewide ''Excellence in Mediation Award'' and was significantly involved in helping to broker the end of the Tampa Bay ''water wars.'' Seibert holds an AV legal rating and has been named one of Florida's ''Legal Elite'' by *Florida Trend* magazine.

Seibert is also a member of the Board of Directors of *The Friends of Florida State Parks*, a member of the Board of Trustees of the Florida Humanities Council and currently serves as the Executive Director of the *Century Commission for a Sustainable Florida.*

John Elkington

Volans Ventures, The Business of Social Innovation: http://www.volans.com/

John Elkington is a Volans Founding Partner and Director. A cofounder of SustainAbility in 1987 (Chair from 1995 to 2005), he is seen as a world authority on corporate responsibility and sustainable development. In 2004, *BusinessWeek* described him as ''a dean of the corporate responsibility movement for three decades.'' John has authored or coauthored 16 books, including 1988's million-selling *Green Consumer Guide* and *Cannibals with Forks: The Triple Bottom Line of 21st Century Business* (1997), and has written or co-written some 40 published reports. He has recently published, with Paula Hartigan of the Schwab Foundation, *The Power of Unreasonable People: How Social Entrepreneurs Create Markets That Change the World.* He is working closely with The Skoll Foundation on a US$1 million, 3-year field-building program in relation to social entrepreneurship.

John is a Visiting Professor at the Doughty Centre for Corporate Responsibility, Cranfield School of Management. He also chairs The Environment Foundation and the Aflatoun Impact and Policy Analysis Steering Group, sitting on advisory boards for the Business & Human Rights Resource Centre, Dow Jones Sustainability Indexes, a new Cleantech Fund developed by Zouk Ventures, Physic Ventures, LP, 2 degrees, Business in the Environment, and Instituto Ethos, Brazil. He has just stood down as Chairman of the Export Credits Guarantee Department's Advisory Council, to allow more time for new ventures. He is also a member of the WWF Council of Ambassadors, the Evian Group Brain Trust, the Tomorrow's Global Company Inquiry Team, the Cambridge Research Advisory Group for the University of Cambridge Programme for Industry (CPI), the United Nations Global

Compact Cities Programme (UNGCCP) International Advisory Council, and the International Judging Panel for the DHL YES Awards, Asia and an advisor to the Fast Company Social Capitalist Awards. John is a Faculty member of the World Economic Forum.

Education

Anthony D. Cortese, ScD
President, Second Nature

Second Nature: http://www.secondnature.org/

Anthony D. Cortese is President of Second Nature, a nonprofit organization with a mission to catalyze a worldwide effort to make healthy, just, and environmentally sustainable action a foundation of all learning and practice in higher education. He is also a codirector of the American College & University Presidents Climate Commitment and cofounder of the Association for the Advancement of Sustainability in Higher Education and the Higher Education Association Sustainability Consortium and a consultant to industry, government, and nonprofit organizations.

Dr Cortese is a frequent presenter and consultant. Among his efforts, he is currently very active with organizations like the National Association of College and University Business Officers, the Society for College and University Planning, the Association of Higher Education Facilities Officers and the National Association of Educational Buyers to promote sustainable design, planning, and purchasing in higher education. He also consults frequently with colleges and universities.

Dr Cortese was formerly the Commissioner of the Massachusetts Department of Environmental Protection. He was the first dean of environmental programs at Tufts University and spearheaded the award-winning Tufts Environmental Literacy Institute in 1989 which helped integrate environmental and sustainability perspectives in over 175 courses and the internationally acclaimed Talloires Declaration of University Leaders for a Sustainable Future in 1990.

Dr Cortese is a founding and current member of the board of directors of The Natural Step US, and a founding member of the Environmental Business Council of New England. He is a Fellow of the American Association for the Advancement of Science. He has been a consultant to UNEP, a member of the EPA Science Advisory Board, and the President's Council on Sustainable Development's Education Task Force. He has been actively engaged in climate change and other large system environmental challenges for 25 years. He is also a founding member of the US Board of Councilors for the China–US Center for Sustainable Development.

His writing can be found in a wide spectrum of publications including *Environmental Science and Technology*, *The Journal of the Association of Governing Boards*, *Planning for Higher Education*, *Facilities Manager*, and in books such as *Ecological Medicine* by Kenny Ausubel as well as the Second Nature website: www.secondnature.org. His articles and essays on Education for

Sustainability serve as foundational reading for anyone striving to transform the process and content of higher education.

Dr Cortese has BS and MS degrees from Tufts University in civil and environmental engineering and a Doctor of Science in Environmental Health from the Harvard School of Public Health.

MaryBeth Burton

Center for Urban and Environmental Solutions at Florida Atlantic University: http://www.cuesfau.org/aboutus_files/staff.asp

MaryBeth Burton served as the Assistant Director for Administration at Florida Atlantic University's now defunct Center for Urban & Environmental Solutions. She was responsible for the regional indicators project and for managing activities in the Ft. Lauderdale office. During her tenure at the Center, she worked on many publications and projects and served as editor of *Florida Connections*, CUES's semiannual newsletter, *CUES News*, CUES's monthly online newsletter, and of CUES websites. Since leaving FAU, she served for 2 years as a full-time volunteer with Trash to Treasure Creative Reuse Center in Fort Lauderdale (www.trash2treasurefl.org). She is currently studying at Broward College to become a registered nurse and plans to continue her education, and to become a nurse practitioner and to provide health care to underserved people around the world.

Leonard Berry, PhD

Director, Florida Center for Environmental Studies (CES)

Florida Center for Environmental Studies: http://www.ces.fau.edu/staff.php?pg=berry

Born in England, Dr Berry studied tropical environments in East and South Asia, and later in Eastern Africa, with 12 years' residence in that area in various university positions. In Africa, he developed an interest in natural resource management and rural development applied problems, including work on regional planning problems for the government of Tanzania. Since coming to the United States in 1970, he has worked on environmental and development training programs for USAID, UNSO, and UNEP; and worked for the World Bank in a number of capacities. Current interests include effective information systems for natural resource management and environmental education.

At Clark University, Massachusetts, in 1970 Dr Berry served as Professor of Geography, Director of the Graduate School of Geography and Provost before leaving Clark for Florida Atlantic University, Boca Raton, in 1987. He was Provost and Vice President for Academic Affairs at FAU 1987–1993.

In 1994, he was appointed Director of the Florida Center for Environmental Studies. The mission of the Center is to collect, analyze, and promote the use of scientifically sound information concerning tropical and subtropical, freshwater and estuary ecosystems. Its role is to bring the full resources of the Florida State University System to bear on the critical environmental management issues of the state and of tropical, subtropical, ecosystems worldwide.

Dr Berry has authored/edited 18 books and over 200 professional papers and reports.

Jaap Vos, PhD

Chair, School of Urban & Regional Planning, Florida Atlantic University: http://wise.fau.edu/caupa/durp/

Dr Jaap Vos, Associate Professor and Chair of the School Urban & Regional Planning, joined the FAU Faculty in 1995. He holds a PhD in Regional Planning from the University of Illinois at Urbana-Champaign and a Master's degree in Environmental Science from Wageningen University in the Netherlands. Dr Vos' main interests include environmental planning, environmental justice, and sustainable development. He has published articles about community participation, environmental justice, and equity in planning. Currently, he is focusing his research on the relationship between Everglades restoration and urban development in southeast Florida.

Judy Walton, PhD

Director of Membership & Outreach, Association for the Advancement of Sustainability in Higher Education: www.aashe.org

Judy Walton is currently the Membership and Outreach Director for AASHE. She was the founding Executive Director of AASHE, and before that the founding Executive Director of Education for Sustainability Western Network (EFS West), which transitioned into AASHE in 2005. She has had a long-standing interest in sustainability, reflected in both her academic work (she played a key role in campus sustainability efforts at Humboldt State University), and her green building consultancy work in Washington state in the mid-1990s. She has delivered presentations to campuses and businesses, assisted campuses with strategic planning, and participated in or helped organize national webcasts on sustainability and higher education. Judy holds a PhD in geography from Syracuse University, an MA in geography from San Diego State University, and a BA in political science from University of California San Diego.

Jean MacGregor

Director, Curriculum for the Bioregion, Washington Center for Improving the Quality of Undergraduate Education, The Evergreen State College

Curriculum for the Bioregion, The Evergreen State College: http://www.evergreen.edu/washcenter/bioregion

Jean MacGregor is Senior Scholar and Project Director of the "Curriculum for the Bioregion" Initiative at The Washington Center for Improving the Quality of Undergraduate Education, at The Evergreen State College. The Curriculum for the Bioregion initiative aims to prepare undergraduates, as well as ourselves, to live in a world where the complex issues of environmental quality, environmental justice, and sustainability are paramount; the project now involves 452 two- and four-year colleges and universities across the State of Washington. Jean also teaches in the Masters of Environmental Studies Program at Evergreen and serves on the Senior Advisory Council to the Association for the Advancement of Sustainability in Higher Education (AASHE).

Jean's formal training is in the field of botany, zoology, and environmental studies (Wellesley College and the University of Michigan). Her professional life has revolved around teaching and community organizing in the fields of higher education innovation and reform, environmental education, community-based learning, and civic engagement. She has strong interests in service and civic learning efforts, and helped to launch the first community-based learning center at Evergreen in the early 1980s. She has taught biology and environmental studies classes (solo and in interdisciplinary teams) at Warren Wilson College in western North Carolina and at The Evergreen State College. Her scholarship and writing have focused on the theory and practice of learning communities (*Learning Communities: Reforming Undergraduate Education*, Jossey Bass, 2004), student intellectual development in the college years, and the pedagogies of collaborative learning, student reflection, and self-assessment. Jean also worked with other Washington Center projects, on cultural pluralism, academic success for students of color, and mathematics and science reform.

Jean has been recognized for her work in environmental education (with the University of Michigan School of Natural Resources Alumni Society Award for Distinguished Service in 1980) and for her national leadership of the learning community movement (with the Virginia B. Smith Innovative Leadership Award given by the Council on Adult and Experiential Education and the National Center for Public Policy and Higher Education). In 1998, *Change* (The Magazine of Higher Learning) named Jean one of eleven "Agenda-Setters" among its 80 "past, present, and future leaders of higher education in the United States."

Daniel E. Meeroff, PhD

Environmental Engineering, Department of Civil Engineering, Florida Atlantic University: http://www.civil.fau.edu/environmental.htm

Daniel Meeroff is an Assistant Professor at Florida Atlantic University's Department of Civil Engineering. His area of specialization is Environmental Engineering, specifically water and wastewater engineering, water quality, environmental microbiology and aquatic chemistry, and pollution prevention. Dr Meeroff is the director and founder of the Laboratories for Engineered Environmental Solutions (Lab-EES) at Florida Atlantic University. His BS (environmental science) was from Florida Tech and his MS (civil engineering) and PhD (civil/environmental engineering) were received from the University of Miami. Since joining FAU, Dr Meeroff has conducted research in water/wastewater technology development, environmental field monitoring, aquatic toxicity, water conservation, contaminant remediation, environmental process modeling, and pollution prevention. In the field of green building design, Dr Meeroff teaches the innovative capstone design course at FAU, which is a two-semester senior level sequence that concentrates on site planning, engineering calculations, and conceptual building design and construction issues of a LEED-certified (Gold level) green building.

Mitchell Thomashow, PhD
President, Unity College, Maine
Unity College: http://www.unity.edu/

Dr Mitchell Thomashow is the President of Unity College in Maine, a small environmental liberal arts college whose mission entails stewardship, sustainability, and service. As a college president, he aspires to integrate concepts of ecology, sustainability, natural history, wellness, participatory governance, and community service into all aspects of college and community life.

He has spent 30 years in the field of environmental studies, promoting an approach that is precisely matched to the unique qualities of Unity College:

- Broadening the constituency for conservation
- Serving the underserved
- Modeling real-time, frugal sustainability
- Emphasizing the outdoors, hands-on, ecological learning experience
- Engaging the regional community in intellectual, artistic, and recreational opportunities

Dr Thomashow is the founder of *Whole Terrain*, an environmental literary publication, originating at Antioch New England Graduate School, and a new publication *Hawk and Handsaw*, a journal of reflective sustainability, published (Summer, 2007) at Unity College. He serves on the advisory board of The Orion Society, the Coalition on Environmental and Jewish Life (COEJL), and the Teleosis Institute. Thomashow is a founding member of the Council of Environmental Deans and Directors (CEDD), a national organization that supports interdisciplinary environmental studies in higher education. He serves on the Steering Committee of the American Colleges and University President's Climate Commitment.

He is also an Associate Faculty Member in the Doctoral Program in Environmental Studies at Antioch New England Graduate School, a program which he founded in 1996.

Academically, Thomashow is interested in developing reflective, interdisciplinary pedagogy for undergraduate and graduate programs in environmental studies. He teaches courses such as Global Environmental Change, Ecological Thought, Cultures of Natural History, and Music and Nature.

Thomashow's book, *Ecological Identity: Becoming a Reflective Environmentalist* (The MIT Press, 1995), offers an approach to teaching environmental education based on reflective practice – a guide to teachers, educators, and concerned citizens alike that incorporates issues of citizenship, ecological identity, and civic responsibility within the framework of environmental studies. His most recent book, *Bringing the Biosphere Home: Learning to Perceive Global Environmental Change* (The MIT Press, 2001), is a guide for learning how to perceive global environmental change. It shows readers that through a blend of local natural history observations, global change science, the use of imagination and memory, and spiritual contemplation, you can learn how to broaden your spatial and temporal view so that it encompasses the entire biosphere. It suggests how global environmental change might become the province of countless educational initiatives – from the classroom to the Internet, from community forums to international conferences, from the backyard to the biosphere. His most recent essay (2007), "The Gaian Generation: A New Approach to Environmental Learning" provides a radical new approach to teaching about global environmental change.

Currently, he is in the initial stages of two writing projects: one a book on the ecology of improvization, linking music, play and sports, and patterns in nature, a second, a book on Abraham Joshua Heschel and his relevance for environmental education.

Thomashow has spent the last 30 years living in the hill country of southwest New Hampshire, in the shadow of Mount Monadnock. Now he is exploring the fields, forests, wetlands, hills, and islands of mid-coast Maine. His recreational interests include basketball, baseball, board games, jazz piano, electronic keyboards, musical composition and recording, guitar, hiking, bicycling, and lake swimming.

Note

1 LEED or Leadership in Energy and Environmental Design is a designation developed by the US Green Building Council to certify sustainable buildings as well as to credential professionals knowledgeable about LEED processes.

References

Allen, D., Allenby, B., Bridges, M., Crittenden, J., Davidson, C., Hedrickson, C., Matthews, S., Murphy, C., & Pijawka, D. (2008). *Benchmarking sustainable engineering education: Final report*. University of Texas at Austin, Carnegie Mellon University, Arizona State University. EPA Grant Number: X3-83235101-0.

Amodeo, R. A. (2005). *Becoming sustainable: Identity dynamics within transformational culture change at Interface* (Doctoral dissertation). Benedictine University, Ann Arbor, MI.

Argyris, C., & Schön, D. (1978). *Organizational learning*. Reading, MA: Addison-Wesley.

AtKisson, A. (2008). *Indicators, systems, innovation, and strategy: Putting ISIS to work to accelerate sustainability*. Stockholm: AtKisson Group, Inc.

Avolio, B. J., & Gibbons, T. C. (1988). Developing transformational leaders: A life span approach. In J.A. Conger, & R.N. Kanungo (Eds.), *Charismatic leadership: The elusive factor in organizational effectiveness* (pp. 276–309). San Francisco: Jossey-Bass.

Baas, M., De Dreu, C. K. W., & Nijstad, B. A. (2008). A meta-analysis of 25 years of mood-creativity research: Hedonic tone, activation, or regulatory focus? *Psychological Bulletin, 134*(6), 779–806. Retrieved from http://psycnet.apa.org/index.cfm?fa=buy.optionToBuy&;id=2008-14745-001

Barabasi, A. L. (2003). *Linked: How everything is connected to everything else and what it means for business, science, and everyday life*. New York: Plume.

Barlett, P. F., & Chase, G. W. (2004). *Sustainability on campus: Stories and strategies for change*. Cambridge, MA: The MIT Press.

Barth, R. (2000). *Improving schools from within: Teachers, parents, and principals can make a difference*. San Francisco: Jossey-Bass.

Bartunek, J., & Koch, M. (1994). Third-order organizational change and the western mystical tradition. *Journal of Organizational Change Management, 7*(1), 24–41.

Bass, B. (1985). *Leadership and performance beyond expectations*. New York: Free Press.

Bass, B., Adams, B., & Webster, S. (1997). *The ethics of transformational leadership*. College Park, MD: The James MacGregor Burns Academy of Leadership Press. Retrieved from http://www.academy.umd.edu/publications/klspdocs/bbass_p1.htm

Bateson, G. (1972). *Steps to an ecology of mind: Collected essays in anthropology, psychiatry, evolution, and epistemology*. University of Chicago Press.

Bennis, W. (2003). *On becoming a leader*. Cambridge, MA: Perseus.

Bertalanffy, L. von. (1950). An outline of general systems theory. *Philosophy of Science, 1*(2), 134–165.

Benyus, J. (2002). *Biomimicry: Innovation inspired by nature*. New York: HarperCollins.

Blake, R. R., & Mouton, J. S. (1964). *The managerial grid*. Houston, TX: Gulf Publishing.

Boyatzis, R., & McKee, A. (2005). *Resonant leadership*. Cambridge, MA: Harvard Business School.

Brown, L. (2006). *Plan B 2.0: Rescuing a planet under stress and a civilization in trouble.* New York: Norton.

Burns, J. (1978). *Leadership.* New York: Harper & Row.

Capra, F. (1996). *The web of life: A new scientific understanding of living systems.* New York: Anchor Books.

Capra, F. (2002). *The hidden connections: A science for sustainable living.* New York: Anchor Books.

Center for Urban & Environmental Solutions. (2008, May). *Preserving paradise: SoFlo's call to action.* Ft. Lauderdale, FL: Florida Atlantic University.

Chopra, D., & Plack, A. (2008). *The soul of healing affirmations: A–Z guide to reprogramming the software of the soul.* SKU: MUS0100012CD.

Cohen, A. (2008). *The world of the authentic self.* Retrieved from http://www.andrewcohen.org/teachings/model-viewer.asp

Cohen, A., & Wilber, K. (2002). *Living enlightenment: A call for evolution beyond ego.* Lenox, MA: Moksha Press.

Collins, J. (2001a). *Good to great: Why some companies make the leap… and others don't.* New York: HarperCollins.

Collins, J. (2001b, January). Level 5 leadership: The triumph of humility and fierce resolve. *Harvard Business Review*, 66–76.

Cortese, A. D. (2003, May). The critical role of higher education in creating a sustainable future. *Planning for Higher Education, 31*(3), 15–22.

Cortese, A. D. (2009, February 18). *Environmental sustainability as a policy issue [Webinar].* Association of Governing Boards.

Costanza, R., Graumlich, L., Steffen, W., Crumley, C., Dearing, J., Hibbard, K., et al. (2007, November). Sustainability or collapse: What can we learn from integrating the history of humans and the rest of nature? *Ambio, 16*(7), 522–527. Retrieved from the Royal Swedish Academy of Sciences Web site http://www.igbp.net/documents/Costanza_2007_Ambio.pdf

Cuginotti, A., Miller, K.M., & van der Pluijm, F. (2008). *Design and decision making: Backcasting using principles to implement cradle-to-cradle* (master's thesis). School of Engineering Blekinge Institute of Technology, Karlskrona, Sweden. Retrieved from http://www.bth.se/fou/cuppsats.nsf/all/018e5c43292a196bc1257463006fbdee/$file/Cuginotti_Miller_van_der_Pluijm_2008.pdf

Crow, M. (2007). *American research universities during the long twilight of the Stone Age. Elaboration on remarks made at the Rocky Mountain Sustainability Summit.* Tempe, AZ: Arizona State University.

Darwin, C. (1859). *On the origin of species by means of natural selection, or the preservation of favoured races in the struggle for life.* London: John Murray.

Day, D. (2001). Leadership development: A review in context. *Leadership Quarterly, 11*(4), 581–613.

Doppelt, B. (2003). *Leading change toward sustainability: A change-management guide for business, government, and civil society.* Sheffield, UK: Greenleaf.

Doppelt, B. (2008). *The power of sustainable thinking. How to create a positive future for the climate, the planet, your organization and your life.* Sheffield, UK: Greenleaf.

Drucker, P. F. (1995). *Managing in a time of great change.* New York: Truman Talley Books/Dutton.

Elkington, J., & Hartigan, P. (2008). *The power of unreasonable people: How social entrepreneurs create markets that change the world.* Boston: Harvard Business School.

Emerson, R. W., & Emerson, E. W. (1979). *Centenary edition: The complete works of Ralph Waldo Emerson.* New York: AMS Press.

Environmental Leader. (2011, March 1). *Walmart, Nike, Gap Create Apparel Index.* Retrieved from http://www.environmentalleader.com/2011/03/01/walmart-nike-gap-create-apparel-index/

Esty, D. C., & Winston, A. S. (2006). *From green to gold: How smart companies use environmental strategy to innovate, create value, and build competitive advantage*. New Haven: Yale University Press.

Ferdig, M. A. (2007). Sustainability leadership: Co-creating a sustainable future. *Journal of Change Management, 7*(7), 25–35.

Ferdig, M. A., & Ludema, J. D. (2005). Transformative interactions: Qualities of conversation that heighten the vitality of self-organizing change. In W. Pasmore, & R. Woodman (Eds.), *Research in organizational change and development* (pp. 171–207). Amsterdam: Elsevier, Ltd.

Flood, R. L., & Romm, N. R. A. (1996). Contours of diversity management and triple loop learning. *Kybernetes, 25*(7/8), 154–163.

Frankl, V. (1984). *Man's search for meaning: An introduction to logotherapy*. New York: Washington Square Press.

Freeman, R. E. (1984). *Strategic management: A stakeholder approach*. Marshfield, MA: Pitman.

Friedman, T. (2005). *The world is flat: A brief history of the 21st century*. New York: Farrar, Straus and Giroux.

Friedman, T. (2008). *Hot, flat, and crowded: Why the world needs a green revolution – and how we can renew our global future*. New York: Farrar, Straus and Giroux.

Giddens, A. (1986). *The constitution of society: Outline of the theory of structuration*. Berkeley, CA: University of California Press.

Gore, A. (2006). *An inconvenient truth: The planetary emergency of global warming and what we can do about it*. New York: Rodale.

Gould, S. J. (2003). *The hedgehog, the fox, and the magister's pox: Mending the gap between science and the humanities*. New York: Three Rivers Press.

Greenleaf, R. (1977). *Servant leadership*. New York: Paulist Press.

Gronn, P. C. (1995). Greatness revisited: The current obsession with transformational leadership. *Leading and Managing, 1*, 14–27.

Hardin, G. (1968). *The tragedy of the commons*. The Garrett Hardin Society. Retrieved from http://www.garretthardinsociety.org/articles/art_tragedy_of_the_commons.html

Harris, A., Day, C., Hopkins, D., Hadfield, M., Hargreaves, A., & Chapman, C. (2003). *Effective leadership for school improvement*. London: RoutledgeFalmer.

Hawken, P. (2007). *Blessed unrest: How the largest social movement in history is restoring grace, justice, and beauty to the world*. New York: Penguin Books.

Hawken, P., Lovins, A., & Lovins, L. H. (1999). *Natural capitalism. Creating the next industrial revolution*. New York: Little Brown.

Holmberg, J., & Robèrt, K.-H. (2000). Back-casting from non-overlapping sustainability principles – a framework for strategic planning. *International Journal of Sustainable Development and World Ecology*, (7), 291–308.

Intergovernmental Panel on Climate Change (IPCC). (2007). *Climate change 2007: The physical science basis*. Retrieved from http://ipcc-wg1.ucar.edu/wg1/docs/WG1AR4_SPM_Approved_05Feb.pdf

International Geosphere-Biosphere Programme. (2007). *Annual report 2007*. Retrieved from http://www.igbp.net/documents/resources/IGBP_AR_2007.pdf

Isaacs, W. (2000). Taking flight: Dialogue, collective thinking, and organizational learning. In R. Cross & Sam Israelit (Eds.), *Strategic learning in a knowledge economy: Individual, collective, and organizational learning process* (pp. 231–252). Woburn, MA: Butterworth-Heinemann.

Jackson, T. (2009). *Growth without prosperity? The transition to a sustainable economy*. UK: The Sustainable Development Commission.

Kania, J., & Kramer, M. (2011). Collective impact. *Stanford Social Innovation Review*, (Winter), 36–41.

Keeley, M. (1995). The trouble with transformational leadership: Toward a federalist ethic for organizations. *Business Ethics Quarterly*, *5*, 67–95.

Koestler, A. (1967). *The ghost in the machine: The urge to self-destruction, a psychological and evolutionary study of modern man's predicament*. New York: Penguin.

Kohlberg, L., Levine, C., & Hewer, A. (1983). *Moral stages: A current formulation and a response to critics*. Basel, NY: Karger.

Kuhn, T. (1962). *The structure of scientific revolutions*. Chicago: University of Chicago Press.

Laszlo, C. (2005). *The sustainable company: How to create lasting value through social and environmental performance*. Washington, DC: Island Press.

Leithwood, K., Seashore Louis, K., Anderson, S., & Wahlstrom, K. (2004). *Review of research: How leadership influences student learning*. Learning from Leadership Project. Ontario Institute for Studies in Education at the University of Toronto. The Wallace Foundation.

Lewin, K. (1951). *Field theory in social science*. New York: Harper & Row.

Link, W. (2006). Inspired pragmatism: Personal experiences and reflections about leadership in the emerging wisdom civilization. In W. Link, T. Corral, & M. Gerson (Eds.), *Leadership is global: Co-creating a more humane and sustainable world* (pp. 33–64). Greenbrae, CA: Global Leadership Network.

Maslow, A. (1943). A theory of human motivation. *Psychological Review*, *50*, 370–396. Retrieved from http://psychclassics.yorku.ca/Maslow/motivation.htm

McDonough, W., & Braungart, M. (1991). *The Hannover principles. Design for sustainability*. EXPO 2000. Hannover, Germany: The World's Fair.

McDonough, W., & Braungart, M. (2002). *From cradle to cradle: Remaking the way we make things*. New York: North Point Press.

McEwen, C., & Schmidt, J. (2007). *Mindsets in action: Leadership and the corporate challenge*. Atlanta, GA: Avastone Consulting.

Meadows, D., Randers, J., & Meadows, D. (2004). *Limits to growth: The 30-year update*. White River Junction, VT: Chelsea Green Publishing.

Meadows, D. H., Meadows, D. L., Randers, J., & Behrens, W. W. (1972). *The limits to growth. A report for the Club of Rome's project on the predicament for mankind*. New York: Universe Books.

Merton, R. (1936). The unanticipated consequences of purposive social action. *American Sociological Review*, *1*(6), 894–904. Retrieved from http://www.jstor.org/stable/2084615

Millennium Development Goals (2000). *End poverty 2015: Make it happen*. Retrieved from http://www.un.org/millenniumgoals/index.shtml

Ospina, M., Bond, K., Karkhaneh, M., Tjosvold, L., Vandermeer, B., Liang, Y., et al. (2007). *Meditation practices for health: State of the research*. Agency for Healthcare Research and Quality: U.S. Department of Health and Human Services. Edmonton, Alberta, Canada: University of Alberta Evidence-based Practice Center.

Peters, T. (1994). *The Tom Peters Seminar: Crazy times call for crazy organizations*. New York: Vintage Books.

Quinn, L. (2007). *Leadership for sustainability and corporate social responsibility*. Greensboro, NC Center for Creative Leadership.

Robèrt, K. H. (1991). Educating a nation: The natural step. In *context, IC 28*, 10. Retrieved from http://www.context.org/ICLIB/IC28/Robert.htm

Robinson, J. (1990, October). Futures under glass: A recipe for people who hate to predict. *Futures*, *22*(9), 820–834.

Romme, A. G., & van Witteloostuijn, A. (1999). Circular organizing and triple-loop learning. *Journal of Organizational Change Management*, *2*(5), 231–252.

Rooke, D., & Torbert, W. (2005, April). *Seven transformations of leadership*. Cambridge, MA: Harvard Business Review.

Rosch, E. (1999). *Primary knowing: When perception happens from the whole field.* Conversation with Professor Eleanor Rosch. University of Berkeley, CA.

Ruf, B., Muralidhar, K., Brown, R. M., Janney, J. J., & Paul, K. (2001). An empirical investigation of the relationship between change in corporate social performance and financial performance: A stakeholder theory perspective. *Journal of Business Ethics, 32*, 143–156.

Sachs, J. (2005). *The end of poverty: Economic possibilities for our time.* New York: Penguin Books.

Santana, L. (2008, June). Integral theory's contribution to leader and leadership development. *Integral Leadership Review III, 3.* Retrieved from http://www.integralleadershi preview.com/archives/2008-06/2008-06-santana.html

Scharmer, O. (2007). *Theory U: Leading from the future as it emerges.* Cambridge, MA: The Society for Organizational Learning.

Scharmer, O. (2009). *Seven acupuncture points for shifting capitalism to create a regenerative ecosystem economy.* Paper presented at the *Roundtable on Transforming Capitalism to Create a Regenerative Economy.* Cambridge, MA: Massachusetts Institute of Technology.

Scharmer, O., Arthur, W. B., Day, J., Jaworski, J., Jung, M., Nonaka, I., & Senge, P. (2002). *Illuminating the blind spot: Leadership in the context of emerging worlds.* Cambridge, MA: Society for Organizational Learning (SOL).

Schmidt, J. D. (2007). Living leadership. *Kosmos: An Integral Approach to Global Awakening, VI*(2), 27.

Schön, D. (1983). *The reflective practitioner: How professionals think in action.* London: Temple Smith.

Seelos, C. & Mair, J. (2005a). Social entrepreneurship: Creating new business models to serve the poor. *Business Horizons, 48*, 241–246.

Seelos, C., & Mair, J. (2005b). *Sustainable development: How social entrepreneurs make it happen* (Working Paper). Barcelona, Spain: IESE Business School, University of Navarra.

Senge, P. (1990). *The fifth discipline.* New York: Doubleday.

Senge, P. (2010). *Building sustainable organizations and communities: Innovation for the world we are now living into.* Global Classroom Seminar. Cambridge, MA: Massachusetts Institute of Technology.

Senge, P., Cambron McCabe, N., Lucas, T., & Kleimer, A. (2000). *Schools that learn: A fifth discipline fieldbook for educators, parents, and everyone who cares about education.* New York: Doubleday.

Senge, P., Kruschwitz, N., Laur, J., & Schley, S. (2008). *The necessary revolution: How individuals and organizations are working together to create a sustainable world.* New York: Doubleday.

Senge, P., Scharmer, C. O., Jaworski, J., & Flowers, B.S. (2004). *Presence: An exploration of profound change in people, organizations, and society.* New York: Doubleday.

Sewell, A., & Salter, J. (1995). Panarchy and other norms of global governance: Boutros-Ghali, Rosenau, and beyond. *Global Governance, 1*, 373–382.

Shriberg, M. (2002). *Sustainability in U.S. higher education: Organizational factors influencing campus environmental performance and leadership* (Unpublished doctoral dissertation). University of Michigan, USA.

Sparks, D. (2005). *Leadership can be taught: A bold approach for a complex world.* Cambridge, MA: Harvard Business School Press.

Stacey, R. D. (2002). *Strategic management and organizational dynamic: The challenge of complexity.* Essex, UK: Pearson Education Ltd, Prentice Hall.

Starr, A., & Torbert, B. (2005). Timely and transforming leadership inquiry and action: Toward triple-loop awareness. *Integral Review, 1.*

Taylor, F. W. (2004). *The principles of scientific management.* Whitefish, MT: Kessinger Publishing, LLC.

Thomashow, M. (2001). *Bringing the biosphere home: Learning to perceive global environmental change.* Cambridge, MA: The MIT Press.

Tichy, N. M., & Devanna, M. A. (1990). *The transformational leader.* New York: John Wiley & Sons.

Trompenaars, F., & Hampden-Turner, C. (2002). *21 Leaders for the 21st century.* New York: McGraw-Hill.

Waters, T., Marzano, R., & McNulty, B. (2003). *Balanced leadership, what 30 years of research tell us about the effect of leadership on student achievement.* Aurora, CO: Mid-continent Research for Education and Learning (McREL).

Wheatley, M. (2004). *Finding our way: Leadership for an uncertain time.* San Francisco: Berrett-Koehler.

Wheatley, M., & Frieze, D. (2006). *Using emergence to take social innovations to scale.* Retrieved from http://www.margaretwheatley.com/articles/emergence.html

Wilber, K. (2000). *A brief history of everything.* Boston: Shambhala.

Wilber, K. (2001). *A theory of everything.* Boston: Shambhala.

Wilber, K. (2007). *The integral vision.* Boston: Shambhala.

Willard, B. (2009). *The sustainability champion's guidebook: How to transform your company.* Gabriola Island, BC, Canada: New Society Publishers.

Williamson, M. (1992). *Return to love: Reflections on the principles of a "course in miracles."* New York: HarperCollins.

World Commission on Environment and Development. (1987). *Our common future. The Brundtland Report to the United Nations General Assembly.* Retrieved from http://www.worldinbalance.net/pdf/1987-brundtland.pdf

Index

For Product Safety Concerns and Information please contact our EU representative GPSR@taylorandfrancis.com
Taylor & Francis Verlag GmbH, Kaufingerstraße 24, 80331 München, Germany

www.ingramcontent.com/pod-product-compliance
Ingram Content Group UK Ltd.
Pitfield, Milton Keynes, MK11 3LW, UK
UKHW021849240425
457818UK00020B/782

* 9 7 8 0 4 1 5 6 9 2 4 5 8 *